SOCIAL WORK PRACTICE

TITLES OF RELATED INTEREST FROM PINE FORGE PRESS

The Social Worlds of Higher Education: Handbook for Teaching,
edited by Bernice Pescosolido and Ronald Aminzade

Adventures in Social Research: Data Analysis Using SPSS®
for Windows95/98™ using Versions 7.5, 8.0, or Higher
by Earl Babbie and Fred Halley

Exploring Social Issues Using SPSS® for Windows95/98™ Using Versions 7.5,
8.0, or Higher *by Joseph Healey, John Boli, Earl Babbie, and Fred Halley*

Social Work in the 21st Century *by Eileen Gambrill and Michael Reisch*

Critical Thinking for Social Workers: Exercises for the Helping Professions,
Revised Edition *by Leonard Gibbs and Eileen Gambrill*

Social Work Practice: Cases, Activities, and Exercises *by Kim Strom-Gottfried*

The Social WorkOut Book: Strength-Building Exercises for the
Pre-Professional *by Alice Lieberman*

Community Resources for Older Adults: Programs and Services in an
Era of Change *by Robbyn Wacker, Karen Roberto, and Linda Piper*

Sociology for a New Century: A Pine Forge Press Series,
Edited by Charles Ragin, Wendy Griswold, and Larry Griffin

Aging, Social Inequality, and Public Policy *by Fred C. Pampel*

SOCIAL WORK PRACTICE
Cases, Activities, and Exercises

Kim Strom-Gottfried

PINE FORGE PRESS
Thousand Oaks ◆ London ◆ New Delhi

For information:

 Pine Forge Press
A Sage Publications Company
2455 Teller Road
Thousand Oaks, California 91320
sales@pfp.sagepub.com

SAGE Publications Ltd.
6 Bonhill Street
London EC2A 4PU
United Kingdom

SAGE Publications India Pvt. Ltd.
M-32 Market
Greater Kailash I
New Delhi 110 048 India

Production Editor: Wendy Westgate
Production Coordinator: Windy Just
Production Assistant: Nevair Kabakian
Designer/Typesetter: Janelle LeMaster
Cover Designer: Ravi Balasuriya
Indexer: Molly Hall

Printed in the United States of America

99 00 01 02 03 04 10 9 8 7 6 5 4 3 2 1

Library of Congress Cataloging-in-Publication Data

Strom-Gottfried, Kim
    Social work practice: Cases, activities, and exercises / by Kim Strom-Gottfried.
        p.   cm.
    Includes bibliographical references and index.
    ISBN 0-7619-8559-X (pbk.: alk. paper)
    1. Social work education.   2. Social service—Problems, exercises, etc.
    3. Social case work—Problems, exercises, etc.   I. Title.
    HV11.S836 1998
    361.3'2—dc21   98-40174

ABOUT THE AUTHOR

Kim Strom-Gottfried, Ph.D., LISW, is Assistant Professor at the University of Minnesota School of Social Work where she teaches social work methods, health and mental health policy, and human resource management. She has taught for over 10 years on both the BSW and MSW levels and has been involved in field practice as an agency field instructor, faculty liaison, and Acting Director of Field Education. Her practice experience includes direct service, administrative, and planning positions in the field of mental health, through nonprofit and public agencies. She is actively involved in continuing professional education, developing and delivering workshops on a variety of topics including training for trainers, ethics, and license exam preparation courses. She is the author of numerous articles and book chapters on private practice, ethics, creative teaching, and the effects of managed care on social work and social work education.

ABOUT THE PUBLISHER

Pine Forge Press is an educational publisher, dedicated to publishing innovative books and software throughout the social sciences. On this and any other of our publications we welcome your comments and suggestions.

Please call or write to:

Pine Forge Press
2455 Teller Road
Thousand Oaks, California 91320
(805) 499-4224
FAX (805) 499-7881
E-mail: sales@pfp.sagepub.com

Visit our World Wide Web site, your direct link to a multitude of online resources:

http://www. pineforge.com

To *George*

BRIEF OUTLINE

CONTENTS

1 UNDERSTANDING SOCIAL WORK

EXERCISE 1
Introductions and Icebreakers   3

This exercise will help you to get to know your classmates and help them to better know you. These exercises can also be adapted for your work with clients. How might you use them in the future?

EXERCISE 2
Putting Systems Theory Into Action   7

Systems theory is an important part of the knowledge base for social work practice. Through three activities, this exercise helps you to understand the concepts that make up the theory and apply them to various situations. The exercise also encourages you to evaluate the advantages and limitations of the theory.

EXERCISE 3
Understanding and Resolving Value Dilemmas   19

Values are our beliefs about how things should be. The complex situations social workers encounter can raise conflicts between professional and personal values and between our values and those of our clients. This exercise presents case scenarios you can use to better understand value dilemmas and develop self-awareness in addressing them.

EXERCISE 4
Understanding and Using the NASW Code of Ethics   26

The Code of Ethics articulates standards of behavior for social workers in their interactions with clients, colleagues, employing organizations, and society at large. This exercise familiarizes you with all aspects of the code and lets you examine how it might guide your actions in a series of cases.

3 GATHERING DATA

EXERCISE 11

Social workers gather case information through interviews with clients, collateral contacts, and other concerned parties. A first step in conducting and evaluating interviews is learning the terminology used to describe communication skills and errors. This exercise allows you to view a videotaped interview, identify the skills used, critique the interview, and re-create it through role play.

EXERCISE 12

This exercise offers you more opportunities to develop your interviewing and observation skills. After identifying helpful and unhelpful interviewer behaviors, you will participate in role plays portraying the client, social worker, and observer. These audio- or videotaped interviews give you an opportunity to develop your skills through immediate feedback and through self-assessment in reviewing the tapes.

EXERCISE 13

This exercise introduces you to the use of a process recording for evaluating interventions. The focus of the recorded interview, a client's perceived racial insult, challenges the skill of his worker, who is different from him in age, gender, and race. Following your analysis of the session, you will have an opportunity to practice your skills in role plays where "difference" is an issue.

EXERCISE 14

Strength-based interviewing allows clients to be "the teachers" in conveying their experiences and life view to the interviewer. Using a case involving suspected child abuse, this exercise helps you develop your investigative interviewing skills in determining whether abuse took place.

EXERCISE 15

Many tools exist to help workers gather information in their cases. This exercise introduces you to eight tools, gives you a chance to experiment with them, and helps you to evaluate their strengths, weaknesses, and the skills needed to use them effectively.

This exercise bridges interviewing and assessment. You and your classmates will collectively act as the social worker, conducting an initial client interview and developing individual preliminary assessments and treatment goals.

In social work with families, you will use different terms and concepts to describe family functioning. As a first step in mastering this knowledge, this activity asks you to reflect on your family of origin and use the professional terminology to describe family relations, decision-making processes, roles, and communications. You'll use these insights to further your self-awareness and to create a genogram and ecomap depicting the family over time and in its relation to other systems.

What are the various forms of diversity represented at your school, workplace, or field placement agency? Does the level of diversity vary among managers, line staff, and clientele? What factors have helped (or are needed) to build a pluralistic workplace? This "audit" helps you examine those questions through an assessment of the organization.

When larger systems factors have a detrimental effect on clients, social workers may focus their intervention on organizational or policy change. As with direct practice, this requires an analysis of the factors affecting the problem and the forces for (or barriers to) change. Based on a case scenario, you will conduct such an assessment and begin to strategize interventions. These techniques could also be applied to change in community settings and in social policy.

When working with committees or community groups, it is often necessary to generate ideas or alternatives (e.g., on ways to address a problem) and then develop priorities on how to proceed. The exercise introduces you to nominal group technique (NGT) and gives you an opportunity to experience and evaluate its usefulness.

Even in long-term work with clients, events arise that cause us to change the focus of our sessions and create new goals for work. This exercise offers three scenarios involving the same client over an extended period of time. It also offers you the opportunity to practice interviewing families and setting mutually acceptable treatment goals.

Goals for service should be mutually developed and spell out the social worker's and client's expectations for services, roles, and tasks. The contacting process can be complicated when there is disagreement about the nature of the problem, when there are differences separating the worker and client, and when the working relationship is not voluntary. This exercise gives you an opportunity to examine and practice goal setting under such conditions.

When clients are being served by multiple systems, those various agendas can affect the type of goals the social worker and client are able to set. This is complicated further when services are mandated and client choice is limited. This exercise offers you various views of a case involving a family that has been referred to child protective services. How will you set goals that are satisfactory to the various systems involved yet are sensitive to your clients' needs and priorities?

6 CREATING CHANGE: INTERVENTIONS

Theoretical frameworks affect the way that social workers view their clients' problems and the services needed to address those problems. This exercise introduces you to a family and requires you to apply one of six theoretical orientations in assessing the family's situation and recommending intervention strategies. How can social workers consciously develop and apply a multitheoretical framework in their professional practice?

Because of the way homosexuality is viewed in our society, gay and lesbian families face particular challenges that are layered on whatever needs bring them in contact with social work services. This exercise offers examples from three practice settings and asks you to craft your interventions with sensitivity to the needs of your clients and the systemic factors affecting them.

In their desire to advocate for their clients, social workers may adopt adversarial stances with other systems' representatives. This may not yield the desired results for the client and may impede future working relationships. This exercise sensitizes you to the importance of empathy in interventions with other professionals and gives you an opportunity to use those skills in an advocacy situation.

This exercise involves a four-session simulation of a parenting group. Over time, you will have the opportunity to practice and examine various group dynamics and leadership skills as they emerge in the extended role play. This activity also highlights the processes, advantages, and disadvantages of group coleadership.

Just as there are a variety of strategies that social workers can employ in direct practice, community workers also must make conscious choices in choosing effective interventions. This exercise introduces you to the process of "constructive controversy" as you and your classmates try to determine the best method for addressing a neighborhood's housing problem.

This exercise helps you synthesize what you have learned about assessments, goal planning, and interventions by applying them to a case that changes over time. The case also challenges your skills in addressing the needs of your primary individual client and those of her family and significant others as she struggles with breast cancer.

Increasingly, social workers must demonstrate the effectiveness of their work to secure funding for programs or reimbursement for individual client services. Similarly, clients want to see progress in their cases and there are other pressures to use effectiveness measures in selecting treatment options. But how do you evaluate progress? This exercise presents two different perspectives for you to critically examine in formulating your own stance on practice evaluation.

Practice evaluation and program evaluation techniques yield information on the impact of social work interventions. The information can
take many forms: unemployment rates, the degree of goal attainment,
scores on self-esteem inventories, and frequency counts, for example,
on compliance with medication, school attendance, meeting curfews,
and so forth. But how does this information get conveyed to demonstrate change and effectiveness? This exercise offers two scenarios
and guides you in graphing the case data and analyzing its meaning.

Process recording is a useful tool for analyzing the interactions in a client
session and uncovering insights about your strengths and weaknesses
as a social worker. This exercise gives you the opportunity to record a
session and do an in-depth analysis of your actions in the session. The
activity also includes case scenarios that can be role-played and videotaped, with analysis of the tape providing a contrasting example of another method for self-evaluation.

8   ENDINGS AND TRANSITIONS

Because social work practice is affected by policies, which are themselves shaped by public opinion and vocal constituencies, it is important
that social workers use their experiences to influence these larger systems. One way of doing this is through letters, for example, to editors,
legislators, or regulatory bodies. This exercise asks you to consider the
qualities of an effective letter and to practice writing and critiquing persuasive letters. Although these skills may be used as part of an advocacy
intervention or in work with organizations and communities, they are included in this section of the workbook because the importance of influencing policy supersedes particular practice situations.

Effective referrals involve knowing the available resources; their
location, operations, and eligibility criteria; and matching those with the
needs of the client system you are seeking to refer. This exercise helps
you to develop your understanding of the available resources for a given
situation and the advantages and limitations of that organization for meeting your client's needs. This exercise also builds appreciation for the
struggles clients encounter in negotiating the maze of services without
guidance or support.

EXERCISE 35
Getting Closure on Unplanned Endings

Closure is an important element of termination, for both the client system and the social worker. This exercise presents you with eight scenarios in which the ending of the working relationship was not planned. You and your classmates will generate and compare ideas for achieving the goals of termination under less-than-ideal circumstances.

EXERCISE 36
Classroom Terminations

The end of a course means termination for the relationships that have developed in the class, in a process somewhat parallel to the endings that occur in social work practice. This exercise offers you several examples for creatively terminating with your classmates and asks you to consider how you might use these exercises, or your adaptations of them, in work with clients.

GUIDE TO EXERCISES

The following table is designed to help you identify exercises that focus on particular client populations, work settings, or forms of practice or that emphasize racial or cultural diversity. The workbook exercises are listed along the left-hand column, with the various areas of focus listed across the top. A check mark in the cell indicates that the exercise's focus, discussion questions, or vignettes offer applications to the particular focus areas. The column "Varies" indicates that the exercise or a portion of it can be varied at the instructor's or students' discretion, depending on the types of examples or resources that are incorporated with the exercise.

Exercise No.	Varies	Individuals	Groups	Families/ Couples	Organi- zations	Commun- ities	Children/ Adoles- cents	Adults	Mental Health	Health	Schools	Corrections/ Courts	Child Welfare	Self- Awareness	Diversity
1	✓		✓				✓	✓						✓	
2	✓	✓	✓	✓		✓	✓	✓	✓	✓				✓	
3	✓	✓		✓		✓		✓	✓	✓	✓			✓	✓
4	✓	✓		✓	✓	✓		✓	✓	✓		✓	✓	✓	✓
5	✓	✓			✓			✓						✓	
6	✓	✓					✓	✓							
7	✓			✓				✓	✓		✓				✓
8		✓					✓	✓	✓			✓		✓	✓
9	✓	✓						✓		✓					
10	✓			✓										✓	✓
11	✓						✓	✓	✓					✓	
12		✓						✓		✓	✓			✓	
13		✓					✓	✓					✓	✓	✓
14						✓	✓							✓	✓
15		✓		✓					✓						✓
16		✓		✓	✓		✓								
17				✓				✓	✓						
18			✓	✓	✓				✓	✓					✓
19				✓	✓				✓						✓
20		✓		✓			✓	✓	✓	✓			✓		✓
21		✓		✓					✓				✓		✓
22				✓			✓				✓	✓	✓		✓
23				✓								✓			
24	✓			✓				✓		✓				✓	
25		✓		✓	✓		✓	✓			✓	✓		✓	
26				✓					✓						
27				✓											✓
28		✓				✓	✓		✓	✓			✓		✓
29		✓		✓				✓	✓	✓			✓		✓
30	✓		✓								✓				
31				✓										✓	
32	✓														
33	✓														
34	✓	✓			✓	✓	✓			✓			✓	✓	
35	✓			✓	✓	✓	✓	✓	✓					✓	
36	✓			✓										✓	

ABOUT THE CONTRIBUTORS

Julie S. Abramson, Ph.D., is Associate Professor at the School of Social Welfare, State University of New York at Albany, where she teaches social work practice and health-related courses. She has over 15 years of social work experience in psychiatric and medical settings. Her research interests include physician/social work collaboration, teamwork, and discharge planning.

Ann Ahlquist, MSW, is on the faculty at the University of Minnesota School of Social Work where she directs the graduate Child Abuse Prevention Studies Certificate program. Ann spent 12 years in child protective services before cofounding, in 1989, CornerHouse, an innovative interagency child abuse evaluation center in Minneapolis, Minnesota.

Anthony Bibus, Ph.D., is Assistant Professor at Augsburg College Social Work Department and contributor to the instructor's manual for *The Reluctant Welfare State* (3rd edition) by Jansson and Cambra. He and Professor Rooney cowrote the article "Multiple Lenses: Ethnically Sensitive Practice With Involuntary Clients," which elaborates on use of the Smith Family exercise.

Craig Boitel, LISW, holds Instructor appointments at the Mandel School of Applied Social Sciences and the School of Medicine, Case Western Reserve University. He is a Ph.D candidate and the Assistant Director of Field Education at MSASS. His practice, teaching, and research interests include clinical social work, affective disorders, and field education.

Lynn Bye, MSW, Ph.D., teaches in the Social Work Program at the College of St. Benedict/St. John's University. Prior to getting her Ph.D. at Rutgers University she was a school social worker for 18 years.

Marcia B. Cohen, Ph.D., is Associate Professor at the University of New England School of Social Work in Biddeford, Maine where she teaches courses in social work practice, social group work, and social welfare policy. Marcia's publications include articles on practice skills, group work issues, and homelessness.

Glenda Dewberry Rooney, Ph.D., is Chair and Associate Professor, Department of Social Work, Augsburg College, Minneapolis, Minnesota. She teaches practice methods and courses related to organizations. Her research interests include practice ethics.

Katherine M. Dunlap, Ph.D., is Associate Clinical Professor at the University of North Carolina at Chapel Hill and Director of the Charlotte MSW Program, an Inter-Institutional Program offered jointly by the Universities of North Carolina at Chapel Hill and Charlotte. Her background is in substance abuse and school and medical social work. Her research interests include preschool and adult education, empowerment of adolescents and families, and homelessness.

Theora Evans, Ph.D., has a joint appointment at the University of Minnesota in the School of Social Work and the Department of Pediatrics, Division of General Pediatrics and Adolescent Health. Dr. Evans conducts research evaluating the psychosocial development of youth with chronic or disabling health conditions. She also studies the role of culture and its impact on health care delivery systems.

Kathleen J. Farkas, Ph.D., LISW, is Associate Professor of Social Work at the Mandel School of Applied Social Sciences where she teaches in both the doctoral and master's degree programs. Her current research and practice interests include the overlap of substance abuse, trauma, and sexual abuse in women and the treatment of substance abuse in the elderly.

Freda J. Herrington is Assistant Professor of Social Work, Central Missouri State University, Warrensburg, Missouri. She came into social work during the social and political turmoil of the early 1970s; much of the work during that time still holds vibrant meaning for her today. Her philosophy is that we each carry responsibility for making our communities genuinely more inclusive and humane for everyone.

Jane Hoyt-Oliver, LISW, ACSW, has taught at Malone College in Canton, Ohio, since 1984. She is a doctoral candidate at Case Western Reserve University's Mandel School of Applied Social Sciences.

Linda E. Jones, Ph.D., is Associate Professor at the University of Minnesota School of Social Work–Twin Cities. She teaches graduate-level research methods, social work ethics, social work teaching methods, and a field seminar and has taught social work practice with lesbians, gays, and bisexuals. Her current research is examining, through in-depth interviews, the experiences of adult sons and daughters who grew up in a home with a gay father or lesbian mother.

Raymond S. Kirk, Ph.D., is Clinical Associate Professor at the School of Social Work and Research Associate in the Jordan Institute for Families at the University of North Carolina–Chapel Hill. He is currently involved in research and evaluation of numerous programs and in developing instruments for assessing child and family risk and family functioning.

Sue Lyman, Ph.D., is Assistant Professor, University at Albany, School of Social Welfare. She has extensive direct practice experience in prevention and treatment of adolescents in the areas of substance abuse and mental health. She conducts her research in the area of child and adolescent mental health with specific emphasis on youth who are in or at risk of being in the foster care system.

Mary L. McCarthy, CSW, is Assistant Dean for Student Services, University at Albany, School of Social Welfare. She teaches micropractice in the MSW program and the undergraduate field seminar. Her practice experience includes over 10 years in child welfare and education prior to coming to the university. Current interests include political practice and public welfare policy.

Megan Morrissey, Ph.D., is Director of Admissions at the University of Minnesota–Twin Cities School of Social Work. She teaches social welfare history and community organizing and does research in the area of social welfare history.

Blanca Ramos, Ph.D., CSW, is Assistant Professor at the University at Albany, School of Social Welfare. She teaches courses in the area of social work practice. Her primary interests are in the treatment of immigrant as well as culturally diverse individuals and families. She has conducted research on acculturation and mental health issues among Hispanics.

James Reinardy, Ph.D., is Assistant Professor at the University of Minnesota–Twin Cities School of Social Work. He does research in the area of aging and long-term care. He teaches in the area of policy formation and analysis and community organizing.

Ronald H. Rooney, Ph.D, is Professor in the School of Social Work, University of Minnesota. He is author of *Social Work With Involuntary Clients* and coauthor with Dean Hepworth and Jo Ann Larsen of the fifth edition of *Direct Social Work Practice.*

Carla Sofka, Ph.D., is Assistant Professor at the University at Albany, School of Social Welfare. She has experience through clinical work and research in the areas of grief, death and dying, and mental health. Current research involves the use of the Internet and World Wide Web as a clinical tool for education and support.

Victoria Van Slyke, MSW, is a full-time faculty member at the University of Minnesota School of Social Work. Her practice experience includes designing and facilitating groups for families of bone marrow transplants, spouses of persons with traumatic brain injury, women in prison, persons with paraplegia and quadriplegia, the dually diagnosed, and homeless adults. She also maintains a practice in clinical social work, specializing in forensic evaluation, consultation, and court testimony.

David Wagner, Ph.D., is Associate Professor at the University of Southern Maine, Portland, Maine, where he teaches in the Departments of Social Work and Sociology. He has written numerous articles and several books, including *Checkerboard Square: Culture and Resistance in a Homeless Community* and *The New Temperance: The American Obsession With Sin and Vice.*

ACKNOWLEDGMENTS

I am grateful to the many people who contributed to the spirit and contents of this text. Those contributing in spirit include the many fine teachers and trainers who have, over the years, inspired my learning and my pursuit of quality instructional methods. In the same fashion, the students who have withstood, critiqued, enjoyed, and learned from so many of the exercises you find here are also contributors to the final product.

I also appreciate the support, feedback, and tangible assistance of many people: my family; my colleagues at the University of Minnesota, including Jeff Edleson, the editor of this workbook series; the staff at Pine Forge Press; the faculty who served as reviewers; the colleagues who contributed chapters; and the members of my writing group, Rosemary Link, Ron Rooney, Tony Bibus, and Maura Sullivan, who reviewed and encouraged the work at every step in the process. Thanks also to the staff at The Meeting Grounds, whose peaceful setting and endless cups of caffeine contributed to my most fruitful and joyful writing experiences. Special thanks to my husband, George, for always offering help and confidence at the moments they were most needed.

INTRODUCTION

How do value differences affect assessments and treatment planning?

Does the Code of Ethics help guide practice?

How can social workers engage with a family whose goals and cultural background differ from the worker's?

How do social workers use tools like genograms and ecomaps in their interviews?

How do organizational and community assessments really work?

How can social workers help a family experiencing a life crisis?

Do evaluation methods really tell us if we're having any effect with clients?

Effective social work practice involves the complex interplay of values, skills, and knowledge. Social work classes teach the theories and processes that guide practice, but sometimes they don't allow the opportunity to put that knowledge into action. This workbook is designed to help overcome that difficulty. Through case examples, individual exercises, group exercises, and discussions, you have the opportunity to "try out" the concepts that you are reading about in other texts. Because you and your classmates are focusing on the same cases and exercises, the workbook has the added advantage of allowing you to explore different perspectives on situations and different approaches to solving difficulties.

Sometimes these exercises can be challenging. They may reveal limits in some of the things you have learned; things that made sense when you read about them may come undone when they are applied to complex client situations. The exercises may also highlight situations where there seem to be no "good" courses of action or where there are many possible choices on how to act. In fact, these experiences mirror what happens in social work practice. Often the analysis of a situation will reveal layers of complexity and various dimensions of things to consider. Learning, in the relative safety of your classroom, how to choose and use various skills will prepare you for those situations when they arise in practice. And the ability to link the concepts from social work knowledge with the demands of practice will serve you well in professional practice throughout your career.

What Does the Book Ask of You?

The book contains 36 exercises, each of which contains an activity or set of activities designed to help you apply a particular set of concepts about social work practice to a particular practice situation. Sometimes, the practice situation is your own class, as with the first exercise on icebreakers and the last exercise on termination exercises. Other exercises will offer vignettes and ask you to answer questions or solve problems related to those scenarios. Other exercises will ask you to review written material and critically examine how the things you're learning apply to those readings. Still others ask you to practice your skills, for example, in role plays or in conducting assessments, and others ask you to examine your biases, strengths, and weaknesses as a developing practitioner.

To use the book effectively, you and your classmates must be working in a climate of trust—where people are willing to share their views, risk trying new skills, and give support and constructive feedback to one another. Part of this trust is a respectful atmosphere where people don't fear ridicule and where they can trust that the views they share are treated confidentially by other class members.

To make the best use of the book, you personally must be familiar with the knowledge and values that guide social work practice, attuned to others' perspectives and opinions, willing to share your own views, open to trying new things, and able to critique the results. The exercises in the workbook will be most useful to you if you continually ask yourself, "How might this be used in other practice settings or with different client populations? What are the limits of using this approach? How does what I'm learning build on other things I've learned?" Such questions are part of being an active learner. They help you to generalize what you've learned from the book to parallel situations you might experience in practice.

Of course, learning extends beyond the classroom and beyond your time in school. We hope the book will be a resource for you and that the exercises, cases, and discussion questions will stimulate your thinking and practice whether or not they are assigned as part of your course work!

What Does the Book Offer?

The book looks at social work practice broadly, defining it not only as practice with individuals but also with groups, families, communities, and organizations. It also incorporates social work practice in an array of settings, such as schools, hospitals, child welfare units, mental health centers, and crisis services. The 36 exercises parallel the process of a working relationship with clients. The first unit, "Understanding Social Work," contains introductions and icebreakers—exercises to help you and your classmates (or any group) get to know each other. Other exercises in this section address systems theory, which undergirds social work practice, and exercises that look at values and ethics as they guide or practice with clients.

The next section, "Getting Started," contains five exercises that focus on different strategies for "tuning in" to clients' needs and for building the rapport that is so essential to the helping relationship.

"Gathering Data" includes five exercises offering different tools and techniques for gathering information on your client system, their strengths, and the nature of their difficulties. It is a good lead-in for the next section, "Making Sense of Data Through Assessment." The four exercises in this unit offer opportunities to practice the skills of turning information gathered about a case into a coherent and valid assessment.

The result of a good assessment is covered in the four exercises of the next unit, "Setting Goals." In this section, you will learn about contracting with clients and the skills and abilities needed when clients are resistant or when clients' goals differ from the ones we want to pursue. This section leads into intervention skills, where we carry out the goals set in the previous stage of work. Intervention skills are addressed even more directly in the following "Interventions" section where six exercises focus on the skills and insights used in the "change" phase of work.

But how do we know that our interventions are any good? In the section "Evaluating Effectiveness," you'll find three exercises that help with assessing your own skills and evaluating the progress in cases. Whether our work has been successful or because we or the clients have chosen to end the relationship or move on, all working relationships are characterized by termination, the topic of the book's final section. In "Endings and Transitions," four exercises address various strategies for effective termination, including different ways to bring closure to the experiences you've shared with your classmates over the duration of the course.

Because the workbook addresses a variety of practice settings and client populations, the Guide to Exercises grid can be used to direct you to exercises that are of particular areas of interest. Thus, you can use it to find exercises that focus on work with diverse populations, for exercises focused on client systems from individuals to communities or from children and adolescents to elderly persons, or in settings from health care to foster care.

The exercises in this book have been contributed by faculty from all over the country who use them in their own teaching. They reflect tried-and-true methods for developing skills and practicing critical thinking. Your own instructor may adapt them further for his or her own teaching objectives. The contributing authors and I are interested in the learning that the book stimulates, the ideas you have for improvements, or the exercises you may have created that could be shared with others. Please contact us in care of Pine Forge Press (see About the Publisher at the beginning of this book). We hope that you get joy, inspiration, and growth as a result of your use of this book.

—KIM STROM-GOTTFRIED
kstrom@che2.che.umn.edu

UNDERSTANDING SOCIAL WORK

EXERCISE 1 *Introductions and Icebreakers*

Kim Strom-Gottfried

Purpose

1. To help you get acquainted with your classmates.
2. To practice exercises useful in work with groups.
3. To help you become comfortable with talking in front of others.

Background

Valuable learning will occur during your courses in social work as a result of your interactions with your classmates. This parallels social work practice, where, for example, clients learn from others in mutual aid groups or workers learn about techniques and resources by networking with their colleagues. "Icebreakers" or introductory exercises help groups of people get to know each other and begin the development of group cohesion. Icebreakers compel participants to get involved and reach out to others, learning more about others in the process. Learning the effective use of icebreakers, and learning different types of icebreakers, will add to the tools you have available to use in your work with clients.

Instructions

Your instructor will guide you through some of the following activities. A variety of options are included in this workbook for you to try in class or adapt for use in your practice.

Excerpts from this chapter reprinted by permission from Haworth Press, 1995, Haworth Press, Binghamton, NY. "Engagement and Termination in the Classroom," *Creative Activities for Beginning and Ending*, 12, 1/2, 39–54.

EXERCISE 1

What's in Your Pocket?

We can learn a lot about each other and what we value by looking more closely at some aspects of our lives that we never thought were very important. Looking at what we carry in our wallets, purses, pockets, or backpacks illustrates this point.

Your instructor will ask you to "take out three things from your wallet (or purse) that reflect things you value or show different aspects of your life that you'll be willing to describe to the rest of us."

When instructed, introduce yourself to the group by stating your name and what the things you've chosen from your wallet say about you, your life, and what you value.

What themes do you see emerging as people share? What are you learning about your classmates that you might not otherwise have known?

Human Treasure Hunt

The purpose of this activity is to help you get acquainted with your classmates in a fun and nonthreatening way. Talk with the others in your class, and try to find *different* people for each of the following categories, then add their names to your sheet.

Find someone who shares your astrological sign:

_____

_____

Find someone who has the same number of children as you:

_____

_____

Find someone who can quote a line from Shakespeare:

_____

_____

Find someone who enjoys a hobby or activity that you do:

_____

_____

Find someone who is ahead in their reading for this class:

_____

_____

Find someone who was born in the same state as you were:

_____

_____

Find someone who is in none of your other classes:

_____

_____

Find someone who was born in the same decade as you were:

_____

_____

Something We Wouldn't Know

Your instructor will provide the directions for this exercise. It involves thinking of and sharing something about yourself that others wouldn't know by spending the course with you. Examples of things you might want to share are hobbies, interests, awards, or accomplishments.

As people share about themselves, consider the following:

- In what ways are there similarities among class members?
- Did anyone mention an interest or experience that coincides with an interest of yours?
- In what ways are the people in the class unique?
- Were you surprised at some people's interests? Were any preconceptions changed by what you heard?

Paired Interviews

Your instructor will provide specific directions for this exercise. In general, it requires you to pair up with a classmate you don't know and "interview" him or her in preparation for introducing him or her to the rest of the class.

After this exercise is concluded, consider the following:

- Did you have difficulty thinking of questions to ask? What do you wish you had asked that you didn't?
- Were you comfortable with your interaction? What factors contributed to your comfort or discomfort?
- How did you feel about the introduction you did following the interview? Do you feel you fairly represented this individual to the class? Did you forget any key pieces of information? What might have contributed to your ability to remember certain aspects of the person and not others?

Pot Luck Supper

"Pot luck suppers" are communal meals where people bring different types of food, and each person creates his or her own meal by trying a little bit of the various foods others have brought. On the first plate below, indicate what special knowledge or skills you can bring to share with this class; on the second, indicate what things you will want to take away at the conclusion of the class.

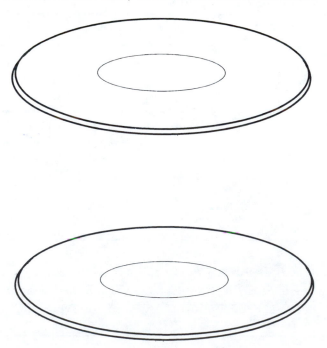

EXERCISE 2 *Putting Systems Theory Into Action*

Katherine M. Dunlap

Purpose

1. To help you understand systems theory.
2. To apply systems concepts to a case, to broader social systems, and to analyze human behavior.

Background

Systems theory forms the foundation for much of social work practice, yet it is highly abstract and often difficult to apply to real-life situations. This series of three activities will give you an opportunity to better understand the theory and examine common situations from this exciting perspective.

First, some information on the theory itself.

Systems theory has been exported into the social sciences from the physical sciences. In its most basic form, a *system* is defined as a whole consisting of interdependent and interactive parts. Each component in the system is related to at least some of the other components in a stable way over a period of time and space.

A *social system* is a special type of system. It is composed of people, or groups of people, who interact and mutually influence each other's behavior. A nation, a public service agency, a school, a married couple, and a young child are all social systems.

Social systems are functional in that they fulfill some task or purpose. In a family system, for example, one adult may assume a task-centered role by earning money for food while another adult accepts primary responsibility for raising children.

All systems have boundaries, energies, tension, and conflict. They accept feedback and use it to achieve *homeostasis,* or a dynamic balance.

Systems theory provides an effective conceptual framework for both macropractice and micropractice settings. With the systems approach, the primary practice arena shifts from past to present—from why things happened to how to facilitate planned change. This approach opens a variety of opportunities for intervention, including environmental change. It removes the notion that conflict and tension represent pathology, and it substitutes the idea that change can be healthy and positive.

A systems approach provides a comprehensive framework that respects the dignity, worth, and capacities of the individual. It promotes client determination with varied alternatives for change. Because systems theory is used by many different professions, it promotes communication between disciplines.

Further information on the theory is available in the Basic Concepts sections and the bibliography at the end of this exercise.

EXERCISE 2

Activity 1

Understanding Systems Theory—"The Poisons of Life"

Purpose: To explore the basic concepts of systems theory.

Instructions: Read the short article "The Poisons of Life" (Foley, 1993) about a young teen living in a public housing project. Then use social systems theory to answer the following questions. Be prepared to discuss your answers when your class reconvenes.

Questions for Reflection

1. Select and define a focal system. What are the component parts of this system? What lies outside the focal system? Draw a diagram to illustrate these relationships. What other focal systems could you have selected?

2. What are the tangible or physical boundaries of the focal system? What are the intangible boundaries?

3. What rules define membership in this system? Are the rules written or unwritten? How are they transmitted? How are they changed?

4. Describe verbal communication patterns in this focal system. Explain the role of negative feedback. Provide an example of positive feedback. Describe the nonverbal patterns of interaction.

5. What is homeostasis for the focal system? What interactions maintain homeostasis? How is balance maintained? What disrupts balance?

6. To what degree is the focal system open? To what degree is it closed? Plot your response on a scale of 1 to 10. What criteria did you use to determine this position? What does a "1" mean? Define a "10." Now define the number you assigned to the focal system.

7. How did this focal system originate? Will it end? How? What promotes synergy within this system? What factors contribute to entropy?

8. How have history and time shaped the life course of this young teen?

The Poisons of Life
by Meg Foley

Teen feels the violence of Earle Village driving him down.

As a lawyer for the Children's Law Center, I've met a lot of kids. At first, he didn't appear any different from many others: 15 years old, black, male. He was having problems—family, emotional, and legal.

But then we got to talking, and I realized how he was able to express himself with beautiful, insightful words. I met him in a psychiatric hospital; he was there because he just couldn't take it anymore.

He compares people to insects and life to pesticides. Some insects and people die, he says, because they can't take the painful poisons of life. Then there are others, like roaches, who get used to the horrible realities and live on. He just couldn't get used to the pain.

He has heard the sound of gunshots in his driveway. He has seen people shot outside his window. He saw a little girl win $20 at a church raffle. Her mother took the $20 to buy crack cocaine. He has seen what drugs and violence do to people's lives.

"It messes up your life. It takes away your future. It takes away your family," he says.

This kid knows who the drug dealers are. He knows them by name and he knows where they hide out. He's amazed that some of them are his own age. Those he doesn't know he recognizes by their cars, their "base" (stereo), their rings, their "gold," and their nice haircuts. He knows that people who have real jobs do not wear all those necklaces or rings on every finger; nor do they have flashing neon or gold around their car license plates.

He feels that Earle Village has scarred him. He says his environment has decayed his inner peace. He believes there are a lot of people in Earle Village who could be successful, but they think no one cares about them. Fights occur because of all the anger that has built up around them and inside of them. Sometimes, the anger gets so powerful they end up killing someone.

He knows his mother is in a predicament. The family used to live in a nicer neighborhood, but his mother lost her job and couldn't afford the rent. He shows me the hole in the bottom of his shoe. He tells me he has to wear his 8-year-old brother's underwear and that it cuts off his circulation and leaves marks on his body.

Holding on to Hope

This 15-year-old loves basketball and track. All summer long he is happy playing basketball and running, just running. He wanted to try out for the basketball and track teams, but his mother couldn't pay for the physical.

He is trying to excel in academics. He wants to be an architect or an engineer and do something exciting, like work on the space shuttle. He earns A's or B's in the fall, but his grades usually drop in the second half of the school year. Last fall he was on the honor roll. He knows that if he got out of his environment he could get all A's.

This young man tries to shut out the noises of his neighborhood—gunshots and small kids running around—so he can focus on his homework.

Over the summer, he heals. Summer brings so much happiness; problems seem to disappear. He plays basketball and runs and runs. He envies his sister, who makes excellent grades and who has been designated academically gifted. He feels his sister has built up a great tolerance to the killing, pesticidal environment in which they live.

NOTE: Meg Foley is a lawyer at the Children's Law Center in Charlotte, North Carolina. Reprinted with permission of the author.

He has tried not to be like his older brother, who is in training school for unlawful, delinquent behavior. He has tried to stay away from that kind of life.

All He Wants Is Out

He's back home with his mom now, but he wants out. He's mad at his mother for getting the family into this situation. He's asking to be placed in a foster home.

He wants away from the overwhelming problems at Earle Village.

"I can't stop the violence," he says. "If I tried, I'd get killed. All those people are involved in drugs. It makes you want to be a part of it, because there's not much else to do in my neighborhood, especially for kids."

His mom tells him to write stories with happy endings. But he can't do that anymore. All his stories end with violence.

Activity 2

Applying Systems Theory—*A Virtuous Woman*

Purpose: To increase your understanding of human behavior in the social environment by applying systems theory to a case study.

Instructions: Your instructor will assign you to a small group for this exercise. Ask one person to be the recorder and another to read aloud the first chapter of *A Virtuous Woman* (Gibbons, 1989). With your group, answer the following questions. Later you will be asked to share your responses with the entire class.

Questions for Reflection

1. What systems are involved in this short vignette? As you answer, think about human systems; the immediate physical environment; and social, organizational, economic, emotional, and cultural systems.

2. Select one of these systems as your focal system.

   a. Describe the focal system as a holon.

   b. What are the goals of your focal system?

   c. What are the tangible boundaries? The intangible boundaries?

   d. What conflicts are apparent in the focal system?

   e. What are some of the ways this system could achieve homeostasis?

3. How does feedback occur between the focal system and larger systems?

4. To what extent are each of these systems open or closed?

Chapter 1 of *A Virtuous Woman*
by Kaye Gibbons

She hasn't been dead four months and I've already eaten to the bottom of the deep freeze. I even ate the green peas. Used to I wouldn't turn my hand over for green peas.

My whole name is Blinking Jack Ernest Stokes, stokes the fire, stokes the stove, stokes the fiery furnace of hell! I've got a nerve problem in back of the face so I blink. June nicknamed me for it when she was little.

My wife's name was Ruby Pitt Woodrow Stokes. She was a real pretty woman. Used to I used to lay up in bed and say, "Don't take it off in the dark! I want to see it all!"

Ruby died with lung cancer in March. She wasn't but forty-five, young woman to die so early. She used to tell me, she'd say, "What's good for the goose is good for the gander. I imagine I'll stop smoking about the time you stop drinking." June's daddy, Burr, told me one time people feed on each other's bad habits, which might could be true except for one thing, I'm not really what I would call a drinking man. I hardly ever take a drink except when I need one.

But Ruby died and they laid her out and crossed her hands over her bosom, and I said to them, "I never saw her sleeping like that." They said but that's the way everybody was laid, so I said, "Fine then, I'll let her be."

I did lean over in the coffin though and fix her fingers so the nicotine stains wouldn't show. Ruby had the creamiest soft skin and I hated to have brown spots ruin her for people. Suppose you went to view somebody who'd died being shot or stabbed somewhere so you'd notice. Don't you know they'd fill in with some kind of spackle and smooth it over to match him? Sure they would! Same thing only different with Ruby's two ashy-smelling fingers.

God, you ought to've seen her in the hospital, weak, trying to sit up, limp as a dishrag. She'd lost down so much, looked like she'd literally almost shook all the meat off, all that coughing and spewing up she'd done. If you want to feel helpless as a baby sometime, you go somewhere and watch such as that. Seemed like every time she'd cough a cold shudder'd run up and down me.

I sat with her long as they'd let me that night, then I had to leave. I stuck my head up under her tent and said to her, "'Night 'night, Ruby. I'm headed back to the Ponderosa with Burr. I'll see you first thing in the morning." Then she put those two ashy-smelling fingers up to her mouth like either she was blowing me a kiss or telling me to hush a little. And while I was looking at her and trying to figure out which one she meant, I realized she wasn't motioning love or to hush to me. She was wanting a cigarette, asking me for one. I thought, Well I will be damned. And I said, Hard as that woman worked to get over too good a life then too bad a life, what a pity, what a shame to see this now.

I hated to but I had to call it selfish, not like the Ruby I knew. But I suppose when you're that bad off and you're not here, not gone either, I suppose you can get to the point that you are all that matters to yourself, and thinking about yourself is the last thing left you can remember how to do. So you're bound to go on and forgive it. And after it all, after it's all said and done, I'll still have to say, Bless you, Ruby. You were a fine partner, and I miss you.

Activity 3

Analyzing Systems Theory—*World News*

Purpose

1. To apply systems concepts to broader social systems.
2. To evaluate the utility of systems theory in analyzing human behavior in the social environment.

Instructions: You will be assigned to a small group to complete this assignment. Your instructor will give you an article from the local newspaper. You have 20 minutes to use systems concepts to analyze this article using systems concepts. Be sure to address Parts A and B below.

A. Use this article to illustrate these concepts:

1. Systems and subsystems
2. Tangible boundaries
3. Intangible boundaries
4. Positive feedback
5. Negative feedback
6. Synergy
7. Entropy
8. Verbal communication patterns
9. Nonverbal communication patterns
10. Homeostasis
11. Goals
12. Functions
13. Tension
14. Change
15. Growth

B. Answer the following questions:

1. In what ways is systems theory helpful in understanding this situation?
2. What are the advantages of using systems theory in this setting?
3. What are the limitations of social systems theory?

Social Systems Theory: Basic Concepts

What Is a System?

A system is a whole consisting of interdependent and interactive parts or relationships. Each component of a system is related to at least some of the other components in a stable way over a period of time and space. A change in one part of the system produces change in the other parts of the system.

A social system is a special type of system. It is composed of people, or groups of people, who interact and mutually influence each other's behavior. Social systems are functional. Together, they must be able to perform some regular task or fulfill some function or purpose. A nation, a public service agency, a school, and a married couple are all systems. So are an individual, an agency, and a college of social work.

The system is a gestalt, and, as such, it is more than the sum of its parts. Just as a poem is more that a collection of words on a page, a system has meaning that surpasses the individual components.

The Holon

The term *holon,* coined by Arthur Koestler, indicates that each system has two qualities: first, the system is composed of smaller systems, and second, the system is part of a larger system. For example, a family is a system composed of individuals. A family is also part of a larger system known as the community. The holon is characterized by the Greek god Janus, who is depicted with two faces looking in opposite directions. Our name for the first month of the year, January, is also derived from this god because January looks back to the old year and forward to the new one.

Subsystems

A subsystem is a secondary or subordinate system—a system within a system. Within a family, the parents form one subsystem and the children form another. Other, more subtle subsystems may also exist. For example, a mother may feel especially close to her oldest daughter, and these two would form a subsystem. In a family with an alcoholic parent, the spouse and children might form a subsystem in coalition against the drinking parent. In an agency, adult intake and treatment workers may form separate subsystems. In a community, separate agencies for mental health and public assistance may form separate subsystems.

The Focal System

The *focal system* is the system or subsystem chosen to receive primary attention; it is the system that sets the perspective for study. If the family is the focal system, then both the individual members and the significant features of the environment—schools, churches, the neighborhood, workplaces, community groups, and the extended family—must all be considered.

Goals and Functions

One of the characteristics of living systems is the purposefulness of their activities. Systems have goals and functions, and they use energy to achieve these. For example, a child uses energy to gain love, status, and position within the family. An organization like the National Association of Social Workers uses energy in the form of dues to promote the profession of social work.

Boundaries of the System

The concept of system implies a boundary within which there is greater interaction and interdependence of members than there is between members and persons outside of the boundary. A boundary specifies the components of the system.

A boundary may exist physically. It may be a tightly corked bottle, the skin of a person, the number of people in a group, or the city limits. Systems can also be delineated in a less tangible way by defining the boundary in less concrete variables. The variables or qualities used to delimit a system may be roles, expectations, communication patterns, spheres of influence, or power relationships. It is important to note that boundaries are not always defined by people and they are not necessarily barriers. Furthermore, different people may define boundaries in different ways. For example, one person may define a family system as including those people related by blood or marriage. Another person may define the family system as all those who spend the night in the house during the week.

Tension and Conflict

The components within a system differ from each other and are not perfectly integrated. The system needs ways of dealing with these differences. The differences among and between the parts lead to varying degrees of tension and subsequent stress that comes from the tension. When tensions and stress build and become opposed along the lines of two or more components, the system experiences conflict.

Tension and conflict are found within all systems and should not be regarded from within or without as shameful, bad, or destructive. What is important is how the tension and conflict are handled. Tension reduction, tension relief, or conflict resolution are usually the working goals of practitioners. Sometimes, however, practitioners increase tension and conflict to facilitate creativity, innovation, and social change.

Change Within the System

Systems tend to achieve a balance among the various forces operating within and on them. A *stationary equilibrium*, or homeostasis, exists when, after a disturbance, the system returns to a fixed point or the same balance previously maintained. A *dynamic equilibrium* exists when, after a disturbance, the system finds a new and different balance. The family as a system seems to be best described by the term dynamic equilibrium. The family must respond in a sensitive fashion to adjust and adapt to the tensions, stresses, and conflicts within and outside itself; to modify its own interactions; to modify the environment impinging on it; to cope; and to accommodate.

Equifinality and *multifinality* are important terms for social workers who use a systems approach. Equifinality is the ability to obtain identical results from different initial conditions. Equifinality means that there is more than one way to skin a cat! Multifinality suggests an opposite principle: similar conditions may lead to dissimilar end states or, as the proverb states, "You can't step into the same river twice." For example, the same intervention will not be equally effective with all families.

Feedback

Systems, especially social systems, receive input from the components within the system and from the environment outside the system. Another word for this type of communication is *feedback*. Feedback is any kind of direct information from an outside source about the effects of a person's behavior. Feedback is an integral part of all therapeutic relationships. It is not merely an echo, like a radar blip, received in response to one's actions; feedback also includes the process of responding to the echo—of staying or correcting the course.

Negative feedback indicates that the system is responding in a way that inhibits goal attainment; it results in a behavioral correction in line with the system's goals. Positive feedback indicates that the system is behaving in accord with its goals; this type of feedback results in more of the same behavior. One example of the use of feedback in social systems is the grading system. High grades tell students that their studying is effective and that they have mastered the material. In other words, high grades say, "Keep it up! You are on target!" Low grades communicate the opposite message by informing students that their performance is not acceptable.

Whether or not a message is positive depends not on the content of the message but on the action it promotes. Positive feedback produces more of the same behavior. Negative feedback promotes a change in behavior.

Open and Closed Systems

No system is completely open or closed. A completely open system would be indistinguishable from the environment around it, whereas a completely closed system would cease to exist at all.

An open system is a growth-oriented system. It has clearly defined boundaries that provide structure for the system, but these boundaries are permeable, not rigid. An open system permits freedom and individuality but it also provides a sense of interdependency. It accommodates change by allowing itself to find a new balance or dynamic equilibrium. Open systems are characterized by *synergy,* increased energy within the system derived from increased interaction among the members of the system.

A closed system is the opposite of an open system. In a closed system, boundaries are rigid and feedback is either nonexistent or filled with static. Stress and tension are usually handled by ignoring, denying, repressing, or defending. There is no room for interdependence within a closed system; instead, members are enmeshed or disengaged. Change usually results in crisis. Rather than finding a dynamic equilibrium, members of a closed system maintain a forced or controlled equilibrium that is stationary. It moves toward *entropy,* or disorganization. In a closed social system, this movement may be expressed through divorce, alcoholism, substance abuse, child abuse, depression, family violence, delinquency, or rebellious running away.

Implications for Practice

Systems theory is highly abstract, and the task of applying it to real-life situations can be immense. It does not explain radical or abrupt change, and it does not tell us how to control phenomena. However, the systems approach provides an effective conceptual framework for both macropractice and micropractice settings. With this approach, the primary arena shifts from past to present—from why things happened to how to facilitate planned change. This approach opens a variety of opportunities for intervention, including environmental change. It removes the notion that conflict and tension represent pathology, and it substitutes the idea that change can be positive and healthy. The systems approach is a comprehensive framework that respects the dignity, worth, and abilities of the individual and promotes client self-determination with varied alternatives for change at many different systems levels.

Social Systems Theory: An Annotated Bibliography

Anderson, R., & Carter, I. (1990). *Human behavior in the social environment* (4th ed.). New York: Aldine.

A Parsonian social systems theory is used for explanation, rather than for intervention. The basic framework is applied to persons, families, groups, organizations, and communities.

Bertalanffy, L. von (1981). *A systems view of man* (P. A. LaViolette, Ed.). Boulder, CO: Westview.

This series of philosophical essays summarizes the major tenets of general systems theory as originally proposed by Bertalanffy.

Brill, N. I. (1990). *Working with people: The helping process* (4th ed.). New York: Longman.

A concrete restatement of the theory with practical application to the helping professions and macropractice.

Bronfenbrenner, U. (1979). *The ecology of human development: Experiments by nature and design.* Cambridge, MA: Harvard University Press.

A clear and engaging application of general systems theory to the human experience.

Chetkow-Yanoov, B. (1992). *Social work practice: A systems approach.* New York: Haworth.

A basic text with ample illustrations and examples from social work.

Garbarino, J. (1992). *Children and families in the social environment* (2nd ed.). New York: Aldine de Gruyter.

Garbarino provides a thorough explanation and application of Bronfenbrenner's approach. This material focuses on the development of children in families.

Germain, C. B. (1991). *Human behavior in the social environment.* New York: Columbia.

Germain was one of the first authors to apply systems theory to social work. This is a comprehensive explanation of social work's traditional person-in-environment approach using systems concepts.

Germain, C. B., & Gitterman, A. (1995). Ecological perspective. In R. L. Edwards (Ed.), *Encyclopedia of social work* (19th ed., Vol. 1, pp. 816-824). Washington, DC: NASW Press.

This article stresses the role of the environment in understanding social systems.

Goldenberg, I., & Goldenberg, H. (1985). *Family therapy: An overview* (2nd ed.). Monterey, CA: Brooks/Cole.

A complete survey of the history, explication, and clinical application of systems theory as applied to family therapy. The tables and diagrams are most helpful.

Greene, R. R. (1993). *Human behavior theory: A diversity theory.* New York: Aldine de Gruyter.

Chapter 9 outlines the basic tenets of general systems theory and applies these tenets to family structure, family therapy, and issues of diversity.

Hanson, B. G. (1995). *General systems theory: Beginning with wholes.* Washington, DC: Taylor & Francis.

A more advanced text, this book addresses content and context, communication patterns, and emotion.

Lippitt, R., Watson, J., & Westley, B. (1958). *The dynamics of planned change.* New York: Harcourt, Brace & World.

A groundbreaking work that rocked the social work profession by using systems theory to analyze individual personality, groups, organizations, and communities.

Martin, P. Y., & O'Connor, G. G. (1989). *The social environment: Open systems applications.* New York: Longman.

In this basic text, the first chapters are dense and dated, but the remainder presents a helpful recapitulation of basic theory.

Merkel, W. T., & Searight, H. R. (1992). Why families are not like swamps, solar systems, or thermostats: Some limits of systems theory as applied to family therapy. *Contemporary Family Therapy, 14*(1), 33-49.

This thoughtful review lists the advantages and limitations of the application of systems theory to human behavior and human agencies.

Pincus, A., & Minahan, A. (1973). *Social work practice: model and method.* Madison: University of Wisconsin.

In this classic text, the authors apply systems theory to social work practice. Their identification of helping systems is particularly relevant to practice.

EXERCISE 3 *Understanding and Resolving Value Dilemmas*

Kim Strom-Gottfried

Purpose

1. To acquaint you with a variety of practice situations in which value dilemmas arise.
2. To help you identify personal values.
3. To help you sort out whose values are in conflict in any given situation.
4. To encourage critical thinking about the competing values and the ethical premises that should guide action in each of the cases.
5. To understand the interface between values and practice actions.

Background

Values are our "preferred conceptions" or beliefs about how things ought to be. The social work relationship is affected by the values held by clients, society as a whole, organizations, and social workers' personal values. The profession of social work has articulated its values and has specified them through the NASW Code of Ethics, but often our personal values are less well examined.

With all the value dimensions at play in any given case, it is essential that social workers have a high level of self-awareness, understand the nature and origins of value conflicts, and understand the impact of values on their case decisions.

Instructions

Review materials in your text about values and value conflicts.

Your instructor will assign each group of 3-4 people one of the cases listed below. For your case, as a group:

AUTHOR'S NOTE: I wish to thank Bonnie Lazar, Barbara Rich, and other faculty at the University of Southern Maine for their contributions to this exercise.

1. Identify any value conflicts or dilemmas that exist for members of your group in regard to the case situations.

2. Identify which values and whose values are at odds in the case. For example, are your values at odds with the client's? With society's? Are your personal values in conflict with those of the profession in this instance?

3. Determine how the values issues you have identified would affect your feelings about and your handling of the case problem.

4. Answer the questions associated with your case.

5. Prepare to discuss your case and the issues that arose with the full class. If you have time left over, begin to examine other cases.

EXERCISE 3

Case Problem 1

You are a social worker at a youth drop-in center. Your client, Ben, is a 16-year-old who has come to you stating that he no longer wants to live at home. He can no longer tolerate his parents' rules and regulations, which include the following: he must keep his hair very short, he must attend church services 2 nights during the week as well as for 3 hours on Sunday, and he cannot date or attend dances or go to movies. Ben agrees to meet with you and his parents. The parents seem concerned about their son. They say they want him to come home. They state that their religious beliefs are the foundation of the rules they expect their son to follow, and it would be a violation of their religious beliefs to be less strict with their son. They say that they love their son and because they love him, they want to give him the benefit of a moral upbringing.

Questions

1. How does the value of self-determination come into this case?

2. Would your values and beliefs affect your handling of this case? If so, how?

3. If Ben had come to you stating that his parents would not let him stay out after midnight and would not lend him the family car whenever he wanted it, how would you have reacted to his statement that he did not want to live at home?

Case Problem 2

You work at a neighborhood health center as a social worker. You are starting a group for women who wish to return to the job market. You discuss the group with Mrs. Ramirez, a shy, passive woman who has three children in school. You know that Mrs. Ramirez went to secretarial school and held a good job before her marriage. Mrs. Ramirez says that she can't join the group because her husband would not allow it; he does not want her to get a job. She adds that her husband has been unemployed for 3 months. She wonders how the family will keep up with mortgage payments. As she leaves your office, Mrs. Ramirez asks you what she should do. Should she sneak out to join the group so that she can get a job? Should she go along with her husband's wishes because he feels so terrible about not being able to get a job that any efforts she makes to get a job will just "destroy" him?

Questions

1. How might cultural differences affect your understanding of the Ramirez family and your approach to the case?

2. How do your feelings about the roles of men and women affect your reaction to this case situation?

3. What advice, if any, would you give to Mrs. Ramirez?

Case Problem 3

You work as a social worker in a mental health center and see some clients who are required to get counseling as a condition of parole. You have been working with Henry for some time and feel that he is making real progress. He developed a serious drug problem while in the armed services and has served time in prison for a drug-related robbery. He is now off all hard drugs and alcohol and states that except for "recreational use of marijuana, I'm clean." Henry has started a good job and is taking courses at vocational school to improve his work skills. He confides in you that he has sold some marijuana to his friends to finance his return to school.

Questions

1. What are your feelings about this case?

2. Would you tell Henry's parole officer about his marijuana use and sale? Why or why not?

3. How would you respond if he were selling "hard" drugs or selling marijuana to minors?

4. What is the role of "informed consent" in situations such as Henry's?

Case Problem 4

You work in a public welfare agency as a social worker in the child protective services division. You worked with Mrs. Gugliotta when her son was in serious conflict with his stepfather. The family worked hard to resolve their problems. Subsequently, Mrs. Gugliotta's husband died, and she applied for financial assistance and food stamps. You run into her one day in her neighborhood and are struck by how hard she is working to keep her family going. She tells you that her two oldest sons have moved in with an aunt in another town to attend an excellent vocational school there. Later on you happen to find out from a co-worker that Mrs. G. is still collecting food stamps for her two sons who no longer live at home.

Questions

1. What feelings do you have about this case?

2. What, if anything, would you do about Mrs. Gugliotta's failure to report that her two sons had moved out of her home?

3. Discuss how you would have responded if Mrs. G. had been a less cooperative client when she worked with you. Would your actions be different if you no longer worked in the public welfare agency?

Case Problem 5

You are a social worker in the field office of a prominent legislator, working primarily on resolving constituent problems. Recently, a man called to complain that his wife, in her second trimester of pregnancy, was drinking heavily, often to the point of blackouts. He is concerned about the welfare of their child, and the possibility that it might be born with fetal alcohol syndrome. His wife insists that he has "forced her" to carry through with an unwanted pregnancy, and she doesn't care about the risk of damage. The caller has tried unsuccessfully to have his wife arrested or committed, so he is requesting your help in drafting a law to allow involuntary commitment under such conditions. The legislator you work for is skeptical of the cost and feasibility of such legislation, but the case is drawing attention from the media, and pressure is mounting to act in such cases.

Questions

1. What are your feelings about this case?

2. What impact would a policy allowing involuntary commitment have on those involved?

3. Would you develop the legislation being requested?

Case Problem 6

You are employed as a community organizer by a citizens' council in a neighborhood of a small city. An organization that serves developmentally delayed adults has purchased a large home in the neighborhood and plans to convert it into a group home for former residents of a state institution for retarded people. After a hearing in which concerns were expressed regarding issues such as safety and property values, the board of directors of the council voted to oppose the establishment of the group home in the neighborhood. You are instructed to "fight" the establishment of the group home. Your first task is to testify before the city's zoning commission at a hearing on the establishment of the group home.

Questions

1. How would you handle the council's instruction?

2. Is the issue of self-determination relevant to this case problem?

3. How would your views or actions differ if the council was predominantly white and those buying the home predominantly people of color? If you were a resident of the neighborhood? If you had a family member with mental retardation?

Case Problem 7

You are a social worker in an elementary school. You are starting a group for fifth graders who have experienced divorce in their families. Jane Yarrow is referred to you as a potential group member. Formerly an excellent student, Jane is now failing several courses. She is withdrawn and distracted and has begun stealing from classmates. Her parents divorced 6 months ago. You contact Mrs. Yarrow to get permission for Jane to join the group. Mrs. Yarrow refuses to allow Jane to join the group, stating that talking about the divorce just "stirs things up." She adds that Jane should forget the whole thing happened and should forget her father because she (Mrs. Yarrow) will never let Jane see her father again because of his leaving his family.

Mrs. Yarrow has left orders at school that her former husband is not to be allowed to see Jane at school. Soon after, Mr. Yarrow calls and asks if you can give him information on how Jane is doing. He states that he has joint legal custody of Jane and is worried about her well-being, stating that Jane has been calling him and begging him to see her.

Questions

1. What are your feelings toward the different members of the Yarrow family? How would these sympathies affect your choices in the case?

2. How would your feelings change if family history revealed that Mr. Yarrow had been abusive to his daughter and wife?

3. What would you do if Jane came to you asking to be allowed to see her father at school?

Case Problem 8

As a hospice worker, you have been assigned to work with Mr. Curtis, a 72-year-old Caucasian man in the end-stage of colon cancer. Your two previous visits with Mr. Curtis have gone well, yet you are troubled by his repeated disparaging and bigoted remarks about homosexuals and people of color. So far, you have tried to ignore his statements or change the subject, but everything—the news, previous workers, entertainers on TV—seems to provide him an opportunity to comment using racial slurs. Today, in discussing his finances, Mr. Curtis referred to his former business partner as a "kike" who "tried to jew me out of our profits." As a Jew yourself, you are troubled by his remark, but unsure whether you should respond, and if so how?

Questions

1. What values are at play in this case?

2. What actions might the social worker take, and what would be the pros and cons of those options?

3. What strategy or strategies might address the competing values in this situation?

Follow-Up

Identify those areas with which you struggled or that caused the most controversy in the class. What aspects are unresolved for you? What made you most uncomfortable? What other situations might involve the same types of issues?

After doing Exercise 4 on the Code of Ethics, return to these vignettes. Discuss the way(s) in which the code helped to clarify your actions in these situations.

_____

_____

_____

_____

_____

_____

_____

_____

_____

_____

_____

_____

_____

_____

_____

_____

_____

_____

_____

_____

_____

_____

EXERCISE 4 *Understanding and Using the NASW Code of Ethics*

Kim Strom-Gottfried

Purpose

1. To help you become familiar with the NASW Code of Ethics.
2. To examine how the code applies to a variety of case vignettes.
3. To determine factors that might lead to ethical concerns in certain cases.
4. To learn ways to practice ethically and avoid or resolve difficulties.

Background

In professions such as social work, ethical codes embody the values of the profession and guide the behavior of members. Our profession uses the Code of Ethics developed by the National Association of Social Workers (NASW). As you will soon see, the code does not always provide clear direction; in fact, sometimes, tenets of the code are in conflict with each other. Yet the code is a useful tool for identifying possible areas of difficulty, and it offers guidelines for social workers as they interact with clients and fellow professionals. "Knowing the code" is an essential first step in using it as a resource for practice decisions.

Instructions

This exercise will walk you through the code section by section. Key segments will be followed by case scenarios. Some of these vignettes demonstrate situations that clearly violate the code. Other scenarios may be less clear and will force you to look at the information from different perspectives, identifying key information that is still needed or identifying competing values at play in the case.

Begin by reading the code's Overview, Preamble, and Purpose and address the questions in the boxes. After that, read each of the following sections and discuss any questions or confusing points with your instructor. After each section, read the case vignette(s) and answer the questions that follow, either in writing or in discussion with your group. As you make decisions on cases, you may want to mark the section of the code on which you based your answer.

EXERCISE 4

Code of Ethics of the National Association of Social Workers
as adopted by the Delegate Assembly of August 1996

Overview

The National Association of Social Workers Code of Ethics is intended to serve as a guide to the everyday professional conduct of social workers. This code includes four sections. Section 1, "Preamble," summarizes the social work profession's mission and core values. Section 2, "Purpose of the Code of Ethics," provides an overview of the Code's main functions and a brief guide for dealing with ethical issues or dilemmas in social work practice. Section 3, "Ethical Principles," presents broad ethical principles, based on social work's core values, that inform social work practice. The final section, "Ethical Standards," includes specific ethical standards to guide social workers' conduct and to provide a basis for adjudication.

Preamble

The primary mission of the social work profession is to enhance human well-being and help meet the basic human needs of all people, with particular attention to the needs and empowerment of people who are vulnerable, oppressed, and living in poverty. A historic and defining feature of social work is the profession's focus on individual well-being in a social context and the well-being of society. Fundamental to social work is attention to the environmental forces that create, contribute to, and address problems in living.

Social workers promote social justice and social change with and on behalf of clients. "Clients" is used inclusively to refer to individuals, families, groups, organizations, and communities. Social workers are sensitive to cultural and ethnic diversity and strive to end discrimination, oppression, poverty, and other forms of social injustice. These activities may be in the form of direct practice, community organizing, supervision, consultation, administration, advocacy, social and political action, policy development and implementation, education, and research and evaluation. Social workers seek to enhance the capacity of people to address their own needs. Social workers also seek to promote the responsiveness of organizations, communities, and other social institutions to individuals' needs and social problems.

The mission of the social work profession is rooted in a set of core values. These core values, embraced by social workers throughout the profession's history, are the foundation of social work's unique purpose and perspective:

- Service
- Social justice
- Dignity and worth of the person
- Importance of human relationships
- Integrity
- Competence

This constellation of core values reflects what is unique to the social work profession. Core values, and the principles that flow from them, must be balanced within the context and complexity of the human experience.

Purpose of the NASW Code of Ethics

Professional ethics are at the core of social work. The profession has an obligation to articulate its basic values, ethical principles, and ethical standards. The NASW Code of Ethics sets forth these values, principles, and standards to guide social workers' conduct. The Code is relevant to all social workers and social work students, regardless of their professional functions, the settings in which they work, or the populations they serve.

The NASW Code of Ethics serves six purposes:

1. The Code identifies core values on which social work's mission is based.

2. The Code summarizes broad ethical principles that reflect the profession's core values and establishes a set of specific ethical standards that should be used to guide social work practice.

3. The Code is designed to help social workers identify relevant considerations when professional obligations conflict or ethical uncertainties arise.

4. The Code provides ethical standards to which the general public can hold the social work profession accountable.

5. The Code socializes practitioners new to the field to social work's mission, values, ethical principles, and ethical standards.

6. The Code articulates standards that the social work profession itself can use to assess whether social workers have engaged in unethical conduct. NASW has formal procedures to adjudicate ethics complaints filed against its members. In subscribing to this Code, social workers are required to cooperate in its implementation, participate in NASW adjudication proceedings, and abide by any NASW disciplinary rulings or sanctions based on it.

The Code offers a set of values, principles, and standards to guide decision making and conduct when ethical issues arise. It does not provide a set of rules that prescribe how social workers should act in all situations. Specific applications of the Code must take into account the context in which it is being considered and the possibility of conflicts among the Code's values, principles, and standards. Ethical responsibilities flow from all human relationships, from the personal and familial to the social and professional.

Further, the NASW Code of Ethics does not specify which values, principles, and standards are most important and ought to outweigh others in instances when they conflict. Reasonable differences of opinion can and do exist among social workers with respect to the ways in which values, ethical principles, and ethical standards should be rank ordered when they conflict. Ethical decision making in a given situation must apply the informed judgment of the individual social worker and should also consider how the issues would be judged in a peer review process where the ethical standards of the profession would be applied.

Ethical decision making is a process. There are many instances in social work where simple answers are not available to resolve complex ethical issues. Social workers should take into consideration all the values, principles, and standards in this Code that are relevant to any situation in which ethical judgment is warranted. Social workers' decisions and actions should be consistent with the spirit as well as the letter of this Code.

In addition to this Code, there are many other sources of information about ethical thinking that may be useful. Social workers should consider ethical theory and principles generally, social work theory and research, laws, regulations, agency policies, and other relevant codes of ethics, recognizing that among codes of ethics social workers should consider the NASW Code of Ethics as their primary source. Social workers also should be aware of the impact on ethical decision making of their clients' and their own personal values and cultural and religious beliefs and practices. They should be aware of any conflicts between personal and professional values and deal with them responsibly. For additional guidance social workers should consult the relevant literature on professional ethics and ethical decision making and seek appropriate consultation when faced with ethical dilemmas. This may involve consultation with an agency-based or social work organization's ethics committee, a regulatory body, knowledgeable colleagues, supervisors, or legal counsel.

Instances may arise when social workers' ethical obligations conflict with agency policies or relevant laws or regulations. When such conflicts occur, social workers must make a responsible effort to resolve the conflict in a manner that is consistent with the values, principles, and standards expressed in this Code. If a reasonable resolution of the conflict does not appear possible, social workers should seek proper consultation before making a decision.

The NASW Code of Ethics is to be used by NASW and by individuals, agencies, organizations, and bodies (such as licensing and regulatory boards, professional liability insurance providers, courts of law, agency boards of directors, government agencies, and other professional groups) that choose to adopt it or use it as a frame of reference. Violation of standards in this Code does not automatically imply legal liability or violation of the law. Such determination can only be made in the context of legal and judicial proceedings. Alleged violations of the Code would be subject to a peer review process. Such processes are generally separate from legal or administrative procedures and insulated from legal review or proceedings to allow the profession to counsel and discipline its own members.

A code of ethics cannot guarantee ethical behavior. Moreover, a code of ethics cannot resolve all ethical issues or disputes or capture the richness and complexity involved in striving to make responsible choices within a moral community. Rather, a code of ethics sets forth values, ethical principles, and ethical standards to which professionals aspire and by which their actions can be judged. Social workers' ethical behavior should result from their personal commitment to engage in ethical practice. The NASW Code of Ethics reflects the commitment of all social workers to uphold the profession's values and to act ethically. Principles and standards must be applied by individuals of good character who discern moral questions and, in good faith, seek to make reliable ethical judgments.

Discussion Questions

1. Why is the Code of Ethics necessary?
2. Who is expected to abide by the NASW Code of Ethics?
3. What steps should be taken when the code offers unclear or conflicting guidelines?
4. What happens when someone violates the Code of Ethics?

Ethical Principles

The following broad ethical principles are based on social work's core values of service, social justice, dignity and worth of the person, importance of human relationships, integrity, and competence. These principles set forth ideals to which all social workers should aspire.

Value: Service

Ethical Principle: Social workers' primary goal is to help people in need and to address social problems.

Social workers elevate service to others above self-interest. Social workers draw on their knowledge, values, and skills to help people in need and to address social problems. Social workers are encouraged to volunteer some portion of their professional skills with no expectation of significant financial return (pro bono service).

Value: Social justice

Ethical Principle: Social workers challenge social injustice.

Social workers pursue social change, particularly with and on behalf of vulnerable and oppressed individuals and groups of people. Social workers' social change efforts are focused primarily on issues of poverty, unemployment, discrimination, and other forms of social injustice. These activities seek to promote sensitivity to and knowledge about oppression and cultural and ethnic diversity. Social workers strive to ensure access to needed information, services, and resources; equality of opportunity; and meaningful participation in decision making for all people.

Value: Dignity and worth of the person

Ethical Principle: Social workers respect the inherent dignity and worth of the person.

Social workers treat each person in a caring and respectful fashion, mindful of individual differences and cultural and ethnic diversity. Social workers promote clients' socially responsible self-determination. Social workers seek to enhance clients' capacity and opportunity to change and to address their own needs. Social workers are cognizant of their dual responsibility to clients and to the broader society. They seek to resolve conflicts between clients' interests and the broader society's interests in a socially responsible manner consistent with the values, ethical principles, and ethical standards of the profession.

Value: Importance of human relationships

Ethical Principle: Social workers recognize the central importance of human relationships.

Social workers understand that relationships between and among people are an important vehicle for change. Social workers engage people as partners in the helping process. Social workers seek to strengthen relationships among people in a purposeful effort to promote, restore, maintain, and enhance the well-being of individuals, families, social groups, organizations, and communities.

Value: Integrity

Ethical Principle: Social workers behave in a trustworthy manner.

Social workers are continually aware of the profession's mission, values, ethical principles, and ethical standards and practice in a manner consistent with them. Social workers act honestly and responsibly and promote ethical practices on the part of the organizations with which they are affiliated.

Value: Competence

Ethical Principle: Social workers practice within their areas of competence and develop and enhance their professional expertise.

Social workers continually strive to increase their professional knowledge and skills and to apply them in practice. Social workers should aspire to contribute to the knowledge base of the profession.

Ethical Standards

The following ethical standards are relevant to the professional activities of all social workers. These standards concern (1) social workers' ethical responsibilities to clients, (2) social workers' ethical responsibilities to colleagues, (3) social workers' ethical responsibilities in practice settings, (4) social workers' ethical responsibilities as professionals, (5) social workers' ethical responsibilities to the social work profession, and (6) social workers' ethical responsibilities to the broader society.

Some of the standards that follow are enforceable guidelines for professional conduct, and some are aspirational. The extent to which each standard is enforceable is a matter of professional judgment to be exercised by those responsible for reviewing alleged violations of ethical standards.

1. SOCIAL WORKERS' ETHICAL RESPONSIBILITIES TO CLIENTS

1.01 Commitment to Clients

Social workers' primary responsibility is to promote the well-being of clients. In general, clients' interests are primary. However, social workers' responsibility to the larger society or specific legal obligations may on limited occasions supersede the loyalty owed clients, and clients should be so advised. (Examples include when a social worker is required by law to report that a client has abused a child or has threatened to harm self or others.)

Self-Determination—Cases 1 and 2

1. Linda is a home health care manager. She has been seeing Mr. and Mrs. Jones for over a year. Mrs. Jones is suffering from advanced stages of dementia, and her husband, age 82, is committed to caring for her at home. Their son lives in another state, they have few friends still living, and Mr. Jones refuses respite services due to his wife's extreme fear of change and of strangers. Due to Mr. Jones's frail condition, Linda has become increasingly concerned about his capacity to care for his wife, yet he has consistently refused to consider other options.

   A. What issues must Linda consider as she attempts to meet her ethical responsibility in this case?

   B. Would Linda be violating the code if she arranged respite care or a placement for Mrs. Jones?

   C. What information or circumstances might move your decision in one direction or another?

   D. What options are available to practice ethically and honor Mr. Jones's wishes?

2. Juan is a social worker in a program for street kids. He has been working with Jim for several months, encouraging Jim to find stable housing and a less self-destructive lifestyle. Jim has told Juan that he is HIV+ and feels his life is, for all intents and purposes, over. Recently, Jim brought his new girlfriend, Karen, in with him for a meal at the shelter. The following day, Juan spoke with Jim about his HIV+ status and Karen's safety. Jim rejected Juan's advice that he tell Karen about his status, but now Juan wonders if he should tell her himself or respect Jim's choice.

   A. Is it ethical to support Jim's self-determination in this case?

   B. Would Juan be violating the Code of Ethics? If so, how?

   C. What information or circumstances might move your decision in one direction or another?

   D. What steps could Juan take to resolve his ethical dilemma?

1.02 Self-Determination

Social workers respect and promote the right of clients to self-determination and assist clients in their efforts to identify and clarify their goals. Social workers may limit clients' right to self-determination when, in the social workers' professional judgment, clients' actions or potential actions pose a serious, foreseeable, and imminent risk to themselves or others.

1.03 Informed Consent

(a) Social workers should provide services to clients only in the context of a professional relationship based, when appropriate, on valid informed consent. Social workers should use clear and understandable language to inform clients of the purpose of the services, risks related to the services, limits to services because of the requirements of a third-party payer, relevant costs, reasonable alternatives, clients' right to refuse or withdraw consent, and the time frame covered by the consent. Social workers should provide clients with an opportunity to ask questions.

(b) In instances when clients are not literate or have difficulty understanding the primary language used in the practice setting, social workers should take steps to ensure clients' comprehension. This may include providing clients with a detailed verbal explanation or arranging for a qualified interpreter or translator whenever possible.

(c) In instances when clients lack the capacity to provide informed consent, social workers should protect clients' interests by seeking permission from an appropriate third party, informing clients consistent with the clients' level of understanding. In such instances social workers should seek to ensure that the third party acts in a manner consistent with clients' wishes and interests. Social workers should take reasonable steps to enhance such clients' ability to give informed consent.

(d) In instances when clients are receiving services involuntarily, social workers should provide information about the nature and extent of services and about the extent of clients' right to refuse service.

(e) Social workers who provide services via electronic media (such as computer, telephone, radio, and television) should inform recipients of the limitations and risks associated with such services.

(f) Social workers should obtain clients' informed consent before audiotaping or videotaping clients or permitting observation of services to clients by a third party.

Informed Consent—Case 3

3. Eileen is a hospital social work intern whose primary responsibility is discharge planning for patients on the medical/surgical units of her facility. Mrs. Rose is a divorced, 40-year-old mother of two who was hospitalized for the removal of a cancerous tumor and her right breast. In meeting with Mrs. Rose following her admission to the hospital, Eileen explains that if there are no complications, she can expect to be discharged the following day. Mrs. Rose expresses alarm at this, raising concerns about her ability to care for herself postoperatively and questioning who is making this decision. Eileen explains that the doctors will make the decision and assures her that she won't be sent home if she's in medical distress, but acknowledges that in part the discharge is determined by her health insurance, which allows only 24 hours of hospitalization for such a procedure. She informs Mrs. Rose of the appeal procedures available within the hospital and within her health plan and suggests that she use them if she is dissatisfied with the care she is given.

   The following day, Eileen is approached by her supervisor, who has been informed by both the hospital quality assurance director and an insurance company representative that Eileen is "stirring up trouble" and "disrupting" Mrs. Rose's care. Her supervisor is concerned that her

---

Informed Consent—Case 3 (continued)

actions reflect negatively on the social services department as a whole, at a time when the hospital is looking for ways to downsize, and she is concerned that the insurance company may make fewer referrals or be less cooperative on future cases, due to Eileen's actions.

A. Do Eileen's actions in this case reflect a violation of the Code of Ethics? If so, how?

B. Are the supervisor's criticisms indicative of a violation of the code? If so, how?

C. What information or circumstances might move your decision in one direction or another?

D. What steps can workers take if they feel their employers' policies are contrary to their professional ethics?

1.04 Competence

(a) Social workers should provide services and represent themselves as competent only within the boundaries of their education, training, license, certification, consultation received, supervised experience, or other relevant professional experience.

(b) Social workers should provide services in substantive areas or use intervention techniques or approaches that are new to them only after engaging in appropriate study, training, consultation, and supervision from people who are competent in those interventions or techniques.

(c) When generally recognized standards do not exist with respect to an emerging area of practice, social workers should exercise careful judgment and take responsible steps (including appropriate education, research, training, consultation, and supervision) to ensure the competence of their work and to protect clients from harm.

1.05 Cultural Competence and Social Diversity

(a) Social workers should understand culture and its function in human behavior and society, recognizing the strengths that exist in all cultures.

(b) Social workers should have a knowledge base of their clients' cultures and be able to demonstrate competence in the provision of services that are sensitive to clients' cultures and to differences among people and cultural groups.

(c) Social workers should obtain education about and seek to understand the nature of social diversity and oppression with respect to race, ethnicity, national origin, color, sex, sexual orientation, age, marital status, political belief, religion, and mental or physical disability.

Competence—Case 4

4. Jackie attended an exciting workshop on the "parentified child" and has come to see that much of her work with women in recovery focuses on this issue. She has done reading on the concept and discusses it regularly over lunch with a colleague who shares her interest. Lately, she has begun to focus her work with clients not on their substance use and relapse issues, but on the childhood issues that she feels may be contributing to their addictive behavior. She feels it would be unethical to continue "treating the symptoms and not the underlying problem."

A. Is Jackie in violation of the Code of Ethics?

B. What activities would assure you that she has met the standard of competence?

1.06 Conflicts of Interest

(a) Social workers should be alert to and avoid conflicts of interest that interfere with the exercise of professional discretion and impartial judgment. Social workers should inform clients when a real or potential conflict of interest arises and take reasonable steps to resolve the issue in a manner that makes the clients' interests primary and protects clients' interests to the greatest extent possible. In some cases, protecting clients' interests may require termination of the professional relationship with proper referral of the client.

(b) Social workers should not take unfair advantage of any professional relationship or exploit others to further their personal, religious, political, or business interests.

(c) Social workers should not engage in dual or multiple relationships with clients or former clients in which there is a risk of exploitation or potential harm to the client. In instances when dual or multiple relationships are unavoidable, social workers should take steps to protect clients and are responsible for setting clear, appropriate, and culturally sensitive boundaries. (Dual or multiple relationships occur when social workers relate to clients in more than one relationship, whether professional, social, or business. Dual or multiple relationships can occur simultaneously or consecutively.)

(d) When social workers provide services to two or more people who have a relationship with each other (for example, couples, family members), social workers should clarify with all parties which individuals will be considered clients and the nature of social workers' professional obligations to the various individuals who are receiving services. Social workers who anticipate a conflict of interest among the individuals receiving services or who anticipate having to perform in potentially conflicting roles (for example, when a social worker is asked to testify in a child custody dispute or divorce proceedings involving clients) should clarify their role with the parties involved and take appropriate action to minimize any conflict of interest.

Dual Relationships—Case 5

5. Professor Salter teaches the only section of a required course in a small MSW program. This fall a student (Jane) whom he had seen in treatment 3 years before is enrolled in his section. Because many of the issues for treatment involved Jane's difficulties with boundaries and authority figures, Professor Salter is apprehensive about what will occur in the class.

   A. Will having Jane as a student constitute a violation of the code? How?

   B. What steps can he take to make sure that their student-teacher relationship is not affected by their previous relationship?

   C. Should Professor Salter discuss the issue with Jane prior to the class?

1.07 Privacy and Confidentiality

(a) Social workers should respect clients' right to privacy. Social workers should not solicit private information from clients unless it is essential to providing services or conducting social work evaluation or research. Once private information is shared, standards of confidentiality apply.

(b) Social workers may disclose confidential information when appropriate with valid consent from a client or a person legally authorized to consent on behalf of a client.

(c) Social workers should protect the confidentiality of all information obtained in the course of professional service, except for compelling professional reasons. The general expectation that social workers will keep information confidential does not apply when disclosure is necessary to prevent serious, foreseeable, and imminent harm to a client or other identifiable persons or when laws or regulations require disclosure without a client's consent. In all instances, social workers should disclose the least amount of confidential information necessary to achieve the desired purpose; only information that is directly relevant to the purpose for which the disclosure is made should be revealed.

(d) Social workers should inform clients, to the extent possible, about the disclosure of confidential information and the potential consequences, when feasible before the disclosure is made. This applies whether social workers disclose confidential information on the basis of a legal requirement or client consent.

(e) Social workers should discuss with clients and other interested parties the nature of confidentiality and limitations of clients' right to confidentiality. Social workers should review with clients circumstances where confidential information may be requested and where disclosure of confidential information may be legally required. This discussion should occur as soon as possible in the social worker-client relationship and as needed throughout the course of the relationship.

(f) When social workers provide counseling services to families, couples, or groups, social workers should seek agreement among the parties involved concerning each individual's right to confidentiality and obligation to preserve the confidentiality of information shared by others. Social workers should inform participants in family, couples, or group counseling that social workers cannot guarantee that all participants will honor such agreements.

(g) Social workers should inform clients involved in family, couples, marital, or group counseling of the social worker's, employer's, and agency's policy concerning the social worker's disclosure of confidential information among the parties involved in the counseling.

(h) Social workers should not disclose confidential information to third-party payers unless clients have authorized such disclosure.

(i) Social workers should not discuss confidential information in any setting unless privacy can be ensured. Social workers should not discuss confidential information in public or semipublic areas such as hallways, waiting rooms, elevators, and restaurants.

(j) Social workers should protect the confidentiality of clients during legal proceedings to the extent permitted by law. When a court of law or other legally authorized body orders social workers to disclose confidential or privileged information without a client's consent and such disclosure could cause harm to the client, social workers should request that the court withdraw the order or limit the order as narrowly as possible or maintain the records under seal, unavailable for public inspection.

(k) Social workers should protect the confidentiality of clients when responding to requests from members of the media.

(l) Social workers should protect the confidentiality of clients' written and electronic records and other sensitive information. Social workers should take reasonable steps to ensure that clients' records are stored in a secure location and that clients' records are not available to others who are not authorized to have access.

(m) Social workers should take precautions to ensure and maintain the confidentiality of information transmitted to other parties through the use of computers, electronic mail, facsimile machines, telephones and telephone answering machines, and other electronic or computer technology. Disclosure of identifying information should be avoided whenever possible.

(n) Social workers should transfer or dispose of clients' records in a manner that protects clients' confidentiality and is consistent with state statutes governing records and social work licensure.

(o) Social workers should take reasonable precautions to protect client confidentiality in the event of the social worker's termination of practice, incapacitation, or death.

(p) Social workers should not disclose identifying information when discussing clients for teaching or training purposes unless the client has consented to disclosure of confidential information.

(q) Social workers should not disclose identifying information when discussing clients with consultants unless the client has consented to disclosure of confidential information or there is a compelling need for such disclosure.

(r) Social workers should protect the confidentiality of deceased clients consistent with the preceding standards.

1.08 Access to Records

(a) Social workers should provide clients with reasonable access to records concerning the clients. Social workers who are concerned that clients' access to their records could cause serious misunderstanding or harm to the client should provide assistance in interpreting the records and consultation with the client regarding the records. Social workers should limit clients' access to their records, or portions of their records, only in exceptional circumstances when there is compelling evidence that such access would cause serious harm to the client. Both clients' requests and the rationale for withholding some or all of the record should be documented in clients' files.

(b) When providing clients with access to their records, social workers should take steps to protect the confidentiality of other individuals identified or discussed in such records.

Privacy and Confidentiality—Cases 6, 7, and 8

6. Gail and Louise are domestic violence workers who provide outreach services at the local courthouse. Because of the lack of an available private office, they conduct their peer supervision at a local coffeehouse, being careful only to identify their clients by their first names.

    A. Does this violate the Code of Ethics?

    B. What information or circumstances might move your decision in one direction or another?

    C. What other choices are available to Gail and Louise?

7. Al saw Dale and his wife for several sessions of couples counseling. The day after one of their sessions, Dale called Al in an agitated state and said he "would not live without his wife." When he hung up abruptly, Al tried to call him back, with no luck. Because he had other clients waiting, he took no further action. Later that night, he found out that Dale had killed his wife and himself. In responding to calls from the local newspaper and the police, Al acknowledged that Dale had called him, distraught, earlier in the day.

    A. Did any of Al's actions or inactions violate the Code of Ethics?

    B. If so, how?

    C. What steps can be taken to practice ethically to decide what actions to take?

8. Refer back to Case 2. How does the information in this section of the code affect your decision making about reporting HIV status to a client's partner?

1.09 Sexual Relationships

(a) Social workers should under no circumstances engage in sexual activities or sexual contact with current clients, whether such contact is consensual or forced.

(b) Social workers should not engage in sexual activities or sexual contact with clients' relatives or other individuals with whom clients maintain a close personal relationship when there is a risk of exploitation or potential harm to the client. Sexual activity or sexual contact with clients' relatives or other individuals with whom clients maintain a personal relationship has the potential to be harmful to the client and may make it difficult for the social worker and client to maintain appropriate professional boundaries. Social workers—not their clients, their clients' relatives, or other individuals with whom the client maintains a personal relationship—assume the full burden for setting clear, appropriate, and culturally sensitive boundaries.

(c) Social workers should not engage in sexual activities or sexual contact with former clients because of the potential for harm to the client. If social workers engage in conduct contrary to this prohibition or claim that an exception to this prohibition is warranted because of extraordinary circumstances, it is social workers—not their clients—who assume the full burden of demonstrating that the former client has not been exploited, coerced, or manipulated, intentionally or unintentionally.

(d) Social workers should not provide clinical services to individuals with whom they have had a prior sexual relationship. Providing clinical services to a former sexual partner has the potential to be harmful to the individual and is likely to make it difficult for the social worker and individual to maintain appropriate professional boundaries.

1.10 Physical Contact

Social workers should not engage in physical contact with clients when there is a possibility of psychological harm to the client as a result of the contact (such as cradling or caressing clients). Social workers who engage in appropriate physical contact with clients are responsible for setting clear, appropriate, and culturally sensitive boundaries that govern such physical contact.

1.11 Sexual Harassment

Social workers should not sexually harass clients. Sexual harassment includes sexual advances, sexual solicitation, requests for sexual favors, and other verbal or physical conduct of a sexual nature.

1.12 Derogatory Language

Social workers should not use derogatory language in their written or verbal communications to or about clients. Social workers should use accurate and respectful language in all communications to and about clients.

1.13 Payment for Services

(a) When setting fees, social workers should ensure that the fees are fair, reasonable, and commensurate with the services performed. Consideration should be given to clients' ability to pay.

(b) Social workers should avoid accepting goods or services from clients as payment for professional services. Bartering arrangements, particularly involving services, create the potential for conflicts of interest, exploitation, and inappropriate boundaries in social workers' relationships with clients. Social workers should explore and may participate in bartering only in very limited circumstances when it can be demonstrated that such arrangements are an accepted practice among professionals in the local community, considered to be essential for the provision of services, negotiated without coercion, and entered into at the client's initiative and with the client's informed consent. Social workers who accept goods or services from clients as payment for professional services assume the full burden of demonstrating that this arrangement will not be detrimental to the client or the professional relationship.

(c) Social workers should not solicit a private fee or other remuneration for providing services to clients who are entitled to such available services through the social workers' employer or agency.

1.14 Clients Who Lack Decision-Making Capacity

When social workers act on behalf of clients who lack the capacity to make informed decisions, social workers should take reasonable steps to safeguard the interests and rights of those clients.

1.15 Interruption of Services

Social workers should make reasonable efforts to ensure continuity of services in the event that services are interrupted by factors such as unavailability, relocation, illness, disability, or death.

Sexual Relationships—Case 9

9. Jack attended a 6-week men's group that Tim facilitated several years ago. Recently, the two met again at the home of a mutual friend, and have since developed an intimate relationship.

   A. Does this relationship constitute a violation of the Code of Ethics?

   B. If the intimacy is not sexual, does that change your decision?

   C. What other information or circumstances might move your decision in one direction or another?

   D. Is there any way for Tim and Jack to have a relationship that is not in violation of the code?

1.16 Termination of Services

(a) Social workers should terminate services to clients and professional relationships with them when such services and relationships are no longer required or no longer serve the clients' needs or interests.

(b) Social workers should take reasonable steps to avoid abandoning clients who are still in need of services. Social workers should withdraw services precipitously only under unusual circumstances, giving careful consideration to all factors in the situation and taking care to minimize possible adverse effects. Social workers should assist in making appropriate arrangements for continuation of services when necessary.

(c) Social workers in fee-for-service settings may terminate services to clients who are not paying an overdue balance if the financial contractual arrangements have been made clear to the client, if the client does not pose an imminent danger to self or others, and if the clinical and other consequences of the current nonpayment have been addressed and discussed with the client.

(d) Social workers should not terminate services to pursue a social, financial, or sexual relationship with a client.

(e) Social workers who anticipate the termination or interruption of services to clients should notify clients promptly and seek the transfer, referral, or continuation of services in relation to the clients' needs and preferences.

(f) Social workers who are leaving an employment setting should inform clients of appropriate options for the continuation of services and of the benefits and risks of the options.

2.10 Incompetence of Colleagues

(a) Social workers who have direct knowledge of a social work colleague's incompetence should consult with that colleague when feasible and assist the colleague in taking remedial action.

(b) Social workers who believe that a social work colleague is incompetent and has not taken adequate steps to address the incompetence should take action through appropriate channels established by employers, agencies, NASW, licensing and regulatory bodies, and other professional organizations.

Impairment of Colleagues—Case 11

11. You are a faculty member at a small school of social work. A student asks to speak with you about another faculty member, who is also the program director. She and her classmates are concerned that on at least two occasions this instructor has come to class intoxicated. The student states they can "smell liquor on his breath," that he repeats himself and his presentations are sometimes incoherent. The student states that on other occasions he is an outstanding teacher and that her main concern is that other students are "planning a revolt" and refusing to accept his grades on assignments, believing that he may have been intoxicated when reviewing their work. You understand the students' concerns. In addition, knowing that the faculty member is in private practice, you are worried that clients may also be adversely affected.

    A. Has the faculty member violated the Code of Ethics?

    B. If so, how?

    C. What information or circumstances might move your decision in one direction or another?

    D. What responsibility does the student have under the code? What responsibility do you have?

    E. What steps should you take to address this colleague's problems, as reported by the student?

2.11 Unethical Conduct of Colleagues

(a) Social workers should take adequate measures to discourage, prevent, expose, and correct the unethical conduct of colleagues.

(b) Social workers should be knowledgeable about established policies and procedures for handling concerns about colleagues' unethical behavior. Social workers should be familiar with national, state, and local procedures for handling ethics complaints. These include policies and procedures created by NASW, licensing and regulatory bodies, employers, agencies, and other professional organizations.

(c) Social workers who believe that a colleague has acted unethically should seek resolution by discussing their concerns with the colleague when feasible and when such discussion is likely to be productive.

(d) When necessary, social workers who believe that a colleague has acted unethically should take action through appropriate formal channels (such as contacting a state licensing board or regulatory body, an NASW committee on inquiry, or other professional ethics committees).

(e) Social workers should defend and assist colleagues who are unjustly charged with unethical conduct.

Incompetence of Colleagues—Case 12

12. Sarah works in a residential facility. For months, she and her colleagues have been complaining about another staff member, Elden. When they come in after his shift, the clients' records are incomplete or in disarray. He seems to allow disputes to escalate among residents, saying it is "reality therapy" for them to work it out among themselves, yet Sarah (and some of the other residents) fear that someone may get hurt if things get out of control. Despite his "hands off" attitude, Elden repeatedly gets into power struggles with the clients, leading to a lot of strife within the residence. Elden's treatment plans seem "off the wall" and are always overruled in team meetings, yet he refuses the input of other workers. The staff is angry at his behavior and frustrated that the director of the facility seems unwilling to do anything about Elden's ineptitude.

A. Is Elden in violation of the Code of Ethics?

B. What information or circumstances might move your decision in one direction or another?

C. What steps should Elden's colleagues take? Should they file an ethics complaint with NASW?

---

3. SOCIAL WORKERS' ETHICAL RESPONSIBILITIES IN PRACTICE SETTINGS

3.01 Supervision and Consultation

(a) Social workers who provide supervision or consultation should have the necessary knowledge and skill to supervise or consult appropriately and should do so only within their areas of knowledge and competence.

(b) Social workers who provide supervision or consultation are responsible for setting clear, appropriate, and culturally sensitive boundaries.

(c) Social workers should not engage in any dual or multiple relationships with supervisees in which there is a risk of exploitation of or potential harm to the supervisee.

(d) Social workers who provide supervision should evaluate supervisees' performance in a manner that is fair and respectful.

3.02 Education and Training

(a) Social workers who function as educators, field instructors for students, or trainers should provide instruction only within their areas of knowledge and competence and should provide instruction based on the most current information and knowledge available in the profession.

(b) Social workers who function as educators or field instructors for students should evaluate students' performance in a manner that is fair and respectful.

(c) Social workers who function as educators or field instructors for students should take reasonable steps to ensure that clients are routinely informed when services are being provided by students.

(d) Social workers who function as educators or field instructors for students should not engage in any dual or multiple relationships with students in which there is a risk of exploitation or potential harm to the student. Social work educators and field instructors are responsible for setting clear, appropriate, and culturally sensitive boundaries.

3.03 Performance Evaluation

Social workers who have responsibility for evaluating the performance of others should fulfill such responsibility in a fair and considerate manner and on the basis of clearly stated criteria.

3.04 Client Records

(a) Social workers should take reasonable steps to ensure that documentation in records is accurate and reflects the services provided.

(b) Social workers should include sufficient and timely documentation in records to facilitate the delivery of services and to ensure continuity of services provided to clients in the future.

(c) Social workers' documentation should protect clients' privacy to the extent that is possible and appropriate and should include only information that is directly relevant to the delivery of services.

(d) Social workers should store records following the termination of services to ensure reasonable future access. Records should be maintained for the number of years required by state statutes or relevant contracts.

3.05 Billing

Social workers should establish and maintain billing practices that accurately reflect the nature and extent of services provided and that identify who provided the service in the practice setting.

3.06 Client Transfer

(a) When an individual who is receiving services from another agency or colleague contacts a social worker for services, the social worker should carefully consider the client's needs before agreeing to provide services. To minimize possible confusion and conflict, social workers should discuss with potential clients the nature of the clients' current relationship with other service providers and the implications, including possible benefits or risks, of entering into a relationship with a new service provider.

(b) If a new client has been served by another agency or colleague, social workers should discuss with the client whether consultation with the previous service provider is in the client's best interest.

3.07 Administration

(a) Social work administrators should advocate within and outside their agencies for adequate resources to meet clients' needs.

(b) Social workers should advocate for resource allocation procedures that are open and fair. When not all clients' needs can be met, an allocation procedure should be developed that is nondiscriminatory and based on appropriate and consistently applied principles.

(c) Social workers who are administrators should take reasonable steps to ensure that adequate agency or organizational resources are available to provide appropriate staff supervision.

(d) Social work administrators should take reasonable steps to ensure that the working environment for which they are responsible is consistent with and encourages compliance with the NASW Code of Ethics. Social work administrators should take reasonable steps to eliminate any conditions in their organizations that violate, interfere with, or discourage compliance with the Code.

3.08 Continuing Education and Staff Development

Social work administrators and supervisors should take reasonable steps to provide or arrange for continuing education and staff development for all staff for whom they are responsible. Continuing education and staff development should address current knowledge and emerging developments related to social work practice and ethics.

Supervision and Consultation—Cases 13 and 14

13. Fred is the administrator of a small nursing home. In his role, he supervises all the managers and many of the clerical staff. Recently, he began dating Jeanine, the facility's MIS (management information system) manager.

    A. Are Fred's actions in violation of the Code of Ethics?

    B. If so, how?

    C. What information or circumstances might move your decision in one direction or another?

    D. How can Fred assure he is not in violation of the code?

14. Alex supervises a unit of 20 child protection workers. The volume of work is such that he often provides supervisory advice "on the run," though he feels he's there when people need him. He also holds biweekly staff meetings that he considers a form of group supervision. Recently, a complaint was lodged against one of his workers by a client, and now the worker is blaming Alex for the mistake.

    A. Are Alex's supervisory practices in keeping with the Code of Ethics?

    B. What information or circumstances might move your decision in one direction or another?

    C. How can busy supervisors assure they are meeting their ethical responsibilities?

3.09 Commitments to Employers

   (a) Social workers generally should adhere to commitments made to employers and employing organizations.

   (b) Social workers should work to improve employing agencies' policies and procedures and the efficiency and effectiveness of their services.

   (c) Social workers should take reasonable steps to ensure that employers are aware of social workers' ethical obligations as set forth in the NASW Code of Ethics and of the implications of those obligations for social work practice.

   (d) Social workers should not allow an employing organization's policies, procedures, regulations, or administrative orders to interfere with their ethical practice of social work. Social workers should take reasonable steps to ensure that their employing organizations' practices are consistent with the NASW Code of Ethics.

   (e) Social workers should act to prevent and eliminate discrimination in the employing organization's work assignments and in its employment policies and practices.

   (f) Social workers should accept employment or arrange student field placements only in organizations that exercise fair personnel practices.

   (g) Social workers should be diligent stewards of the resources of their employing organizations, wisely conserving funds where appropriate and never misappropriating funds or using them for unintended purposes.

   3.10 Labor-Management Disputes

   (a) Social workers may engage in organized action, including the formation of and participation in labor unions, to improve services to clients and working conditions.

(b) The actions of social workers who are involved in labor-management disputes, job actions, or labor strikes should be guided by the profession's values, ethical principles, and ethical standards. Reasonable differences of opinion exist among social workers concerning their primary obligation as professionals during an actual or threatened labor strike or job action. Social workers should carefully examine relevant issues and their possible impact on clients before deciding on a course of action.

Commitments to Employers—Case 15

15. Andrew is a social work student placed in a small group mental health practice. The practice has recently been accepted as a preferred provider for a large managed care firm. In a staff meeting where the procedures for the managed care contract were discussed, the administrator described the records that the firm would keep on the practice. To assure that they were providing effective and efficient services, their service statistics would be compared with other providers and their performance would be rated from time to time in a "report card."

    Later that month, as part of his community relations responsibilities at the agency, Andrew spoke with a group of parents of severely disturbed adults about the nature of mental illness and the services his organization offered. Several of the families followed up with phone calls to the agency to seek services, yet Andrew was surprised to find that none were offered intake appointments. When he asked the administrator about this, he was told, "They're not the kind of people we want to serve. We know they need help and are eligible for our services, but our effectiveness ratings will go way down if we take multiproblem cases like that. Then we won't get to serve anybody."

    A. In what areas is this case in violation with the code?

    B. How can Andrew maintain his commitment to his employer if he feels the employer's policies are unfair?

    C. Who should Andrew talk with about his concerns?

---

4. SOCIAL WORKERS' ETHICAL RESPONSIBILITIES AS PROFESSIONALS

4.01 Competence

(a) Social workers should accept responsibility or employment only on the basis of existing competence or the intention to acquire the necessary competence.

(b) Social workers should strive to become and remain proficient in professional practice and the performance of professional functions. Social workers should critically examine and keep current with emerging knowledge relevant to social work. Social workers should routinely review the professional literature and participate in continuing education relevant to social work practice and social work ethics.

(c) Social workers should base practice on recognized knowledge, including empirically based knowledge, relevant to social work and social work ethics.

4.02 Discrimination

Social workers should not practice, condone, facilitate, or collaborate with any form of discrimination on the basis of race, ethnicity, national origin, color, sex, sexual orientation, age, marital status, political belief, religion, or mental or physical disability.

4.03 Private Conduct

Social workers should not permit their private conduct to interfere with their ability to fulfill their professional responsibilities.

4.04 Dishonesty, Fraud, and Deception

Social workers should not participate in, condone, or be associated with dishonesty, fraud, or deception.

4.05 Impairment

(a) Social workers should not allow their own personal problems, psychosocial distress, legal problems, substance abuse, or mental health difficulties to interfere with their professional judgment and performance or to jeopardize the best interests of people for whom they have a professional responsibility.

(b) Social workers whose personal problems, psychosocial distress, legal problems, substance abuse, or mental health difficulties interfere with their professional judgment and performance should immediately seek consultation and take appropriate remedial action by seeking professional help, making adjustments in workload, terminating practice, or taking any other steps necessary to protect clients and others.

4.06 Misrepresentation

(a) Social workers should make clear distinctions between statements made and actions engaged in as a private individual and as a representative of the social work profession, a professional social work organization, or the social worker's employing agency.

(b) Social workers who speak on behalf of professional social work organizations should accurately represent the official and authorized positions of the organizations.

(c) Social workers should ensure that their representations to clients, agencies, and the public of professional qualifications, credentials, education, competence, affiliations, services provided, or results to be achieved are accurate. Social workers should claim only those relevant professional credentials they actually possess and take steps to correct any inaccuracies or misrepresentations of their credentials by others.

4.07 Solicitations

(a) Social workers should not engage in uninvited solicitation of potential clients who, because of their circumstances, are vulnerable to undue influence, manipulation, or coercion.

(b) Social workers should not engage in solicitation of testimonial endorsements (including solicitation of consent to use a client's prior statement as a testimonial endorsement) from current clients or from other people who, because of their particular circumstances, are vulnerable to undue influence.

4.08 Acknowledging Credit

(a) Social workers should take responsibility and credit, including authorship credit, only for work they have actually performed and to which they have contributed.

(b) Social workers should honestly acknowledge the work of and the contributions made by others.

Responsibilities as Professionals—Case 16

16. Rolanda is a social worker at an agency that recently received a large federal grant to implement a "Return to Work" program as part of welfare reform. Although the evaluation protocol is very clear about what constitutes "work," the agency is pressuring Rolanda and her co-workers (none of whom are social workers) to count clients' volunteer efforts and other nonpaying jobs as "work" to ensure that this valuable program will continue. The agency maintains that paying jobs are hard to find, so clients who are actively working, even in noncompensated jobs "fit the spirit, if not the letter of the law."

A. Is Rolanda being asked to violate the Code of Ethics?

B. If her colleagues aren't social workers, should they share her concern about the agency's practices?

C. What information or circumstances might move your decision in one direction or another?

D. What steps should Rolanda take to resolve this dilemma?

5. SOCIAL WORKERS' ETHICAL RESPONSIBILITIES TO THE SOCIAL WORK PROFESSION

5.01 Integrity of the Profession

(a) Social workers should work toward the maintenance and promotion of high standards of practice.

(b) Social workers should uphold and advance the values, ethics, knowledge, and mission of the profession. Social workers should protect, enhance, and improve the integrity of the profession through appropriate study and research, active discussion, and responsible criticism of the profession.

(c) Social workers should contribute time and professional expertise to activities that promote respect for the value, integrity, and competence of the social work profession. These activities may include teaching, research, consultation, service, legislative testimony, presentations in the community, and participation in their professional organizations.

(d) Social workers should contribute to the knowledge base of social work and share with colleagues their knowledge related to practice, research, and ethics. Social workers should seek to contribute to the profession's literature and to share their knowledge at professional meetings and conferences.

(e) Social workers should act to prevent the unauthorized and unqualified practice of social work.

5.02 Evaluation and Research

(a) Social workers should monitor and evaluate policies, the implementation of programs, and practice interventions.

(b) Social workers should promote and facilitate evaluation and research to contribute to the development of knowledge.

(c) Social workers should critically examine and keep current with emerging knowledge relevant to social work and fully use evaluation and research evidence in their professional practice.

(d) Social workers engaged in evaluation or research should carefully consider possible consequences and should follow guidelines developed for the protection of evaluation and research participants. Appropriate institutional review boards should be consulted.

(e) Social workers engaged in evaluation or research should obtain voluntary and written informed consent from participants, when appropriate, without any implied or actual deprivation or penalty for refusal to participate; without undue inducement to participate; and with due regard for participants' well-being, privacy, and dignity. Informed consent should include information about the nature, extent, and duration of the participation requested and disclosure of the risks and benefits of participation in the research.

(f) When evaluation or research participants are incapable of giving informed consent, social workers should provide an appropriate explanation to the participants, obtain the participants' assent to the extent they are able, and obtain written consent from an appropriate proxy.

(g) Social workers should never design or conduct evaluation or research that does not use consent procedures, such as certain forms of naturalistic observation and archival research, unless rigorous and responsible review of the research has found it to be justified because of its prospective scientific, educational, or applied value and unless equally effective alternative procedures that do not involve waiver of consent are not feasible.

(h) Social workers should inform participants of their right to withdraw from evaluation and research at any time without penalty.

(i) Social workers should take appropriate steps to ensure that participants in evaluation and research have access to appropriate supportive services.

(j) Social workers engaged in evaluation or research should protect participants from unwarranted physical or mental distress, harm, danger, or deprivation.

(k) Social workers engaged in the evaluation of services should discuss collected information only for professional purposes and only with people professionally concerned with this information.

(l) Social workers engaged in evaluation or research should ensure the anonymity or confidentiality of participants and of the data obtained from them. Social workers should inform participants of any limits of confidentiality, the measures that will be taken to ensure confidentiality, and when any records containing research data will be destroyed.

(m) Social workers who report evaluation and research results should protect participants' confidentiality by omitting identifying information unless proper consent has been obtained authorizing disclosure.

(n) Social workers should report evaluation and research findings accurately. They should not fabricate or falsify results and should take steps to correct any errors later found in published data using standard publication methods.

(o) Social workers engaged in evaluation or research should be alert to and avoid conflicts of interest and dual relationships with participants, should inform participants when a real or potential conflict of interest arises, and should take steps to resolve the issue in a manner that makes participants' interests primary.

(p) Social workers should educate themselves, their students, and their colleagues about responsible research practices.

Evaluation and Research—Case 17

17. Richard wants to assess his effectiveness in conducting family sessions, but he fears that if clients know they are being taped, their behaviors will change, and his findings will be distorted. He will only use the tapes for his own development, viewing them himself and sharing them in supervision. He feels that because he discusses cases with his supervisor, showing the tapes without clients' knowledge or permission will be acceptable as well.

   A. How are Richard's actions a violation of the code?

   B. How can Richard meet the requirements of evaluation, competence, and professional development while maintaining ethical practices?

---

6. SOCIAL WORKERS' ETHICAL RESPONSIBILITIES TO THE BROADER SOCIETY

6.01 Social Welfare

Social workers should promote the general welfare of society, from local to global levels, and the development of people, their communities, and their environments. Social workers should advocate for living conditions conducive to the fulfillment of basic human needs and should promote social, economic, political, and cultural values and institutions that are compatible with the realization of social justice.

6.02 Public Participation

Social workers should facilitate informed participation by the public in shaping social policies and institutions.

6.03 Public Emergencies

Social workers should provide appropriate professional services in public emergencies to the greatest extent possible.

6.04 Social and Political Action

(a) Social workers should engage in social and political action that seeks to ensure that all people have equal access to the resources, employment, services, and opportunities they require to meet their basic human needs and to develop fully. Social workers should be aware of the impact of the political arena on practice and should advocate for changes in policy and legislation to improve social conditions in order to meet basic human needs and promote social justice.

(b) Social workers should act to expand choice and opportunity for all people, with special regard for vulnerable, disadvantaged, oppressed, and exploited people and groups.

(c) Social workers should promote conditions that encourage respect for cultural and social diversity within the United States and globally. Social workers should promote policies and practices that demonstrate respect for difference, support the expansion of cultural knowledge and resources, advocate for programs and institutions that demonstrate cultural competence, and promote policies that safeguard the rights of and confirm equity and social justice for all people.

(d) Social workers should act to prevent and eliminate domination of, exploitation of, and discrimination against any person, group, or class on the basis of race, ethnicity, national origin, color, sex, sexual orientation, age, marital status, political belief, religion, or mental or physical disability.

Discussion Questions

1. Did reading the code make you aware of practices that might raise ethical questions?

2. Which elements of the code might be the most difficult for you to adhere to? Why?

3. Identify any of the case vignettes that involved "competing principles" where different elements of the code were in conflict.

4. When there were conflicting principles, how would you choose one action over another?

5. What ideas do you have about resolving ethical concerns that arise in your practice as a social worker?

EXERCISE 5 *Examining the Values and Ethics Reflected in Policy Decisions*

Glenda Dewberry Rooney

Purpose

1. To help you understand the policies and procedures that govern client services in your school or social services agency.
2. To understand how policies and procedures influence the interactions between professionals and clients.
3. To examine the extent that organizational policies and procedures support or constrain social work values and ethics.

Background

Social work practice occurs in an organizational context and is governed by a set of agency policies and procedures. Just as social workers may experience ethical conflicts in their client interactions, so too may they experience conflicts with their agencies' actions or policies. In particular, dilemmas may arise when the commitment to an employer conflicts with responsibilities to clients.

This exercise encourages you to examine an organizational policy for the messages it sends to workers and clients and for the dilemmas it may create.

Instructions

Identify a policy or procedure in your practicum agency that deals with clients' services. Some sample policies include

- Eligibility criteria for services
- The types of proof required to get services or benefits
- Rules governing clients' behavior in residential or institutional settings
- Rules related to access to services, for example, that a family can use a food shelf only once per month, or that welfare benefits are limited to a specified period of time

- Policies around missed appointments or failure to follow through with treatment recommendations
- Procedures for developing treatment plans
- Policies about client access to records
- Policies requiring that the client be given a diagnosis or special education label

If you are not currently in placement or working in a human service setting, you may want to examine a policy of your school of social work, or a policy provided by your instructor. Assess the policy using the following questions and be prepared to summarize and discuss your findings in class.

EXERCISE 5

Questions

1. Discuss the origin, ideology, and values that appear to have influenced the policy. Include in the discussion the intended and potential unintended consequences of the policy's application.

_____

_____

_____

_____

_____

_____

_____

2. To what extent is the policy and what it expects of clients influenced by societal ideology (e.g., worthy and unworthy poor, social control, compliance)?

_____

_____

_____

_____

_____

_____

_____

3. What is the image of clients and practitioners portrayed by the policy?

_____

_____

_____

_____

_____

_____

4. What does the policy demand of clients and practitioners?

_____

_____

_____

_____

_____

_____

5. What are client reactions to the policy?

_____

_____

_____

_____

_____

_____

6. Assess the extent to which the policy and its procedures support or constrain social work values, ethics, and social justice concerns.

_____

_____

_____

_____

_____

_____

7. Does the NASW Code of Ethics offer you any guidance about the appropriateness of the policy? In what way(s)?

_____

_____

_____

_____

_____

_____

_____

2 GETTING STARTED

EXERCISE 6 *Building Rapport*

Glenda Dewberry Rooney

Purpose

1. To develop understanding about the feelings and reactions experienced by clients during the initial contact with professional helpers.

Background

People seek help for a variety of reasons. They may need help in resolving life difficulties or in finding resources, or they may be reluctant participants in the change process. Applicants for services experience anxieties about what will transpire between themselves and the social worker. Talking to a stranger and revealing intimate details about their lives increases anxieties. These anxieties may be about differences in status, race, gender, and class; how they will be viewed or accepted; the extent of control they will have over their lives; what their rights are; whether the social worker is able to separate who they are from their current difficulties; and what attributes will be assigned to them. Exploring our own experiences as a stranger in need of assistance provides valuable insights into how clients may feel in their initial contact with us as professional helpers.

This is a reflective exercise that builds on the strengths perspective. The aim is to highlight what social workers can do to set a tone of acceptance in the initial contact with clients that aids in establishing rapport.

Instructions

Pause for a moment and imagine yourself in one of the scenarios below, then address the questions that follow. Be prepared to discuss your thoughts and reactions with your classmates.

In each of these settings you are required to disclose information about yourself as a part of the application/selection process and the individual(s) with whom you are meeting will make a decision affecting your future.

You are applying for your first social work job and are about to be interviewed by the program director.

You are meeting with a committee that is screening applicants for the school of social work.

You are meeting with the field supervisor at a placement where you'd really like to work.

You are a social work student seeking help from the college counseling service to deal with the stresses of balancing school with your job and family responsibilities.

EXERCISE 6

Questions

1. What initial reactions, anxieties, feelings, and expectations do you experience?

_____

_____

_____

_____

_____

_____

_____

2. What actions would make you feel comfortable and welcomed?

_____

_____

_____

_____

_____

_____

_____

3. What concerns might you and the interviewer have about each other?

_____

_____

_____

_____

_____

_____

4. What would you want the individual to know about you (attributes, strengths, resources)?

_____

_____

_____

_____

_____

_____

5. Based on your physical characteristics or the reasons you are applying, what attributes or stereotypes might be assigned to you?

_____

_____

_____

_____

_____

_____

6. What would you want to know about this individual and the organization?

_____

_____

_____

_____

_____

_____

7. How might this individual go about engaging and showing a genuine interest in you?

_____

_____

_____

_____

_____

_____

EXERCISE 7 *Tuning in Through Guided Visualization*

Kim Strom-Gottfried

Purpose

1. To help you tune in to the experience of seeking help.
2. To help you develop anticipatory empathy.
3. To help you identify the qualities clients need in a helper.
4. To help you identify the priorities to address in the initial session with a client.

Background

The first meeting with a new client usually requires addressing a number of issues: understanding the difficulty that brings them in for service, getting to know a bit about them, providing information on your role and other items as necessary for informed consent, making sure forms are completed, and so forth. When social workers are new to practice, first sessions can be intimidating. Conversely, when people have been in practice a while, first sessions can become routine. In either case, it is easy to forget about the uniqueness of the client and how it may feel to be in the position of seeking help from a formal system you barely understand. "Tuning in" or anticipatory empathy allows us to think ahead about the upcoming client meeting and to "put ourselves in the client's shoes," preparing our interview accordingly. Ultimately, it helps us answer the question, "What will this client need from me in the time we have together?"

Instructions

Close your eyes and get in as comfortable position as possible. You may want to put your head on your desk. Your instructor will read a scenario to you. Try to imagine yourself as the person described in the visualization. When the visualization concludes, answer the following questions. When your classmates discuss their reactions, jot them down and compare them with your own.

EXERCISE 7

Questions

1. What feelings did you experience, imagining yourself as this client?

_____

_____

_____

_____

_____

_____

_____

2. How do you want the social worker who has just come out to greet you to behave?

_____

_____

_____

_____

_____

_____

_____

3. What actions or statements by the social worker do you *not* need at this point?

_____

_____

_____

_____

_____

_____

4. What questions do you need to have addressed at this session?

_____

_____

_____

_____

_____

_____

5. What other reactions, thoughts, feelings, or observations do you have at this point?

_____

_____

_____

_____

_____

_____

6. As a professional, how can you keep yourself attuned to the needs and questions clients bring, especially to first sessions?

_____

_____

_____

_____

_____

_____

EXERCISE 8   Looking for Assets

Kim Strom-Gottfried

Purpose

1. To develop a preliminary understanding of the strengths at play in a case.
2. To understand the ways in which social workers' roles and settings affect the way they might view a client's situation.

Background

Because much of our work with clients is focused on the particular difficulties they are having, it is easy to dwell on their shortcomings and problems and overlook the "assets" at play in their lives. These assets can include clients' personal strengths, abilities, and accomplishments; their social support networks; and their material resources. Sometimes, the *absence of difficulties* in a particular area of functioning may constitute a strength. Yet often we overlook these resources or we minimize their importance. And when we work in settings where our focus is narrow, when our time with the client is short, or where we are interacting with only an element of the client system, our understanding of the strengths in place may be further limited. Exploring and using strengths in the helping process takes a conscious and concerted effort!

Instructions

Your instructor will assign you to a social work role and setting. Read the case material provided for that setting and determine the strengths and areas of concern for the family, based on what you've read. List your findings on the page following your case.

When instructed to do so, form a small group with the others who were assigned to view the case from the same role and setting. Compare notes with the others in your group. Did some people identify assets that others reviewing the case missed? Were things that were listed as strengths by some people listed as weaknesses by others? List these findings in the space provided. As a group, develop a comprehensive list of the family's strengths and vulnerabilities, based on what you've read. Be prepared to share your findings with the entire class.

Following the full-class discussion, address the following questions:

How did your assessment of your assigned client and the other family members change when more information or viewpoints were provided?

In what ways does the labeling of things as a "strength" or "weakness" depend on the values of the person doing the labeling?

What strengths were identified that could be used as resources in the change effort if the social workers had a broader understanding of the family?

EXERCISE 8

Therapist—Family and Children's Service Agency

The Carr family consists of Eleanor, age 35, her children Artie, Phil, and Lorene, and her estranged husband, Arthur Sr. Mr. Carr is currently in the state prison, serving the first year of a 9-year sentence for the sexual abuse of Phil. Phil, now age 11, is in the fifth grade and receiving weekly therapy for the anger and aggression he has demonstrated since his abuse. Artie, age 19, is on probation for a burglary conviction and has recently received a drunken driving conviction. He lives with his mother and siblings and works doing automobile repair at the family's home. Lorene is 9 years old, a B/C student who is well liked by her teachers, but somewhat ostracized by her classmates because of poor hygiene.

You are a social worker at the local Family and Children's Service Agency and have been working with Phil for 2 months. Phil's mother referred him for counseling after he displayed angry outbursts at school and at home, beginning at about the same time as Mr. Carr's sentencing. Phil had refused to seek counseling about his abuse, and he is not very verbal in his sessions with you, but he does enjoy playing games, solving word puzzles, and drawing. He impresses you as a shy boy whose aggression is a way of warding off further abuse. Still, you worry that he may hurt someone when he becomes angry, and you wonder if he may be abusive toward his younger sister or the family pets. So far, he refuses to even approach these topics.

You know the family is struggling financially and that they have lots of dogs and Phil's older brother living with them in their tiny home. It isn't the focus of your work, but you wonder about the expense of all these "family members" and if they are taking away from the family's ability to meet some of Phil's material and emotional needs.

Phil has always struggled with schoolwork, due in part to difficulty concentrating, but he has passed all of his classes and has usually received good marks for his behavior. The Carr family is very involved in their parish church, and members there have paid for Phil to take a karate class at the local Y. He lights up when he talks about the class, says he "likes the showers at the Y," and enthusiastically shows you the moves he has learned in class that week.

Strengths/Assets You've Identified

_____

_____

_____

_____

_____

_____

_____

_____

_____

_____

Needs/Vulnerabilities You've Identified

_____

_____

_____

_____

_____

_____

_____

_____

_____

Strengths/Assets Identified by Others

_____

_____

_____

_____

_____

_____

_____

_____

_____

_____

Needs/Vulnerabilities Identified by Others

_____

_____

_____

_____

_____

_____

_____

_____

_____

Probation Officer—Department of Corrections

The Carr family consists of Eleanor, age 35, her children Artie, Phil, and Lorene, and her estranged husband, Arthur Sr. Mr. Carr is currently in the state prison, serving the first year of a 9-year sentence for the sexual abuse of Phil. Phil, now age 11, is in the fifth grade and receiving weekly therapy for the anger and aggression he has demonstrated since his abuse. Artie, age 19, is on probation for a burglary conviction and has recently received a drunken driving conviction. He lives with his mother and siblings and works doing automobile repair at the family's home. Lorene is 9 years old, a B/C student who is well liked by her teachers, but somewhat ostracized by her classmates because of poor hygiene.

You work for the Department of Corrections and have been assigned as the probation officer for Artie. Your role is to generally monitor him, making sure he is completing the conditions of probation and staying out of trouble.

Artie's original offense was 9 months ago when he and some friends broke into a local appliance store. Artie maintained he was drunk at the time and "just went along with them for the heck of it." Although he was considered an adult at the time of the offense, because it was his first arrest, he received probation. The conditions of probation include receiving treatment for chemical dependency, maintaining a job, and checking in regularly with the probation department. Artie is faithful in maintaining contact with probation, but he has had trouble keeping a job and recently was arrested for driving while intoxicated. Artie expresses interest in attending Alcoholics Anonymous, but his follow-through is poor. Although he dropped out of his high school vocational program at age 16, he is a talented mechanic who knows a lot about various makes and models of cars and enjoys drawing detailed drag racer designs. Some people think Artie is stubborn, but when it comes to his work on cars, he is dogged in his determination to find and solve problems. Because of this, people are willing to go out of their way to have him work on their cars. Artie is known for his jokes and humor, which win him a wide array of friends but have caused difficulty in school and on jobs, as he has a hard time staying with his work tasks.

Artie admits to you that he is very angry with his father, although he won't be more specific. He seems to be proud of his new role in "taking care of the family" but is disappointed in himself, stating, "When I screw up now, it hurts them, too." You think Artie means well, and you will not revoke his probation despite the driving conviction. You know a little bit about his family, and even though it's none of your business, you wonder if Artie's father didn't abuse him as well.

Strengths/Assets You've Identified

_____

_____

_____

_____

_____

_____

_____

_____

_____

_____

Needs/Vulnerabilities You've Identified

_____

_____

_____

_____

_____

_____

_____

_____

_____

_____

Strengths/Assets Identified by Others

_____

_____

_____

_____

_____

_____

_____

_____

_____

_____

_____

Needs/Vulnerabilities Identified by Others

_____

_____

_____

_____

_____

_____

_____

_____

_____

_____

_____

Parent Aide—County Home Health Service

The Carr family consists of Eleanor, age 35, her children Artie, Phil, and Lorene, and her estranged husband, Arthur Sr. Mr. Carr is currently in the state prison, serving the first year of a 9-year sentence for the sexual abuse of Phil. Phil, now age 11, is in the fifth grade and receiving weekly therapy for the anger and aggression he has demonstrated since his abuse. Artie, age 19, is on probation for a burglary conviction and has recently received a drunken driving conviction. He lives with his mother and siblings and works doing automobile repair at the family's home. Lorene is 9 years old, a B/C student who is well liked by her teachers, but somewhat ostracized by her classmates because of poor hygiene.

Ten months ago, you were assigned by child protective services to work with Mrs. Carr on her inability to protect Phil from her husband's abuse. Although you have formally closed the case, Mrs. Carr calls you occasionally when crises arise. You enjoyed your interactions with Mrs. Carr and believe she is working very hard to meet her family's needs, so you try to offer support when you can.

The Carr family was poor even before Mr. Carr was sent to jail. The family's home is run-down and in a desolate part of town, but it is paid for and has a large lot of adjacent land. The Carrs are currently on public assistance, which is supplemented by Artie's income from auto repair work and Mrs. Carr's occasional income from providing child care for friends.

The home is small and cluttered, with several roof and wall leaks, but Mrs. Carr invests a lot of energy in keeping it clean and her brothers help with emergency repairs. The hot water has broken down repeatedly, which limits how often the family can take showers and do dishes. Although she is generally unperturbed about family crises, in a recent call, Mrs. Carr was frantic about how she will pay to replace the water heater before winter.

Mrs. Carr disapproves of Artie's drinking and his legal difficulties, but she is generally proud of her children and spends a lot of energy worrying about them and trying to provide for them. Because she does not drive and Artie has lost his license, she spends a lot of time arranging transportation for Phil's karate classes and therapy appointments and Lorene's Girl Scout meetings. Sometimes the plans she arranges fall through, as on a recent day when a relative forgot to pick Lorene up from her church meeting, but the family is used to the unpredictability and manages somehow.

Mrs. Carr is angry at her husband for "leaving her with this mess" and is also concerned about Phil, but to a lesser degree, alluding that her husband had a history of "funny business," though "never with his own family." She would like to maintain contact with him, though transportation is a problem, as are her limited literacy and financial problems. Mrs. Carr has worked as a data entry operator in the past, but she blames her time outside the home for "what happened with Phil" and quit the job to better attend to her family's needs.

Mrs. Carr is an Irish American and devout Catholic who attends church nearly every week. She is discouraged that, of her children, only Lorene shares her devotion, because she feels her faith helped her deal with health problems and a miscarriage 15 years ago and could be helpful to Phil and Artie for their difficulties.

Strengths/Assets You've Identified

_____

_____

_____

_____

_____

_____

_____

_____

_____

Needs/Vulnerabilities You've Identified

_____

_____

_____

_____

_____

_____

_____

_____

_____

Strengths/Assets Identified by Others

_____

_____

_____

_____

_____

_____

_____

_____

_____

Needs/Vulnerabilities Identified by Others

_____

_____

_____

_____

_____

_____

_____

_____

_____

School Social Worker—Local Middle School

The Carr family consists of Eleanor, age 35, her children Artie, Phil, and Lorene, and her estranged husband, Arthur Sr. Mr. Carr is currently in the state prison, serving the first year of a 9-year sentence for the sexual abuse of Phil. Phil, now age 11, is in the fifth grade and receiving weekly therapy for the anger and aggression he has demonstrated since his abuse. Artie, age 19, is on probation for a burglary conviction and has recently received a drunken driving conviction. He lives with his mother and siblings and works doing automobile repair at the family's home. Lorene is 9 years old, a B/C student who is well liked by her teachers, but somewhat ostracized by her classmates because of poor hygiene.

You are a social worker at the middle school where Lorene is a fourth-grade student. Her homeroom teacher has referred her to your "Friends" group because she seems lonely and sad and is picked on by other class members. Lorene is a small girl with glasses, whose clothes are often too small, mismatched, and smelly. When the school nurse called Mrs. Carr about this problem, she became quite angry and defensive. The teachers wanted to talk with her at parent-teacher conferences, but Mrs. Carr never came in. Considering her brothers' problems, which are well known in the school, Lorene is a good student. She completes her assignments on time, her work is neat, and she performs reasonably well, though her reading is poor and that affects many of her classes. She seems to be in good health, and may get an award at the end of the school year for perfect attendance.

Lorene loves animals and has three dogs and a cat at home. She reports playing games with them on weekends and vacations. She is somewhat shy, but is eager to be friendly and helpful when people show an interest in her. Sadly, other girls will pretend to be friends with her, then treat her cruelly when she returns their interest. She has better relationships with adults in the school, particularly the school librarian, whom she helps by collecting books during study hall. Lorene eats lunch with one or two other girls who are generally considered to be "outcasts" and who will also be joining the Friends group.

Lorene's Phys Ed teacher reports that she has a real talent for gymnastics, doing flips and tumbles easily without instruction. The teacher would like her to join the gymnastics group that meets after school, but Lorene's mother will not allow it, saying "she has to come home on the bus."

Strengths/Assets You've Identified

_____

_____

_____

_____

_____

_____

_____

_____

_____

_____

Needs/Vulnerabilities You've Identified

_____

_____

_____

_____

_____

_____

_____

_____

_____

Strengths/Assets Identified by Others

_____

_____

_____

_____

_____

_____

_____

_____

_____

Needs/Vulnerabilities Identified by Others

_____

_____

_____

_____

_____

_____

_____

_____

_____

Group Findings

(Use this space for notes on your group's list of the family's strengths and vulnerabilities)

_____

_____

_____

_____

_____

_____

_____

_____

_____

_____

_____

_____

_____

_____

_____

_____

_____

_____

_____

EXERCISE 9 *Understanding Loss*

Jane Hoyt-Oliver

Purpose

1. To assist you in getting in touch with the dynamics of loss and the emotions accompanying grief.
2. To observe how reactions to loss vary from individual to individual.
3. To understand the needs of people experiencing grief.

Background

Social work practice frequently involves assisting clients with issues of grief and loss. Grief reactions may be triggered by divorce, the death of a loved one, the loss of a job, diminished physical or mental capacities as a result of illness, the loss of friends as a result of moving or a change in roles, or the loss of a pet, home, or business following a fire or natural disaster. Losses can cause multiple reactions. Often, losses may trigger not only the pain of the moment but will trigger grief reactions to other, unresolved losses experienced earlier in life. In addition, loss may be complicated by issues outside the loss that affect the individuals' ability to function in carrying out their day-to-day responsibilities.

This exercise is designed to help you get in touch with how a loss is experienced and to stimulate discussion about how to help individuals experiencing various forms of loss.

Instructions

Your instructor will guide you through this exercise. To begin, use the following page to write down 10 things that are important to you. These items do not have to be in order (i.e., most important to least important). Not all the items you list have to be people; some might be such things as a job, education, or a special pet. Try to think of the things that are *really most important to you right now.*

This exercise sometimes brings up feelings for students that they have not completely thought through. If in the next few days you find yourself thinking about the exercise, or one particular aspect of the exercise process, plan to talk to your professor, a professional helper, or a person you trust about your concerns.

EXERCISE 9

What is important to me?

1. _____

_____

2. _____

_____

3. _____

_____

4. _____

_____

5. _____

_____

6. _____

_____

7. _____

_____

8. _____

_____

9. _____

_____

10. _____

_____

Questions for Reflection and Discussion

1. How did it feel to have items taken away from your list? Did the way you lost an item make a difference in how you reacted?

_____

_____

_____

_____

_____

_____

2. Did some things on your list matter less than others? Was there one item that was most painful? Why might this be the case?

_____

_____

_____

_____

_____

_____

3. Were you able to "keep" what was most important in your life? How did this feel?

_____

_____

_____

_____

_____

4. Ask each member in your group to describe in one or two sentences why an item was particularly meaningful. Was there an item on one person's list that he or she found particularly difficult to give up that might have been easier for other group members? What might account for these different reactions?

_____

_____

_____

_____

_____

_____

5. What do your experiences in this exercise tell you about loss and grief?

_____

_____

_____

_____

_____

_____

6. What assistance might be helpful to people experiencing losses of various types?

_____

_____

_____

_____

_____

_____

_____

EXERCISE 10

Engaging a Family Who Has Not Asked for Help

Marcia B. Cohen

Purpose

1. To become familiar with the processes of engagement and exploration with a family system.
2. To help you understand what impact the degree of client choice (or "voluntariness") has on the helping relationship.

Background

People need to be engaged in the helping relationship before they can truly be considered clients. How we engage people depends, in part, on whether services are *sought* by them, *offered* to them, or *imposed* on them. The engagement process, particularly where services are not sought voluntarily, includes clarification of the agency's function, the social work role, and the services being offered. Effective engagement requires offering concrete, jargon-free descriptions of social work services and professional purpose that take into account the person's values and lifestyle. Clients are far more likely to become engaged in a helping relationship if the services being offered match their felt needs.

Identifying a fit between client needs and the available services requires skill in tuning in to the person's life space and exploring individual concerns, strengths, obstacles, and resources. When the client system is a family, the worker has the additional challenge of tuning in to each family member as well as the system as a whole.

Instructions

The class is divided into three groups: a family group (consisting of six members), a patient group (size is optional), and a social worker group (size is optional). Read the description of the setting and roles for whichever group you are assigned. Each member of the family group should choose a family role to portray. Patients (all of whom are in the role of Johnny) and family members should familiarize themselves with the role descriptions of other family members as well as prepare to portray their own characters. The social worker should tune in to what he or she perceives as the general concerns of the patient and his family (he or she does not yet know enough about the family to tune in to their individual concerns).

After preparation and getting "into role," each group will spend 15 minutes discussing several questions in their small groups from the vantage point of their assumed roles. Following this discussion, one member of the social worker group, one member of the patient group, and all six members of the family group will role-play the social worker's initial entry into the case while the remaining class members observe. If time allows, this exercise can be repeated with new "patients" and "social workers" adopting those roles. Following the role play, the class as a whole will discuss the exercise.

Case Material

Setting

The setting is a pediatrics unit of a large teaching hospital. The patient is 13-year-old Johnny Salvatore. Johnny has bone cancer and needs to have his left leg amputated. Johnny's parents have been staying with him around the clock since his hospitalization earlier in the week. They have refused to leave his bedside, even briefly, to let the nurses and doctors examine him in private. They often answer for Johnny when people ask him questions, and they do not use the word *cancer* or refer to the impending amputation. While Rosa, Johnny's mother, cries (not usually in front of him), his father Frank tells the family they must be strong. Other relatives have also been coming to visit and staying in the room. A nurse, fairly new to the unit, has tried to give Johnny an injection; several family members watch over her work carefully, telling Johnny how to behave (and thereby impeding the nurse's work). The nurse tells the parents that only two visitors are allowed in the room at a time. This is a hospital policy because the patient is on isolation precautions for infection. The nurse says gently but firmly that all but two family members must leave. Frank quietly but firmly argues with her. When the nurse tries to explain why they must go, Frank asks to see someone who can help him. The nurse finds the unit social worker, gives him/her a brief description of the situation, and tells him/her to get the family out of there.

Roles

Stephanie Butler: Stephanie is a 26-year-old, white, Protestant social worker on the pediatrics unit of a large teaching hospital where she has worked for the past 2 years.

Johnny Salvatore: Johnny is a 13-year-old boy, second-generation Italian American, recently diagnosed with bone cancer. Johnny's condition is such that his left leg must be amputated. He has been in this hospital for several days, having been transferred from another hospital where he was diagnosed. Johnny has not been told his diagnosis. He fears the worst and is terrified but is trying not to show it.

Rosa Salvatore: Rosa is Johnny's mother, a first-generation Italian American woman in her mid-30s. She is extremely upset by the situation and finds it hard not to cry.

Frank Salvatore: Frank is Johnny's father, a first-generation Italian American in his early 40s. He is terrified that his only son may die but feels he has to appear strong and unafraid. It is important to Frank that his son not find out what is wrong with him and he worries his wife will inadvertently say something.

Daria Salvatore: Johnny's 11-year-old sister. She does not know what is wrong with Johnny but she can tell that her parents are very afraid. This scares her, particularly because no one will tell her anything.

Angela Salvatore: Angie is Johnny's 15-year-old sister. She has overheard her parents talking about the amputation and has her suspicions about the diagnosis. She is worried about her brother and concerned about how her mother is holding up.

Serafina Salvatore: Fina is Frank's mother, a very religious Italian-born widow in her 60s. She is overwhelmed by the hospital routine but is not as frightened as the other family members because she is convinced Johnny will get well.

Josephine Salvatore: Josephine is Johnny's aunt and Fina's daughter. She was born in Italy and raised in the United States. Johnny is her favorite nephew and she is quite upset about his illness. She tries not to think about what is wrong with him and prays for the best.

Questions for Johnny

1. What has the experience of your illness and hospitalizations been like for you?
2. What are your biggest problems and concerns right now?
3. In view of these concerns, how can the social worker be of help to you?

Questions for Family Members

1. What has the experience of Johnny's illness and hospitalizations been like for you?
2. What are the major problems you are facing now?
3. In view of these problems, what would you find most helpful from a social worker?

Questions for Social Workers

1. What might this patient/family see as their most pressing problems and needs?
2. Will the fact that neither the patient nor his family requested your services influence how you begin?
3. How can you engage this patient and family?
4. What obstacles to engagement and exploration do you anticipate?

3 GATHERING DATA

EXERCISE 11 *Video Analysis and Interview Practice*

Kim Strom-Gottfried

Purpose

1. To help you understand interviewing techniques by identifying them in a videotaped interview.
2. To develop skills at constructively critiquing an interview.
3. To develop interviewing skills.

Background

Most social work practice books describe interviewing skills and give examples of these skills, yet it can be difficult to understand the importance of these techniques unless you are able to see them in use. Knowing what various skills (and common errors!) are called, knowing how they are used, and being able to use them effectively yourself are the communication "building blocks" that make up an interview.

Instructions

1. Look over the interviewing skills listed in the blocks below. Look up definitions of any that are unfamiliar to you or ask your instructor for assistance.
2. Your instructor will assign you to look for one or more of the skills in a videotaped interview. When you see the skill, jot it down in the block.
3. When the video is over, answer the questions on the following page.
4. Based on what you've seen and your analysis of the interview, be prepared to participate in a role play recreating the situation depicted in the video.

EXERCISE 11

Questions

a. Were the skills you noted used effectively in the interview? How could you tell?

_____

_____

_____

_____

b. Was the interview, overall, effectively done? What was effectively done and what could be strengthened?

_____

_____

_____

_____

_____

c. What would you do differently?

_____

_____

_____

_____

Leading Question	Attending

Minimal Encourager	Summarizing

Shared Feelings	Open-Ended Question

Empathy	Closed Question

Focusing	Advising

Probe Statement/Question	Supportive Statement

Clarification	Accent
Seeking Feedback	Paraphrasing
Confusing Term or Statement	Nonverbal Communication

Seeking Concreteness	Self-Involving Statements

Giving Information	Stacked Questions

Reflecting Content	Focusing

Interpretation	Use of Silence

Confrontation	Reflecting Feelings

Personal Self-Disclosure	Sanctioning Feelings

EXERCISE 12 *Practicing and Analyzing Interviews*

Craig Boitel and Kathleen J. Farkas

> Listen or thy tongue will keep thee deaf.
> —American Indian proverb

Purpose

1. To help you to become aware of the elements in the interview process.
2. To help develop listening and interviewing skills.
3. To foster your self-awareness about strengths and weaknesses as an interviewer.

Background

Listening involves attending to, synthesizing, and analyzing *what* is said, *how* it is said, and *why* it is said. Listening means reconciling manifest and latent content; it includes actively developing, testing, and revising hypotheses about what contributes to and lies behind the client's verbal behavior (questions, statements, use of language) and nonverbal behavior (eye contact, silence, posture, gestures, etc.).

The experienced interviewer purposefully engages with the client, generally talks less than the client, sees strengths and weaknesses as well as themes and patterns, and makes full use of the client's participation to assess the accuracy of the social worker's perceptions. Effective listeners simultaneously organize what is being communicated and suspend assumptions about the material. Conclusions are considered tentative at best and are aided by paraphrases and reflective statements that involve the client. Effective listeners encourage the client to allow his or her story to unfold and they make use of regular checks about language to note what particular words or phrases mean to the client.

In this exercise, three activities build on each other. They use small group dynamics; offer a "safe" role play experience within the small group that does not require exposure to the entire class; make increasing demands on participants; and use peer, self-, and instructor feedback. The exercises focus on basic skill identification and skill development with particular emphasis on client cues and the skill of listening.

EXERCISE 12

Activity 1: Best and Worst Helping Relationships

Instructions

Review material in your text on interviewing or another source, such as Ivey (1994) or Kadushin and Kadushin (1997). To begin the exercises, your instructor will divide you into small groups of three. You will stay in the same small group to complete all three exercises.

Please think about any helping relationships in which you were the recipient. Some examples might be seeing a physician for a medical problem, talking with a teacher or coach, seeking a friend's advice, or seeing a counselor for career or personal issues. Try to identify and discuss the key features of your "best" and "worst" experiences. Please think about both the qualities of the helper, that is, what behaviors you found helpful or unhelpful, and your personal responses to those behaviors and list them on the chart below. Be prepared to discuss your observations with others in the group.

Best Helping Behaviors	*Worst Helping Behaviors*
1. _____	1. _____
2. _____	2. _____
3. _____	3. _____
4. _____	4. _____
5. _____	5. _____
6. _____	6. _____
7. _____	7. _____
8. _____	8. _____
9. _____	9. _____
10. _____	10. _____

What helper behaviors were most helpful and why?

_____

_____

_____

_____

_____

How did that which was helpful contribute to your level of comfort and participation?

_____

_____

_____

_____

_____

What helper behaviors were most detrimental and why?

_____

_____

_____

_____

How did that which was not helpful contribute to your level of comfort and participation?

_____

_____

_____

_____

Activity 2: Initial Interview

Instructions

For the next activity, please rejoin your small group. In this 1½- to 2-hour exercise each person will take a turn as interviewer, interviewee, and observer. The interviewee's task is to take either a prior or current personal situation/problem and, in an *initial interview at a family service agency,* present this information. Use this personal experience as the basis for discussion. The expectation is *not* for an intense level of personal disclosure—the interviewee should select an area that he or she feels comfortable discussing. The interviewee should *not* attempt to thwart the interviewer or make his or her job difficult. If possible, each 15-minute interview will be audio- or videorecorded. The observer will evaluate the interview using the Interview Skills Checklist, and discuss it with and give it to the interviewer. The interviewee's impressions can also be very helpful. Each small group should use the last 15-20 minutes to discuss their feedback with one another. The information below, on giving effective feedback, may be helpful in critiquing the interviews. Your instructor will circulate among the groups as you participate in the exercise. When you are finished, please rejoin the large group.

Tips on Giving Effective Feedback

1. Describe rather than pass judgment. When you describe your feelings and reactions, the listener can then react as he or she sees fit. Give feedback about what was said or done and how it was said or done, but not why it occurred.

2. Be as specific as possible. Rather than saying, "You dominated the interview," say "You interrupted when the client was starting to tell about her experience."

3. Consider the needs of the receiver. How much can the listener hear, accept, and handle at any given point in time?

4. Check to see if your feedback is understood. Perhaps you should restate your point or ask others to help clarify by adding their perspectives.

5. Expect trust to develop slowly. As trust grows, so does the willingness to risk, make errors, and offer and accept constructive criticism.

6. Share information rather than give advice.

Tips on Receiving Feedback

1. Try to be open and nondefensive. Don't blame or look for quick explanations.

2. Ask for specific examples of areas for improvement.

3. Share your feelings about the feedback with those who are offering it.

4. Remember, it is up to you to decide how to act on the feedback you are given.

NOTE: Adapted from the Field Education handbook, University of Minnesota.

Interview Skills Checklist

Interviewer _____ Interviewee _____ Observer _____

Skill Area	Yes	No	Comments
Introduction			
"Client's" name	☐	☐	
"Social worker's" name	☐	☐	
Discloses student status	☐	☐	
States purpose	☐	☐	
Puts client at ease	☐	☐	
Invites client to talk	☐	☐	
Conveys genuineness	☐	☐	
Attends to client			
Eye contact	☐	☐	
Facilitative body language	☐	☐	
Solicits client's view of problem	☐	☐	
Shows interest in client	☐	☐	
Solicits client's feedback	☐	☐	
Listens to client			
Balances talk time	☐	☐	
Hears *what* is said	☐	☐	
Hears *how* it is said	☐	☐	
Hears *why* it is said	☐	☐	
Paraphrases	☐	☐	
Reflects feeling	☐	☐	
Clarifies meaning	☐	☐	
Facilitative comments	☐	☐	
Tolerates silence	☐	☐	
Tolerates client's affect	☐	☐	
Questions			
Appropriate to content	☐	☐	
Appropriate to process	☐	☐	
Uses open-ended questions	☐	☐	
Responds to client questions	☐	☐	
Appropriate self-disclosure	☐	☐	
Focuses questions	☐	☐	
Other			
Gives advice	☐	☐	
Interrupts	☐	☐	
Reassures too quickly	☐	☐	
Makes smooth transitions	☐	☐	
Structures the interview	☐	☐	
Paces the interview	☐	☐	
Closes the interview	☐	☐	
Themes			

Activity 3: With Cases

Instructions

Your instructor will assign one of the following cases to each member of the small group. This time, repeat Activity 2, basing your interview on the role assigned. Again, the interviews should be audio- or videorecorded, if possible. Your instructor will circulate among the small groups. The class will reconvene when you are finished and discuss the similarities and differences between the first and second interviews.

Case 1

Interviewee: You are a 39-year-old mother of four who is hospitalized for psychiatric evaluation following an aspirin overdose.

Interviewer: You are the social worker on the inpatient psychiatry service.

Interviewee's Background Information: This is your first psychiatric hospital admission. Your only previous hospitalizations were for the births of your children, now ages 5, 10, 15, and 19. A male child was delivered stillborn at 5 months gestation 17 years ago; he lived for 1 hour.

You have been married for 20 years. During this marriage you and your husband have separated three times. Currently, you are separated and this separation began 1 month ago. Your husband abuses alcohol and recently entered treatment for this. This is the second time he has sought formal treatment for his alcohol problems. Your parents both live nearby, but they have been divorced for 30 years. You were 9 years old when they divorced. You are the fourth of six children. You feel that your childhood was cold and impoverished and you feel your mother was abusive to you and your brothers and sisters. Your father, you feel, was detached and uninterested in you. As a parent, you have devoted yourself to your children and husband to the point that you often neglect your own needs and desires. You have not worked out of the home since you were married.

You say that you have had "no clue" that you were depressed and that your siblings have been taken "completely by surprise" by your actions because you have always been the "strong one" who has taken care of everyone else. Your siblings, as well as your parents, have expressed interest in talking to the hospital staff.

Case 2

Interviewee: You are a 15-year-old male who has come to a family service agency for evaluation at your parent's insistence.

Interviewer: You are a member of the social work staff at a family service agency.

Interviewee's Background Information: You have reluctantly shown up for an initial interview at the family service agency in your neighborhood. Your parents have been interviewed by the social worker previously.

You and your parents have been having a lot of problems getting along. These problems have always been there, but lately they have gotten worse. There are frequent arguments about how much time you spend away from home and your choice of friends. During an argument 5 months ago your mother asked if you wanted to remain a member of the family and you said no. You and your father have physically fought on one occasion. In the interview with the social worker, your parents have described you as defiant, provocative, unwilling to pitch in, irresponsible, and a negative influence on your 12-year-old twin sisters.

You are a capable student and a voracious reader. However, you rarely work to your capacity and have consistently, after a positive start, managed to alienate your teachers. This is a long-standing problem and has marked your school career. In high school, however, your adjustment problems have increased to the point where expulsion from your private school is likely.

You were adopted as a young child and your parents waited for several years to adopt you. Within months of your adoption, both of your adoptive parents lost their fathers. Your adoptive father has not had any contact with his mother since his father's death. Your early relationship with your parents was smooth, and they enjoyed spending time with you and they say they fell in love with you as soon as they saw you. They have said they felt your problems began when you entered school.

Case 3

Interviewee: You are a 19-year-old female seeking information from the college counseling center.

Interviewer: You are the social worker at the counseling center.

Interviewee's Background Information: You are a college student who is beginning her sophomore year at school. For the past 6 weeks you have been feeling distracted and irritable and not at all like your usual self. You are troubled by these feelings, but are not sure what they are about. During the past month you have experienced several panic attacks and now leave your dorm room only to go to class and to eat meals. You find yourself worrying about things you normally do not worry about: your mother's health, fires at home, the well-being of the family pets. You have had trouble sleeping and are worried about how these problems will affect your academic work and your grades.

You did well academically during your first year at this prestigious school. You are enrolled in several honors seminars and enjoy these classes. You worked hard to gain admission to this particular college because it has a special curriculum that interests you. Your two older siblings did well in college and now are in graduate school. Both of your parents are well educated and have successful careers. You have friends at school and felt that you adjusted well during the first year.

You spent the summer at home with your parents and high school friends and enjoyed it. During this visit, your mother made frequent references to how far away your school is from home. You have felt guilty about being so far away and have considered transferring to a school closer to home.

Interview Skills Checklist

Interviewer _____ Interviewee _____ Observer _____

Skill Area	Yes	No	Comments
Introduction			
"Client's" name	☐	☐	
"Social worker's" name	☐	☐	
Discloses student status	☐	☐	
States purpose	☐	☐	
Puts client at ease	☐	☐	
Invites client to talk	☐	☐	
Conveys genuineness	☐	☐	
Attends to client			
Eye contact	☐	☐	
Facilitative body language	☐	☐	
Solicits client's view of problem	☐	☐	
Shows interest in client	☐	☐	
Solicits client's feedback	☐	☐	
Listens to client			
Balances talk time	☐	☐	
Hears *what* is said	☐	☐	
Hears *how* it is said	☐	☐	
Hears *why* it is said	☐	☐	
Paraphrases	☐	☐	
Reflects feeling	☐	☐	
Clarifies meaning	☐	☐	
Facilitative comments	☐	☐	
Tolerates silence	☐	☐	
Tolerates client's affect	☐	☐	
Questions			
Appropriate to content	☐	☐	
Appropriate to process	☐	☐	
Uses open-ended questions	☐	☐	
Responds to client questions	☐	☐	
Appropriate self-disclosure	☐	☐	
Focuses questions	☐	☐	
Other			
Gives advice	☐	☐	
Interrupts	☐	☐	
Reassures too quickly	☐	☐	
Makes smooth transitions	☐	☐	
Structures the interview	☐	☐	
Paces the interview	☐	☐	
Closes the interview	☐	☐	
Themes			

Summary Assignment

The final assignment of the interviewing module is for you to listen to your tape recordings or to view your video recordings and then compare and contrast your two interviews and the skills they reflect. Prepare a two-page self-assessment of areas of strength and areas needing improvement and be prepared to submit it to your instructor and/or discuss it in class. How will you use the insights you've gained in these activities to enhance your work with clients?

References

Ivey, A. (1994). *Intentional interviewing and counseling: Facilitating client development in a multicultural society* (3rd ed.). Belmont, CA: Brooks/Cole.

Kadushin, A., & Kadushin, G. (1997). *The social work interview: A guide for human service professionals* (4th ed.). New York: Columbia University Press.

EXERCISE 13 *"Hanging in There" When Differences Between Client and Worker Are at Issue*

Julie S. Abramson

Purpose

1. To identify direct and indirect cues indicating that race or other areas of difference are at play in the client-practitioner relationship.
2. To develop comfort in addressing such cues.
3. To be able to respond genuinely and quickly "on one's feet" to emotionally charged issues.

Background

Even seasoned practitioners tend to be cautious rather than confident when dealing with racial issues, especially when the client and social worker are racially different. Fears arise in such circumstances that any interventions other than efforts to clarify the client's statements may be misinterpreted, seen as insensitive to the client's reality, or perceived as racist. Similar feelings occur in dealing with other emotionally charged differences such as sexual orientation, gender, or sometimes, age. Yet unless the social worker demonstrates willingness to address the difference directly by reaching for underlying issues or responding genuinely and directly to the client's concerns about difference, the essence of the client-social worker relationship will be undermined.

This exercise provides you with the process recording of a social work student's interaction with a client in her field placement and asks you to evaluate it using discussion questions. The review is followed by an opportunity to practice the skills called for when working across differences.

AUTHOR'S NOTE: I wish to acknowledge Kristen Kurien Spear's contribution of a process recording to this exercise.

EXERCISE 13

Activity 1: Review of Student Process Recording

Instructions

Read the following process recording and address the discussion questions that follow. The first column of the recording can be used for your notes and thoughts.

After you have made notes to yourself regarding the questions, review the questions with other students in your group. Try to share your thoughts openly and encourage others to do so as well.

The following process recording was done with a 47-year-old African American male recovering from an amputation. The student social worker is in her first MSW field placement. The client was interviewed at a hospital. This was the fourth contact with the client.

Reviewer's Comments	Content—Narrative (W = Social worker; C = Client)	Student Feelings
	W: *Hi Mr. Curtis.*	He seems happy to see me. Felt good.
	C: Hi. C'mon over and have a seat. Mr. Curtis pulled a chair over closer to him. I sat down in the chair.	
	W: *You're a hard man to find.* *You weren't in your room again today.*	I'm trying to be funny to break the ice. I'm still a bit unsure of our rapport.
	C: I was in there a little while ago. I come in here to have a cigarette.	
	W: *Well, I'm glad I found you.* *How are you today?*	
	C: I'm doing good.	
	W: *How is your leg? Is it draining?*	
	C: Yes, it's draining a little. It's much better than last week.	
	W: *Was it draining more last week?*	
	C: Yes, it was draining more.	
	W: *Did you go to PT today?*	
	C: Yes, I went two times today.	

Reviewer's Comments	Content—Narrative (W = Social worker; C = Client)	Student Feelings
	W: *How did it go?*	
	C: Good, but two times ain't enough. That's only an hour a day. I'd rather be home than sitting around here if I'm only getting an hour. Now I'm going to go to a group to walk.	Good for him! I'm glad he's advocating for himself. It would be great if more clients did it!
	W: *So that will be another half hour of PT?*	
	C: Yes.	
	W: *Will that be enough?*	
	C: I think so.	
	W: *If it gets you too tired or you have chest pains again, though, you should tell Christine.*	I hope he does.
	C: Yes, I will.	
	W: *Did you go to OT this morning?*	
	C: Yes. At 11 o'clock.	
	W: *11 o'clock? I thought it was at 10 o'clock, right after PT?*	
	C: Well today they done it different.	
	W: *Maybe that's because we had rounds this morning.*	
	C: I don't know. There was a pause in the conversation and then Mr. Curtis began shaking his head. C: That lady in the kitchen made me so mad though.	What should I bring up next? How should I lead into asking him about his story?
	W: *The occupational therapist made you mad?*	Mad? This doesn't seem like someone who gets mad easily.
	C: No, that lady in the cafeteria made me mad.	
	W: *What happened?*	What will happen if I ask? Have to ask.

(continued)

Reviewer's Comments	Content—Narrative (W = Social worker; C = Client)	Student Feelings
	C: I go down there to get 4 or 5 or 2 dollars change. Today I go down there and she looked at me. Then I asked her for change of a dollar and she said no. She told me I have to go ask the nursing station. But she looked at me like I just come out of the jungle.	As soon as he said "jungle," I knew it was a racial issue. I wanted him to tell me that though.
	W: *The jungle?*	
	C: Jungle.	
	W: *So you were upset because of the way she looked at you?*	
	C: I know that look. I seen that look a hundred times before. She's lucky I need a leg because if I didn't need a leg then I would have told her just what I thinked.	I knew what was coming next. I started to feel anxious and wondered how to handle what was seeming increasingly inevitable.
	W: *What did you think?*	I knew I had to ask.
	Mr. Curtis paused and looked away.	
	C: I don't want to say what I think. Pause. C: She be looking at me like I'm a nigger. I know what she be thinking. You can tell the difference between that look and any other look.	I knew he wanted to say more. I decided just to wait. OK, he said it. I guess we need to explore this. Oh boy, he's really getting angry!
	W: *So you felt like she was looking at you a certain way because you're black.*	
	C: I know she was. I knowed what she was thinking. If I was her I would've said, "Can I help you?" She helped the white man in front of me, then she just looked at me and didn't say nothing. Then I asked her for change for a dollar and she said no. I was so mad, I just turned my chair around and wheeled right out of there. I wheeled out of there so fast my two front wheels went right up in the air.	I was really hoping that he was wrong about what she was thinking. Either way, this was an incredibly uncomfortable position for me.

Reviewer's Comments	Content—Narrative (W = Social worker; C = Client)	Student Feelings
	W: *You must have been very angry to wheel out of there so fast.*	
	C: You don't know how lucky she is that I need a leg. If I didn't need nothing, then I would've told her, then Charles would have to come get me because they would call the police.	I'm glad he's venting. Maybe this is good that I'm here for him to talk with rather than stuffing his feelings. I hope I'm helping.
	W: *What did you think: if you told her what you thought you'd get in trouble?*	
	C: I been in the county jail for a year because somebody called me a nigger.	I was caught off guard here. My thought was to control my facial expression.
	W: *You went to jail because someone called you a nigger?*	I wanted to know more about his past.
	C: These men was in a car next to mine then passed me. They thought their car was better than mine. So I passed them then pulled in front of them and stopped my car. They called me a nigger. I took off my work boot and broke up they windshield. Cut them up real bad. It was 1984. Then I spent 1 year in the county jail. I don't care though because I done right. I was raised up that you say what you think no matter what. Don't matter none—you got to say what you think.	This story was somewhat confusing, but I got the basic point. I was surprised that this relatively harmless looking man who had been so pleasant to me could have such a past. To top it off, I'm a white middle-class female social worker.
	W: *It sounds like being called a nigger really upsets you and I can imagine why. I don't think I'd care to be called names.*	He probably thinks I'm full of it. I feel like there's something "right" to say and this isn't it.
	C: I been called nigger, coon, burrhead, and all like that. I don't care but nobody going to look at me like that.	I am uncomfortable hearing these words. I feel empathy toward the client.
	W: *Did you get your change, Mr. Curtis?*	
	C: I got it at the nurse's station. I ain't never going back to that kitchen. That lady ain't never going to see me again. From now on, Charles going to bring me change or I get it from the nurse's station.	I really hope that this wasn't the case. I don't know if it's true. There are a number of other possibilities. How can I bring them up without sounding like I'm sticking up for her?

(continued)

Reviewer's Comments	Content—Narrative (W = Social worker; C = Client)	Student Feelings
	W: OK, Mr. Curtis, I understand that you think Carol looked at you a certain way, but can I suggest that maybe it wasn't you? It might be that she was having a bad day or that she was angry at someone else.	
	C: Then she don't have to take it out on me.	
	W: You're right. She shouldn't have taken it out on you.	
	C: She wasn't having no bad day. She was polite to the white man in front of me. I'm so mad my blood is boiling.	He thinks I don't understand. I feel like I should be able to communicate better with him.
	W: She's given you change before though with no problem, right?	
	C: You don't know. You aren't 47 years old. You were raised up in a different time than me.	He's right. I don't know. I wonder how he would react if I just talk completely openly.
	W: You're absolutely right, Mr. Curtis. I'm not your age, I'm not black, and I didn't grow up in the South. It would be foolish of me to pretend I know what it's like. The only thing I can tell you is that I'm sorry it happened.	I want to say something that is genuine. I'm feeling very genuine.
	C: Well, that's OK. Nothing you can do.	
	W: I'm very uncomfortable with this, Mr. Curtis. I'm obviously white and I hope you don't think I look at you that way.	I am uncomfortable! I hope I don't sound patronizing. I don't know what else to say about this.
	C: I know you don't look at me that way. There's bad people in all colors. Bad blacks and bad whites too. Don't matter. All colors got bad in 'em. Nothing you can do about it. Mr. Curtis is paged over the loud speaker to come to PT. He looks at his watch. C: Must be time for me to go.	I believe that he means this. He's trying to make me feel OK about this. Now I feel like I dumped on him. Oh, thank God!

Reviewer's Comments	Content—Narrative (W = Social worker; C = Client)	Student Feelings
	W: *Yes, it's 2:30.* Mr. Curtis and I ride down to PT. W: *OK, Mr. Curtis, this wasn't what I had in mind for us to do today, but I'm glad we talked. I'm glad you told me what was on your mind*	Uncomfortable silence. I don't know what to say, so I say nothing. Might as well be honest. I am glad he told me. I feel like he trusts me at some level and maybe I helped by letting him vent.
	C: That's OK. Do you have to go now?	He doesn't want me to go!
	W: *Yes, I have to meet with my supervisor.*	
	C: OK.	
	W: *I'll be back on Friday. I'll come back and see you then.*	
	C: Yes, OK.	
	W: *Good. Take care, Mr. Curtis.*	Whew! I'm glad that's over. I wonder how he's feeling. He seems OK with the conversation. I wonder if there's something I could have done differently so that I could be more sure I acted in the best professional capacity.

Discussion Questions

1. How do you think you might have reacted if *you* were the student social worker listening to this client's story? What would have been the most difficult parts for you? Why?

_____

_____

_____

_____

_____

_____

_____

2. Using the section of the process recording that deals with the incident in the cafeteria, identify three of the social worker's responses that seemed very in tune with the client. Explain why they seemed effective.

_____

_____

_____

_____

_____

3. Identify three responses or statements where you feel the student social worker took a risk that might have been difficult for you. Analyze why each would have been hard for you to do. Were the social worker's efforts effective with this client?

_____

_____

_____

_____

_____

4. Identify three of the student social worker's statements that you feel were not as in tune with the client. Analyze why these responses were not effective and suggest a more appropriate response for each.

_____

_____

_____

_____

_____

_____

5. What are some of the issues for this student (or for you) in dealing with a client's attribution of someone's behavior to racial prejudice?

_____

_____

_____

_____

_____

_____

_____

6. Are you comfortable with the approach taken by this student social worker? If not, why not and what alternative approaches would you support?

_____

_____

_____

_____

_____

_____

7. If you feel that her approach was effective, what were the key elements that made it work?

_____

_____

_____

_____

_____

_____

8. What issues related to differences in age and gender between the social worker and the client might have affected their interaction? Did the student address these, and if so, were her interventions effective?

_____

_____

_____

_____

_____

_____

Activity 2: Practicing "Hanging in There" When Race Is an Issue

Instructions

Form groups of three students. Using the scenario you are assigned by your instructor, take turns role-playing the client, the social worker, and the observer until everyone has played all three roles. Keep each turn under 5 minutes. As the social worker, pay particular attention as to responding to the client's race-related comment genuinely and openly. Try to develop an empathic understanding of the meaning of the client's comment.

As the client, try to put yourself emotionally in the client's shoes and experience directly the impact of the social worker's comments on you to provide genuine feedback to the student social worker.

As the observer, listen acutely and provide direct, honest, but sensitive feedback that acknowledges the difficulties we all face in dealing with racial issues.

Scenario 1

A white social worker in a mental health clinic is doing an intake interview with a 33-year-old African American woman with a diagnosis of chronic undifferentiated schizophrenia and a history of periods of delusional thinking, sometimes resulting in hospitalization. The client has completed several years of college and has had several jobs over the past 10 years as a clerk in the medical records departments of various local hospitals. She had previously been seen at the clinic after her last hospitalization 2 years ago but had stopped coming to treatment over a year ago. Her prior social worker has left the clinic, and she has requested a new one.

The client reports at the beginning of the interview that she is under more stress at work recently since a new director of medical records has been hired. She describes the woman as very demanding and critical; the director is reorganizing the record retrieval system and making other changes as well. The client shares several incidents where she was taken to task by the director in front of other employees. When the social worker asks the client to tell her a little more about the woman, she says, among other things, that the woman is white and doesn't like people "like her" (the client).

Scenario 2

A white social worker works in a residential youth treatment center where the clients are mostly minority youth with unstable family situations and with histories of acting out, poor school performance, and minor delinquency. The social worker has been working with a 15-year-old African American boy, Lionel, since his admission to the program last month. Lionel was admitted to the treatment center after he got into a fight with his mother's boyfriend. The boyfriend was arrested for child abuse, but Lionel's mother refused to allow Lionel to remain at home, saying that he was unmanageable, hanging out with friends until very late at night, refusing to go to school, and threatening her if she tried to discipline him.

In the first of the three sessions the social worker has had with Lionel, he was initially very quiet. Once she reassured him that she wasn't going to report everything he said to the staff or to his mother (explaining under what limited circumstances she might have to), he began to tell her a little about his family situation. He opened up a little further over a game of pool, presenting himself as the victim of various injustices at home and at school. In the third session, while Lionel and the social worker are taking a walk together, he begins telling her about things that go on in his neighborhood, both with his friends and with local drug dealers. Suddenly he stops short, turns, and looks at the social worker and says, "I don't know why I'm telling you this stuff. . . you wouldn't understand."

Scenario 3

A white social worker in a foster care agency who is doing screening interviews for new foster families plans to meet an African American potential foster family in their home. When she comes to their door, Mrs. Williams greets her and invites her in. The social worker notices that when Mrs. Williams first catches sight of her, a look of surprise goes over the client's face. However, she recovers quickly and is gracious in offering the social worker coffee and cookies. However, when the social worker begins the screening process, Mrs. Williams interrupts her, saying that she is surprised that the agency sent this social worker because all their other social workers have been black. Her husband seems startled by this comment and says that it doesn't matter.

EXERCISE 14   *"Stations": Ethnographic Strength-Based Interviewing*

Ann Ahlquist

Purpose

1. To help you develop strength-based interviewing skills.
2. To develop insight about the ways that a social worker's agenda influences the process and outcome of an interview.

Background

Social work practice requires effective interviewing skills. The notion of *discovery* is an essential component of an effective interview, as social workers discover from clients what their dilemmas might be, and discover what capacities they possess for resolution. The ability to ascertain both of these elements through the interview process is a challenge, one requiring the ability to listen and pay keen attention. Respectful attention-giving and empathic listening are social work skills that sound simple, but are, in practice, extremely difficult. These skills are often compromised, sometimes by an overreliance on checklists or preformulated questions, which are both intended to be guides for social workers but often act more like girdles. When checklists or formats are used in a rigid or exclusive manner, the scope of an interview decreases and issues that may be most pressing to the client are ignored. Ethnographic and strength-based interviewing posits that the social worker role is one of learning *from* the client what their experience is and what it means to them.

Instructions

This interviewing exercise requires two groups: interviewers (Group A) and interviewees (Group B). Group A participants will do social work assessment interviews, and members of Group B will role-play a 15-year-old client. The "social workers" will interview the client about reported abuse, and at the end make a determination about the abuse. Prior to the interview, your groups will be separated and you will review information relevant to your role.

Preinterview

Group A: Read Child Protection Social Worker Interviewer material. After reading material, divide into small groups of 3-5 and create six essential questions to ask during the interview. Remember, you are responsible for making a determination about abuse after talking to this client. After discussion, each person should make a copy of these essential questions so they can use them during the role play. There will be paper and markers for your use at the interview station.

Group B: Read Hannah (Hank) role material. After reading the case, divide into pairs. Quiz one another about the role to help commit information about your role to memory. You will be given additional information by the instructor.

Interview

Each interviewee and interviewer will be assigned to a prearranged "station" in the room by instructor. Each station will have paper, pens, and markers for the interviewers' use. Your six essential questions may be used as a guide during the interview. You may begin interviewing immediately.

Postinterview

Return to classroom without discussion between interviewer and interviewee. Bring all notes or materials you completed during the interview.

Group A Reading Material:
Child Protection Social Worker Interviewer

You are a social worker with child protective services and are assigned to interview children about allegations of child maltreatment. You will be responsible for determining the answer to the following two questions at the end of the interview:

1. Did child maltreatment occur?
2. Who was responsible?

Your client will be Hannah (or Hank), age 15. Hannah is presently at Rarig Shelter for Women and Children. She was brought to Rarig last night by the police on a 72-hour "health and welfare" hold. The report you received states Hannah's brother, Patrick, age 6, called police and reported he had seen Hannah and their stepfather, Harold, "naked in bed." Officer Jim visited Hannah's home yesterday. His report states Hannah told him of "sexual abuse for a long time." Officer Jim arrested

Harold, who is now in jail. According to the police report, Hannah's mother, Jennifer, was at home during the sexual abuse but would not talk to the police. Officer Jim wrote in his report that he removed Hannah and Patrick from the home "for their health and welfare."

You have no previous reports about this child or her family. According to the police report, the family consists of Hannah, age 15, Patrick, age 6, stepfather Harold, age 36, and mother, Jennifer, age 33. The family has lived at their present address for 3 months, living at six other addresses in the city during the past 4 years. Both parents list themselves as unemployed. They have no telephone. Hannah is in 10th grade at school, Patrick is in first grade. School attendance is poor; however, you learn from Hannah's school that her grades are outstanding. You attempted to reach Hannah's mother at home but were unsuccessful.

You are now to interview Hannah at Rarig Shelter for Women and Children to make a determination regarding abuse of Hannah. Be sure to take your six essential questions to the interview.

Group B Reading Material:
Hannah (Hank) Role

Your name is Hannah. (If male, you may wish to change your name to Hank and alter aspects of the case below as needed.) You are 15 years old and are in 10th grade. Currently, you are staying at the Rarig Shelter for Women and Children after being placed on a 72-hour police "health and welfare" hold. Your brother, Patrick, age 6, is also at the shelter. Yesterday, Patrick called 911 after he saw you and your stepfather, Harold, naked in a bed together. An officer came to your house last night and you told the police that your stepfather had done "lots of sexual things to you" since he moved in with the family 7 years ago.

You have lived with your mother, Jennifer, since birth. You do not know your father. Your mother works "when she can," but mostly "lives on welfare." You take care of your mother often as she has always been sickly. When you were 8 years old, Harold moved into your home. You liked him at first because he paid lots of attention to you. He gave you special presents, read you stories, let you watch TV with him, and took you to movies. You are afraid of him now because he yells frequently, throws knives when he is angry, and sometimes points a gun at your mother when he has been drinking. Harold started coming into your bedroom when you were 8. He read to you and then rubbed your back. Then he started to rub your crotch, and make you rub his penis, which he called "his dick." You did not tell anyone at first, but then you told your mother. She yelled at Harold, but he denied everything. Your mother told you to "lock your door at night." Harold started taking you to movies and for rides in his black truck. He would often take your hand and make you rub "his dick." He put his fingers in your crotch, which he called "your pussy."

You saw movies at school about good touch-bad touch, but you never told anyone else. You "just lived through it" and "went on with your life." Sometimes you pretended you were somewhere else when it was happening. Harold was often angry and drunk and you tried to stay away from him. He took you into the truck about once a week, and sometimes gave you $10.00. Yesterday, he took you into the bedroom and took all your clothes off, and made you "diddle" (masturbate) him. He gave you $20.00. Harold had sent Patrick out to play yesterday, but he came back in and walked into the bedroom. Patrick called 911. Your mother was out in the kitchen at the time. You are not sure what she was doing. Your stepfather told you to "shut up if the police come," and he ran out. Your mother was furious and cried hysterically. When the police came, you shook your head affirmatively when they asked you if your stepfather had "abused you." Your mother would not talk to you or the police. You feel "numb" and afraid.

Reread the information about Hannah, then pair up with another interviewee to query each other about the role. Your instructor will give you further instructions before the actual interview.

EXERCISE 15 *Beyond Interviewing: Data Collection Methods for Individuals, Families, Organizations, and Communities*

Kim Strom-Gottfried

Purpose

1. To introduce you to methods for gathering information that expand on interviews.
2. To allow you to practice an interview using a data collection tool.
3. To develop your ability to think critically about the relative strengths and weaknesses of different data collection methods.

Background

By now you are familiar with the use of interviews to gather information on clients and their situations. Tools such as those introduced in this exercise help to supplement interviews by graphically displaying information on the clients' support systems or history or by providing quantifiable information about the level of difficulty experienced. Sometimes, using these tools in an interview can put the client at ease or help a reluctant client to open up.

This exercise gives you a chance to try out a tool for data collection and assess the tool's usefulness for various populations or situations. Through discussion with your classmates, you will be introduced to a range of methods, evaluate their advantages and disadvantages, and consider the methods' usefulness for your future practice.

Instructions

Your instructor will divide the class into pairs or small groups, give you the role of social worker or client, and assign you to try one of the following data collection methods in a role-played interview.

AUTHOR'S NOTE: I wish to thank James McDonell, Ph.D., from whom the structured community analysis was adapted.

If you are the social worker: Read the instructions for the data collection method you are assigned and think about how you will describe it to your client and use it in the interview.

If you are the client: You can portray yourself, make up a fictionalized client, or act out some combination of the two. Think about yourself as the client, anticipating your situation and role prior to the interview.

When you are both ready, begin the role play. Remember that the purpose of the exercise is to try out the data collection tool and examine its strengths and limitations.

When the interview is over, each participant should address the following questions and be prepared to discuss them with the class.

EXERCISE 15

Questions

1. Describe, briefly, the data collection method you used.

_____

_____

_____

_____

2. How did the method used "feel" to you as the "client"? As the social worker?

_____

_____

_____

_____

3. In what ways was the tool useful in gathering information and building the helping relationship?

_____

_____

_____

_____

4. What were the limitations in the tool for gathering information or building the relationship? What other sources of information might you need to supplement what this technique helped you learn about your client?

_____

_____

_____

_____

_____

5. With what client populations and situations might this tool work best?

_____

_____

_____

_____

_____

6. With what situations or clients would you *not* want to use this method?

_____

_____

_____

_____

_____

7. What particular skills do social workers need to use this tool effectively?

_____

_____

_____

_____

_____

Tools for Collecting and Organizing Data:
Rapid Assessment Instruments

Rapid assessment instruments (RAIs) are brief, questionnaire-like instruments that ask clients questions about the degree, severity, or magnitude of specific problems in social functioning. The responses on each of the questions are calculated and yield a score that represents the client's level of difficulty with the particular issue being measured, for example, marital relations, substance use, or self-esteem. The instruments demonstrated here were developed for social workers who need an easy-to-use method for evaluating and tracking client functioning. These scales have several important characteristics: they can be administered repeatedly, they use similar directions, and they are scored in the same manner, on a 1-100 scale, where a low score reflects the relative absence of a problem and a high score indicates the presence of a more severe problem. For many of the scales "clinical cutting scores" have been established, so that a score of 30 or higher indicates a clinically significant problem in the area being measured.

There are also some cautions in using the measures. These scales were not intended to be used by persons under 12 years of age, due to the level of literacy, cognitive development, and ability to integrate affective content that the scales require. For similar reasons, the scales should also not be used with persons who have severe cognitive impairments such as retardation, senility, active psychosis, or brain damage. Whereas "cognitive impairment" refers to a continuum of functioning, the scales may not be valid, if due to the impairment, the client cannot understand and properly complete the list of items. In addition, the scales should be used with caution in circumstances where the social worker can give or withhold something of value to the client. The answers a client provides on the scales may not be valid if he or she is attempting to influence the worker's decisions. Finally, the scales are targeted for use by those who have grown up or been socialized in a Western culture, and the validities of the scales were established based on a population of individuals who have grown up in the United States. Therefore, the scales may not be effective or appropriate for use with persons from other cultures.

The instruments shown in Figure 15.1 reflect only 5 of the 20 questions that would normally appear on each scale. Therefore, your role play will involve exploring the "client's" presenting problem, introducing the use of RAIs, and asking him or her to complete the abbreviated versions contained here. What apprehensions might a client experience in using such an instrument and how would you address such concerns?

For information on the psychometric characteristics of these instruments or to order the complete scales, contact WALMYR Publishing Co., P.O. Box 6229, Tallahassee, FL 32314-6229; (850) 656-2787; e-mail: scales@walmyr.com.

For information on other RAIs, see Fischer and Corcoran (1994).

INDEX OF FAMILY RELATIONS (IFR)

Name: _____ Today's Date: _____

This questionnaire is designed to measure the way you feel about your family as a whole. It is not a test, so there are no right or wrong answers. Answer each item as carefully and as accurately as you can by placing a number beside each one as follows:

    1 = None of the time
    2 = Very rarely
    3 = A little of the time
    4 = Some of the time
    5 = A good part of the time
    6 = Most of the time
    7 = All of the time

1. The members of my family really care about each other.   _____
2. I think my family is terrific.   _____
3. My family gets on my nerves.   _____
4. I really enjoy my family.   _____
5. I can really depend on my family.   _____

GENERALIZED CONTENTMENT SCALE (GCS)

Name: _____ Today's Date: _____

This questionnaire is designed to measure the way you feel about your life and surroundings. It is not a test, so there are no right or wrong answers. Answer each item as carefully and as accurately as you can by placing a number beside each one as follows:

    1 = None of the time
    2 = Very rarely
    3 = A little of the time
    4 = Some of the time
    5 = A good part of the time
    6 = Most of the time
    7 = All of the time

1. I feel powerless to do anything about my life.   _____
2. I feel blue.   _____
3. I think about ending my life.   _____
4. I have crying spells.   _____
5. It is easy for me to enjoy myself.   _____

Figure 15.1.   Sample Items From Two Rapid Assessment Instruments

SOURCE: Copyright © 1990 by Walter W. Hudson. Used with permission of WALMYR Publishing Co.

Tools for Collecting and Organizing Data:
Life History Grid for Adolescents
by James E. Anderson and Ralph A. Brown

Notes for Practice

A "life history grid" is a means to elicit the life history of a client in graphic form during an initial interview. It is a therapeutic, task-oriented tool that helps build the client-worker relationship, correlate items of the client's life history, identify periods of crisis, and summarize the formal written record.

The authors developed the grid from early attempts to summarize in chronological order facts contained in various documents (from schools, physicians, social workers, probation officers, and so forth) in preparing presentence reports on youthful offenders. Presentation of facts in tabular form uncovered important information and correlations that were "hidden" within specialized reports. Certain facts became available at a glance. Information from a single report was not necessarily significant on its own, but when correlated with information from several other reports, its significance in the client's life emerged.

After a year of constructing such grids, the authors realized the obvious: the grid should be done by the client. It soon became clear that with the client's participation, the grid's benefits were greater than originally thought.

The importance of the initial interview is well known, as are the difficulties encountered when the client is an adolescent who is a reluctant participant. The life history approach has been described elsewhere, as has a technique in which adolescents participate in the writing of their own reports. In addition, a task-oriented approach has proved successful. Reid and Epstein state, "It is apparent . . . that children and adolescents can identify pertinent target problems. They can be committed to task-structured work to reduce problems." Garvin believes that "performing tasks comes naturally to adolescents since they must engage in planful action in order to embark on new roles." He uses an "abbreviated life story" in his initial work with groups of adolescents and believes that adolescents can be helped to accomplish tasks with instruments such as a "work sheet." Finally, Bass supports the authors' view that some structure in working with adolescents gives them a level of comfort in interviews and gives the practitioner a sense of being in control of the treatment process. The structure provides both a format for direction and a reminder of tasks. The life history grid combines all these advantages in working with adolescent clients.

Initial Interview

The initial interview begins with the client and practitioner sitting together at a small desk with a large ruled sheet of paper. After a brief introduction, the practitioner describes the grid along the following lines.

> *You and I are going to try to summarize your whole life up to now on one sheet of paper. The left-hand column will be the years of your life. Let's see, you were born in 1961, so you were 1 in 1962, 2 in 1963, and so on. Perhaps the next column can be for geography—where you've lived and traveled. The next column will be for schools—how you did in each grade and the names of the schools you attended. How should we label the other columns?*

The client then designates topics for the other columns, such as family, friends, sports, and health, while the practitioner writes the headings in as dictated.

When the blank grid has been prepared, the practitioner, acting as recorder, asks the client to identify events in his or her life. Recording events in chronological order is less successful than allowing the client to start anywhere, letting associations stimulate memory. Gradually the squares fill up, usually with some corrections in dates and sequences. The authors' experience has been that the client will retrace previous events in the grid later in the interview, adding more personal and perhaps more painful insights to those earlier years. An observer might describe this activity as two people trying to solve an intriguing puzzle together. The client and practitioner then study and discuss the finished grid.

The discussion may focus on the data as a whole or on particular events in the client's life. The practitioner should help the client make connections that have not been made to date between experiences. The structure of the grid allows the client to point concretely to areas that need to be discussed or that require further attention in subsequent interviews.

Therapeutic Tool

The life history grid is currently used during initial interviews with clients at Adolescent Services, Chedoke Hospitals, Hamilton, Ontario, Canada, a program to which young people are referred who have been through a multiplicity of services and agencies. Most of these clients arrive suspecting they are going to be subjected to yet another "shrinking session." In working with the grid during the initial interview, however, the adolescent is caught off guard in something new and involving.

Adolescents are notoriously difficult to engage in treatment, especially if they have been exposed to many agencies. Because the grid represents a task-oriented approach, it facilitates the initial, tenuous relationship between the adolescent and practitioner, especially because it allows the adolescent a sufficient degree of distance. When the client can devote attention to the grid, for example, he or she does not have to make continual eye contact with the practitioner. This protects the client from being overwhelmed by the practitioner. In addition, the client can test the practitioner by gradually revealing pieces of information in response to questions about the grid and by seeking intermittent assistance from the practitioner.

The grid brings structure to the interview in that an uncomplicated guideline for gathering data is provided. This can reduce the practitioner's anxiety about interviewing adolescents. It is common for the client to pull his or her chair closer to the practitioner and pick up the grid while speaking, often making corrections such as "No, my brother left home back here when I was 11, not 13," or "Oh, I forgot to say, when I was in Grade 5, my father drank a lot and used to hit my mother."

Case History

The grid can assist some clients identify crisis periods in their lives. A "bad year" can be recognized by negative entries in two or more columns of the grid and subsequent deterioration of behavior. David, a 17-year-old high school student whose grid is shown in Figure 15.2, is an example of a client whose behavior was clarified through the use of the grid.

Presenting Problem. David was arrested for causing a disturbance at a rock concert and assaulting an officer while resisting arrest. Prior to the concert, David had consumed six bottles of beer and 50 mg. of diazepam.

Geography. David was born in 1956, six months after his parents' marriage, in the small Canadian town of Hillfield where his father had a small insurance and real estate agency. In 1959, the family moved to Peterboro, where his father purchased a large real estate company. They moved to Hamilton in 1968 when David's mother became a high school teacher to support the family.

Family. David was living with his parents, a sister aged 14, and brother aged 8. The father's alcoholism caused him to lose his business in Peterboro. The family moved to Hamilton so that David's mother could work. In January 1971 David's mother stopped working because his father had joined Alcoholics Anonymous and began working again as a realtor.

DATE	AGE	GEOGRAPHY	FAMILY	SCHOOL	HEALTH	ACTIVITIES	OTHER
3 JUNE 1956		HILLFIELD	FATHER:21 GEORGE MOTHER:20 JOAN				
'57	1	↓					
'58	2						
'59	3	↓ PETERBORO	♀ KAREN BORN				
'60	4				ASTHMA: → HOSP. 3 DAYS		
'61	5			K			
'62	6			I			
'63	7			II	APPENDIX		
'64	8			IV (SKIPPED)		CUBS	
'65	9	→ SMALLER HOUSE	♂ DONALD BORN FATHER ALCOHOLIC	V NEW SCHOOL ↓		↓ ALL BADGES SUNDAY SCHOOL	
'66	10			III			
'67	11			VII		SCOUTS ↓	INTEREST IN READING
'68	12	↓ HAMILTON	DAD "FIRED" MOTHER WORKING	VIII		NEW FRIENDS PAPER ROUTE DELIVERY WATER POLO BASKETBALL SWIM	
'69	13			IX ↑ HONOR STUDENT			
'70	14	↓	FATHER: AA + JOB	X INTEREST ↓	ASTHMA ↓	FRIENDS ↓	↓ MARIJUANA
'71	15		MOTHER STOPS WORK	XI 60%	EMERGENCY INJECTIONS ✱✱		LSD × 5 ALCOHOL
'72	16			XII 60%	✱✱		
'73	17	↓		XIII 55%		DAILY ↓	WINE + VALIUM → VIOLENCE → COURT

Figure 15.2. David's Life History Grid
SOURCE: Anderson and Brown (1980). Used with permission.

School. David had a measured IQ of 125. He skipped Grade 3 and was successful in school until Grade 10 when his grades fell from 82% to 60%. Since then, David's motivation had been low, and his grades were barely passing. He was doing poorly in his final year of high school (Ontario has 13 grades).

Health. David's medical history showed a brief hospitalization for asthma early in 1960 when he was almost 4 years old. Asthma became a problem again in 1970 and he had been seen in emergency rooms six times since then for acute attacks, which were treated by injections. He also had an appendectomy in 1963.

Activities. Until Grade 10, David has been active in sports, particularly swimming, water polo, and basketball. He spent 3 years in Cub Scouts and earned as many badges as possible. He was in scouts until moving to Hamilton, where he had two paper routes and made deliveries for a drugstore on weekends to assist the family financially. He no longer needed a part-time job when his father resumed work. Formerly, David had a wide range of friends, but this had narrowed to three male classmates who spent their time together mainly talking and listening to records. He knew some girls but had not dated alone.

Drug Use. David was introduced to marijuana in the fall of 1970 and was smoking daily, usually with his friends. He had used LSD five times. On one occasion, he mixed wine and diazepam and became violent, destroying furniture in a friend's recreation room. He tried the combination again with similar effects, which led to his involvement with the court.

Discussion. David was a tall, handsome, shy young man who came to the interview well dressed and scared. Figure 15.2 summarizes the events of his life. In subsequent meetings, he described the difficult years during which he had contributed to the family financially, assisted in raising his younger siblings, and provided support for his mother, who shared her worries and feeling of loneliness with him each night after the other children were in bed. He pointed out proudly that he had done well in school and sports in spite of this. As he studied the grid, he noted that "things went downhill after things got better at home." He described with anger how his mother "dropped me, once *her husband* cleaned up his act." For the first time, he realized that his father's return, his poor grades at school, the recurrence of asthma, his changing friendships, his quitting sports, and his use of marijuana all occurred within the space of a few months.

This case example illustrates the benefits of using the life history grid. The grid helped David and the practitioner assess the interrelationships among various areas of David's life. The grid helped David develop insight and identify issues, such as things getting worse after things got better at home, which could be discussed.

The life history grid summarizes a case quickly because data are recorded on one page in chart form. Furthermore, each grid is unique, having a character of its own. Because the grid is not a standardized form, but rather is created for each client, the size of the columns will vary in relation to each client's needs and wishes. One client may request that the column for "social life and activities," for example, be larger than the other columns. Another client may wish to emphasize academic involvement rather than other areas of activity.

The life history grid is a useful supplement to the formal written record in that the practitioner can quickly review a case without having to read long anecdotal narratives. The practitioner has a readily available guideline for issues needing to be entered into the formal record or for presenting the case to colleagues.

In summary, the life history grid is a task-oriented tool for involving a client in treatment, thus improving cooperation and rapport. It is a device for correlating the various aspects of a client's life history and, in some cases, identifying crisis periods. It is a therapeutic tool that helps the client survey the events of his or her life and interpret their significance. Finally, the life history grid is an easily consulted summary of the formal written record, summarizing a client's life history in graphic form. The following is a blank grid to use for your interview.

A grid to use for your interview

Year	Age	Family	School	Health	Friends	Interests	Other

Tools for Collecting and Organizing Data: Ecomap

Using an ecosystemic perspective, the social worker looks at and addresses the interacting factors that make up the client's environment. In an ecosystemic assessment, the clinician collects data useful in creating a picture of the client within his or her environmental context. One tool that helps in this process is the ecomap, in which the social worker and client identify, organize, and depict relevant environmental factors affecting the client's individual or family context. Ecomaps are useful in clarifying data related to the supports and stresses in the client's environment. The ecomap reveals patterns such as social isolation. It also shows the direction in which resources flow (e.g., if client gives but does not receive support). Doing an ecomap can also facilitate the helping relationship, as the process of actively drawing or filling in the information can dissipate the tension that sometimes accompanies a verbal interview.

Typically, the social worker will explain the ecomap to the client and describe how it helps in getting a better picture of their current situation. Then, with the interviewer's prompting and assistance, the client can begin to provide the information and fill in the map. As an alternative, the social worker can begin to draw the depictions and then turn it over to the client as he or she becomes more comfortable with the process. Often, both the process and the visual depiction of the situation allow the client to recognize patterns or develop insights that he or she might not have previously considered.

In the map, the social systems that affect (or could potentially affect) the client/family are placed within circles. These circles are arranged in a circle. The individual or the family unit is placed within a circle in the middle of the other circles. The interaction between the individual or family and these social systems is indicated by symbols. These symbols include: ———— strong relationship; - - - - - tenuous relationship; -/-/-/-/- stressful or conflictual relationship.

A sample ecomap (see Figure 15.3) and a blank one, to use in your interview, are included here.

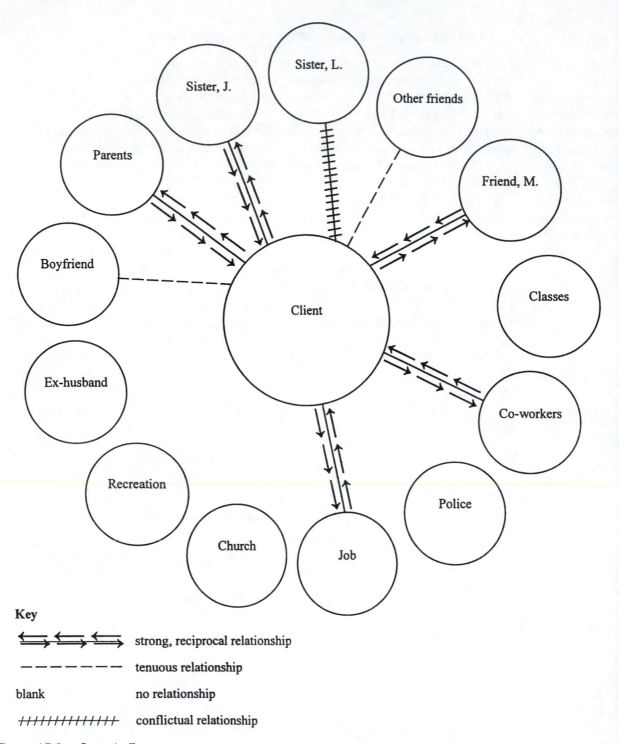

Key

$\Longleftrightarrow \Longleftarrow \Longleftarrow$ strong, reciprocal relationship

— — — — — — —   tenuous relationship

blank   no relationship

+/+/+/+/+/+/+/+/+   conflictual relationship

Figure 15.3.   Sample Ecomap

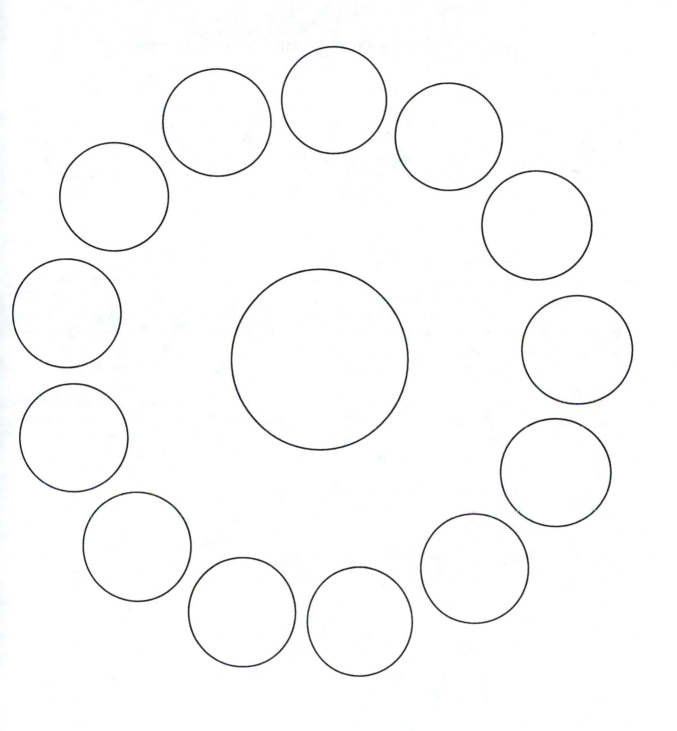

Tools for Collecting and Organizing Data: Genogram

Using an ecosystemic perspective, social workers look at and address the interacting factors that make up the client's environment. In an ecosystemic assessment, the interviewer collects data useful in creating a picture with the client of his or her environmental context. One tool for understanding the person in his or her family context is the genogram. This tool can be used to identify and organize some of the historical information and familial patterns that may influence present interactions in a client's life. The process of completing a genogram can facilitate the helping relationship, because the process of actively drawing or filling in the information can dissipate the tension that sometimes accompanies a verbal interview.

Typically, the social worker starts by explaining the genogram to the client and describing how it can help to give a picture of the client's current situation and family history. Then, with the interviewer's prompting and assistance, the client can begin to provide the information and fill in the chart. As an alternative, the social worker can begin to draw the depictions and then turn it over to the client as he or she becomes more comfortable with the process. Often, both the process and the visual depiction of the family allow the client to recognize patterns or develop insights that he or she might not have previously considered.

The genogram diagrams the client in his or her generational context, taking into account family history and current members and events. Genograms typically include information on births, deaths, occupations, education, illnesses, alcoholism, divorce, separations, adoptions, and hobbies or interests as they have occurred over time. Additionally, patterns of past, current, and intergenerational family interaction are revealed.

Some of the common symbols used to signify family events and relationships in a genogram are indicated in Figure 15.4. It is best not to get too caught up in drawing it perfectly. Let the client start with whatever family segment is easiest. The important thing is the information it generates, whether or not the chart itself is easy to read. A blank page follows on which you can construct the genogram from your interview.

Genogram format

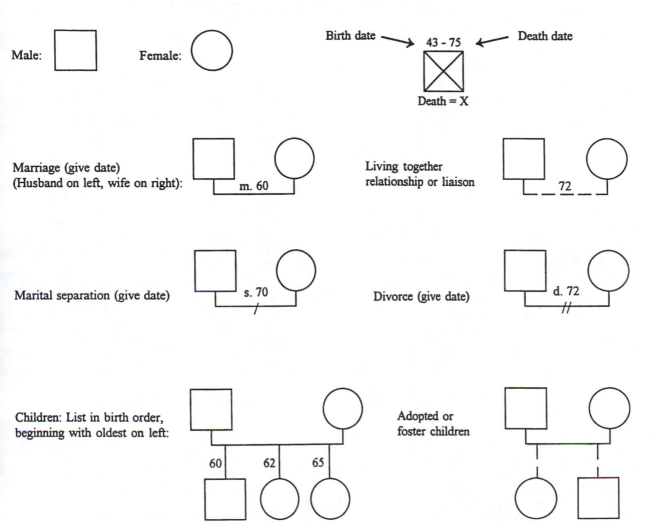

Male:

Female:

Birth date → 43 - 75 ← Death date

Death = X

Marriage (give date)
(Husband on left, wife on right):

m. 60

Living together
relationship or liaison

72

Marital separation (give date)

s. 70

Divorce (give date)

d. 72

Children: List in birth order,
beginning with oldest on left:

60   62   65

Adopted or
foster children

Figures 15.4.   Sample Genogram

GENOGRAM FOR YOUR INTERVIEW

Tools for Collecting and Organizing Data:
Social Network Map

Social networks are the interconnected systems with which a client interacts. Social support networks refer specifically to those relationships that provide support and encourage successful coping with one's life. Clients receive support informally from family, friends, and community members. These relationships are generally reciprocal and have an egalitarian quality, making them a uniquely powerful resource for clients. Social support may take such forms as encouragement and validation, advice-giving, education/resource-sharing, guidance, and concrete assistance.

In social work practice, attention to existing and potential sources of social support is vital, both for assessment and intervention planning. The social network map allows the client and social worker to work together actively in examining what social supports are available and how they function in the client's life. The assessment of social supports addresses existing and potential formal and informal resources, the barriers to involving social supports, and the factors to be considered when incorporating informal resources in the formal service plan.

The social network map has two parts. A circle mapping technique is used to record network membership. Dimensions on the map include household, family, friends, work/school, clubs/organizations/religious groups, neighbors, and agencies/formal service providers. Significant members of these groups are listed in the pie diagram (see Figure 15.5).

The second part of the map is a grid (see Figure 15.6) that is used to record information about the supportive (and unsupportive) roles of various elements of the social network. The individuals listed on the pie chart are indicated on the first column of the grid. The rest of the grid then includes information, for that person, on the quantity and quality of the specific kinds of support (e.g., concrete, emotional, informational/advice) they provide, the direction of support, the degree of closeness of relationship, the frequency of contact, the length (duration) of the relationship, and the amount of criticism in the relationship.

The following questions are useful in translating the data obtained on the map into service goals:

- Who is/could be in the network?
- What are the strengths and resources of the social network (generally and specifically)?
- Are there gaps in areas of needed support? What are they?
- Is there a balanced exchange of support? Reciprocity? Is the client overburdened? Are others overburdened? What changes could promote balance/reciprocity?
- Which network members are particularly responsive, effective, and dependable? Are there a sufficient number of members meeting these criteria?
- Which network members are critical/demanding in a stress-producing, unproductive way?
- What are the barriers to using social support resources?
- How are social support needs prioritized in relation to other client needs?

Family Support Project Social Network Map

Date: ___/___/___
Respondent: _____
ID: _____

Figures 15.5. Family Support Project Social Network Map
SOURCE: Tracy and Whitaker (1990, p. 463). Used with permission of Families International, Inc.

The social network map has two parts. A circle mapping technique is used to record network membership. Dimensions on the map include household, family, friends, work/school, clubs/organizations/religious groups, neighbors, and agencies/formal service providers. Significant members of these groups are listed in the pie diagram (see Figure 15.5).

ID _____	Areas of life	Concrete support	Emotional support	Information/ advice	Critical	Direction of help	Closeness	How often see	How long known
Respondent _____	1. Household 2. Other family 3. Work/school 4. Organizations 5. Other friends 6. Neighbors 7. Professionals 8. Other	1. Hardly ever 2. Sometimes 3. Almost always	1. Hardly ever 2. Sometimes 3. Almost always	1. Hardly ever 2. Sometimes 3. Almost always	1. Hardly ever 2. Sometimes 3. Almost always	1. Goes both ways 2. You to them 3. They to you	1. Not very close 2. Sort of close 3. Very close	0. Does not see 1. Few times/yr. 2. Monthly 3. Weekly 4. Daily	1. Less than 1 yr. 2. 1-5 yrs. 3. More than 5 yrs.
1-6	7	8	9	10	11	12	13	14	15

Figure 15.6.   Family Support Project Social Network Grid

SOURCE: Tracy and Whitaker (1990, p. 466). Used with permission of Families International, Inc.

Tools for Collecting and Organizing Data:
Observing Organizations' Nonverbal Messages

Organizations, like people, communicate nonverbally. Through their locations, their physical setup, the behaviors of their staff, and the promotional materials they share with the public, they convey a variety of messages to prospective clients, other organizations, and society as a whole. Select an organization in your community, preferably one you know little about, and make a brief visit to learn what you can about it.

Note your observations below, then address the questions that follow.

Observations

_____

_____

_____

_____

_____

_____

_____

_____

1. What are your impressions of this agency, its clientele, and staff, based on your visit?

_____

_____

_____

_____

_____

_____

_____

_____

_____

2. What physical characteristics might impede or facilitate clients in accessing this agency's services?

_____

_____

_____

_____

_____

_____

_____

_____

_____

_____

3. How do the agency's brochure and other promotional materials fit with your experience in visiting the site?

_____

_____

_____

_____

_____

_____

_____

_____

_____

4. How might the time or day that you were visiting or the nature of your visit have affected your experience?

_____

_____

_____

_____

_____

_____

_____

_____

_____

5. If you were consulting with this organization, what recommendations would you make to improve the "messages" it is giving to the community?

_____

_____

_____

_____

_____

_____

_____

_____

_____

Tools for Collecting and Organizing Data:
Structured Community Observation

Observation is an important skill in assessing the vitality and functioning of any client system. In this exercise, you will use observation to gather information on a neighborhood or community. Your task is to do structured observation, where the qualities you examine and evaluate are guided by the following questionnaire.

Structured Community Observation Questionnaire

I. Select a neighborhood that encompasses residential and commercial (business) elements, preferably one with which you are unfamiliar. Read through the following sections and follow the directions for each. If you are unable to answer certain items, note that on your form, providing explanations as necessary.

II. Start with a house or an apartment building as a reference point, and, by walking, driving, or taking public transportation, go to each of the services or amenities listed below. Note your observations about these sites and their accessibility.

1. Public transportation

_____

_____

2. Grocery store

_____

_____

3. Discount merchandise store

_____

_____

4. Pharmacy

_____

_____

5. Bank

_____

_____

6. Church

_____

_____

7. Hospital/clinic/medical care

_____

_____

8. Park/play area

_____

_____

9. School

_____

_____

10. Restaurant

_____

_____

11. Library

_____

_____

12. Other relevant services/amenities

_____

_____

III. Rate the physical appearance of the neighborhood along the following dimensions, using the additional space to note your observations

1. Residences/businesses
   are in poor repair   1   2   3   4   5   Residences/businesses
   are in good repair

2. Residences/businesses are
   not attractive in appearance   1   2   3   4   5   Residences/businesses are
   attractive in appearance

3. Yards are poorly kept   1   2   3   4   5   Yards are well kept

4. Streets are in poor repair   1   2   3   4   5   Streets are in good repair

5. Sidewalks are in poor repair   1   2   3   4   5   Sidewalks are in good repair

6. Residential/business area
   is full of trash   1   2   3   4   5   Residential/business area is
   free of trash

7. Low occupancy rate in
   buildings   1   2   3   4   5   High occupancy rate in
   buildings

8. Local school is in poor repair   1   2   3   4   5   Local school is in good repair

9. School yard is full of trash   1   2   3   4   5   School yard is free of trash

10. School has poor play
    equipment   1   2   3   4   5   School has good play
    equipment

11. Park/play area is in poor repair   1   2   3   4   5   Park/play area is in good repair

12. Park/play area is full of trash   1   2   3   4   5   Park/play area is free of trash

IV. Rate the social appearance of the neighborhood along the following dimensions, using the space provided to elaborate on your observations and ratings.

1.	Residential area uncrowded	1	2	3	4	5	Residential area crowded
2.	Commercial area uncrowded	1	2	3	4	5	Commercial area crowded
3.	Residential area quiet	1	2	3	4	5	Residential area noisy
4.	Low barrier density between residences	1	2	3	4	5	High barrier density between residences
5.	People not engaged socially in residential areas	1	2	3	4	5	People engaged socially in residential areas
6.	People not engaged socially in business areas	1	2	3	4	5	People engaged socially in business areas
7.	Businesses not busy	1	2	3	4	5	Businesses are busy
8.	Business are not inviting	1	2	3	4	5	Businesses are inviting
9.	Children's activity not apparent in residential areas	1	2	3	4	5	Children's activity apparent in residential areas
10.	Park/play areas not easily accessible	1	2	3	4	5	Park/play areas easily accessible
11.	Park/play areas uncrowded	1	2	3	4	5	Park/play areas crowded

12.	Park/play area is unsafe	1 2 3 4 5	Park play area is safe
13.	School area is unsafe	1 2 3 4 5	School area is safe
14.	Residential area is unsafe	1 2 3 4 5	Residential area is safe
15.	Neighborhood is alienating	1 2 3 4 5	Neighborhood is welcoming
16.	Neighborhood seems unpleasant to live in	1 2 3 4 5	Neighborhood seems pleasant to live in

V. Choose a business to enter. Rate the physical and social appearance along the following dimensions, using the space provided to elaborate on your ratings.

1.	Interior is in poor repair	1 2 3 4 5	Interior is in good repair
2.	Interior is dirty	1 2 3 4 5	Interior is clean
3.	Interior is uncrowded	1 2 3 4 5	Interior is crowded
4.	People not engaged socially	1 2 3 4 5	People engaged socially
5.	Interior is quiet	1 2 3 4 5	Interior is noisy
6.	Staff are discourteous	1 2 3 4 5	Staff are friendly
7.	Staff are not helpful	1 2 3 4 5	Staff are helpful

VI. Please respond to the following questions

   1. What factors might have influenced your observations and ratings of the neighborhood?

     _____

     _____

     _____

     _____

     _____

     _____

   2. Would you live in the residential neighborhood chosen? Please state the reasons for your response.

     _____

     _____

     _____

     _____

     _____

     _____

   3. Would you do business in the commercial neighborhood chosen? Please state the reasons for your response.

     _____

     _____

     _____

     _____

     _____

     _____

4. Would you own a business in the commercial neighborhood chosen? Please state the reasons for your response.

_____

_____

_____

_____

_____

_____

Tools for Collecting and Organizing Data: Unstructured Community Observation

Observation is an important social work skill. Seeing a client in a natural setting, such as on the job or in the classroom, gives social workers valuable information to use in assessment and intervention planning. Similarly, observation skills can be used with larger systems, such as groups, organizations, and communities. In this activity, you will tour the community or neighborhood that you have been assigned and use your eyes and ears to develop impressions of the strengths and weaknesses of the area. Although you may tour the neighborhood on foot or by car with a classmate who is using structured observation methods, the two of you should not compare notes or discuss what you are observing. Address the following questions after completing your observations.

Questions

1. What are your impressions of this community, based on your observations? (What are its assets and needs? Would it be a comfortable community in which to live? work? play? with which to do community organizing?)

_____

_____

_____

_____

_____

_____

_____

2. What observations or interactions influenced your opinions?

_____

_____

_____

_____

_____

_____

_____

3. What previous knowledge or experience did you have with the "community" you were observing?

_____

_____

_____

_____

_____

_____

4. How did previous knowledge or experience affect your observations—both what you observed and what sense you made of what you saw? What other variables might have affected your observations?

_____

_____

_____

_____

_____

_____

References

Anderson, J. E., & Brown, R. A. (1980, July). Notes for practice: Life history grid for adolescents. *Social Work,* pp. 321-323.

Fischer, J., & Corcoran, K. (1994). *Measures for clinical practice.* New York: Free Press.

Tracy, E. M., & Whitaker, J. K. (1990, October). The social network map: Assessing social support in clinical practice. *Families in Society,* pp. 463, 466.

4 MAKING SENSE OF DATA THROUGH ASSESSMENT

EXERCISE 16 *Roundtable Interview*

Kim Strom-Gottfried

Purpose

1. To practice the skills needed in an initial interview.
2. To practice writing assessments based on the information and impressions gathered in an initial interview.
3. To critically examine the impressions formed in a first interview.

Background

Initial interviews allow clients the opportunity to share information and feelings about their situation and the difficulties for which they are seeking your help. Generally, first interviews will give you an impression of the client, their needs, and your ability to assist them. The questions you ask should be targeted at helping you to achieve this goal.

First interviews also provide the foundation for *assessment:* the social worker's understanding about the important features of the case and the way that various factors contribute to the client's current difficulties.

Instructions

In this exercise, you and your classmates will work together to be the "collective social worker" interviewing your instructor as he or she portrays a client seeking assistance at a rural mental health center. Sit in a circle or horseshoe shape with your instructor sitting so that everyone can see him or her. After your instructor gives you background information on the case, you and your classmates should ask questions appropriate to an initial interview. Because all of you are participating as one social worker, you cannot control the pacing or sequencing of questions. However, you do have control over your body language and the phrasing of your questions and can construct them based on what you've read in your text on interviewing.

At the conclusion of the interview, address the items below. Write a brief (2-3 paragraph) assessment and a sentence or two indicating what your treatment plan would be at this point and how long you expect to see the client.

Following this, your instructor will debrief with the class and discuss your impressions on the case.

EXERCISE 16

Missing Information

What else do you wish you'd asked? What more do you need to know?

_____

_____

_____

_____

_____

_____

_____

_____

Assessment

What is the presenting problem? What is the problem for work? Is anyone else involved? How is the client functioning? What strengths are evident?

_____

_____

_____

_____

_____

_____

_____

_____

Assessment (continued)

_____

_____

_____

_____

_____

_____

_____

_____

_____

Treatment Plan

_____

_____

_____

_____

_____

_____

_____

_____

_____

_____

EXERCISE 17 *Assessing Your Family of Origin*

Mary L. McCarthy, Blanca Ramos, Carla Sofka, and Sue Lyman

Purpose

1. To apply the concepts used in family assessments to your family of origin.
2. To look at your own family experience and the role it played in creating your current values, attitudes, and biases.
3. To think about and discuss the ways your family experience may influence your social work practice.

Background

The assessment of families relies on different concepts to describe the functioning of the family unit, its relationship with the external environment, and the interactions among individual members. A first step in applying these concepts to the families in our practice is applying them to that family with which we are most familiar—the one in which we grew up. Not only does this examination help us understand the different ways that families work, but it also helps us to look at our own development, thereby fostering self-awareness.

Self-awareness is a critical component of social work practice. Self-awareness influences all aspects of our work including initial engagement, how we listen to clients, our communication with others, our approach to intervention, and our ability to practice in an ethical and competent manner. Family experience plays a crucial role in the development of our personal values, attitudes, and biases. Understanding ourselves by looking at our family of origin can assist us in understanding the ways our current values, attitudes, and beliefs may influence our social work practice.

Instructions

This assignment requires that you examine your family of origin and be able to describe it in light of the family concepts discussed in your texts. Your family of origin refers to those people with whom you spent your childhood. You may have come from a traditional nuclear family;

you may have experienced diverse forms of family life as a child. Most families have both "functional" and "dysfunctional" aspects to them, but all of these features contribute to your view of relationships and family life. Unless instructed otherwise by your teacher, you will not be asked to share this information in class.

After this reflection, you will complete a genogram about your own family of origin and an ecomap of your current life situation. To complete the genogram and ecomap, you must spend some time thinking about your family experience and the role these experiences played in creating your current values, attitudes, and biases regarding family dynamics. You will use these tools in class, discussing with a classmate the ways your family experience may influence your practice.

If you have concerns about your ability to complete this assignment based on your family history, please see your instructor.

The following readings will assist you with this assignment if you are not yet familiar with some of the terms used to describe family structure and functioning:

References

Hartman, A. (1978). Diagrammatic assessment of family relationships. *Social Casework, 59,* 467-474.

Hepworth, D. H., Rooney, R. H., & Larsen, J. A. (1997). Assessing family functioning in diverse family and cultural contexts. In *Direct social work practice: Theory and skills* (5th ed., pp. 276-316). Pacific Grove, CA: Brooks/Cole.

McPhatter, A. (1993). Assessment revisited: A comprehensive approach to understanding family dynamics. In J. Rauch, *Assessment: A sourcebook for social work practice* (pp. 31-45). Milwaukee, WI: Families International.

In Preparation for Class

a. Reflect on your family of origin and address the questions on concepts in assessing families. Unless your instructor says otherwise, these will be your private notes and will not be collected.

b. Complete an ecomap of your *current* family situation, using the space provided.

c. Complete a genogram of your family based on information that you already have, going back to your maternal and paternal grandparents.

d. In class, you will be paired with a fellow classmate. Briefly describe your family to your partner, using the concepts for family assessment and the ecomap and genogram. Address primarily those things that you think are important to understanding your own strengths, needs, and areas for growth as a social worker. After your partner has described his or her own family, take turns discussing the following questions.

I. How do you think that your upbringing, culture, or ethnicity influences your style of relating to clients? Discuss the impact of these aspects of your heritage on your work with clients.

II. Your personal style of dealing with problems or concerns in your life has an impact on your work. Describe how your own coping style might influence the way you interact with clients, your supervisor, and/or your co-workers.

III. As a result of personal beliefs, values, and ethnic/cultural heritage, what value-oriented or ethical dilemmas may arise in your work with clients? Can you think of any particular group or population that has triggered feelings of uneasiness or discomfort? Are there situations in which you are fearful of something or someone who is different from yourself or your experiences? Identify and discuss potential dilemmas that you have faced or anticipate in your work with clients. Briefly describe potential strategies for dealing with such dilemmas.

IV. What have you learned about yourself that you didn't realize before you did this exercise that will strengthen your work with clients? How will these insights assist you in family assessments? What concepts have you discovered that can be applied to your assessment of other families?

EXERCISE 17

Concepts in Assessing Families

1. What were the internal boundaries in your family? Were there subgroups or alliances in your family? Did the subgroups include extended family members? How did the alliances affect the functioning of the family?

2. What was the power structure in your family? Who had the most influence? Were there different domains of influence for different people? How was the balance of power maintained?

3. What formal and informal roles did the individual members of the family play? Did these roles contribute to or impede your family's functioning? Were roles adopted or ascribed? Did they contribute to the growth of the individuals in the family or restrict that growth?

4. How were decisions made in your family? Were the needs of all family members considered or were there family members that participated in the decision making by agreeing, submitting, or discounting their own needs? Was there a dominant figure or subgroup that made decisions with no room for negotiating or consideration of the needs of others? Was there a style of decision making in your family where no one's needs were considered and decisions were avoided?

5. How were feelings expressed in your family? Was it safe to talk about feelings or was it taboo? What was the affect and range of feeling expressed in your family?

6. Did your family have goals? What were they? Were they shared by all of the members? How did these goals affect family life?

7. What did your family believe in?

8. What were the myths in your family? Did they contribute to the health of the family? Did they facilitate the growth of the individual members of the family or did they restrict that growth?

9. How did your family members communicate with one another? Was it effective?

10. Identify the strengths that you saw in your family.

11. How do you think your family experience influenced you as an individual today?

12. Did you come away from your childhood with strong feelings regarding family-related issues?

13. Did your early experience with your family create any issues that you feel may affect how you deal with clients? Are these issues that you need to address or resolve? How would you go about addressing or resolving them?

Specify issues that you feel will be particularly challenging or difficult:

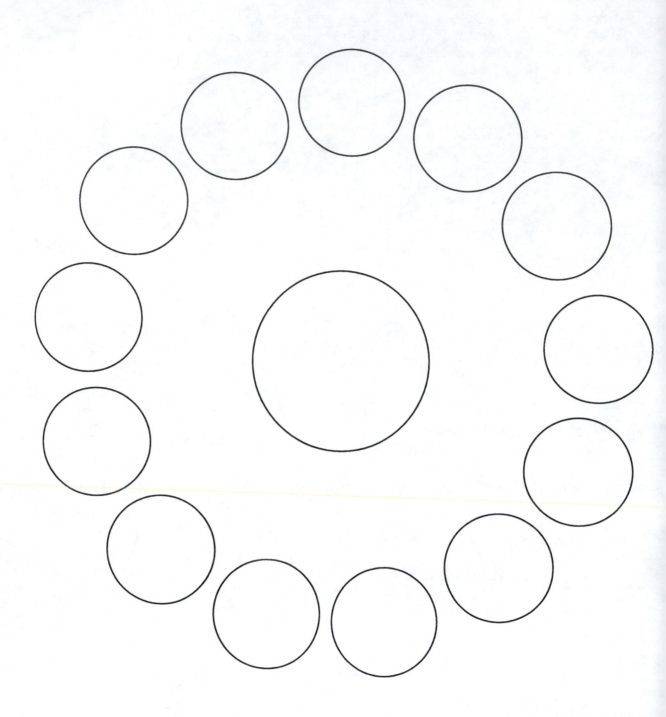

GENOGRAM OF YOUR FAMILY

EXERCISE 18 *The Organizational Diversity Audit*

Kim Strom-Gottfried and Megan Morrissey

Purpose

1. To encourage you to look at the various forms of diversity among clientele and personnel at your field placement or workplace.
2. To develop impressions about your organization based on the process and findings of this exercise.

Background

Social work agencies are committed to diversity, both to competently serve clients from a variety of racial and cultural backgrounds and because staff diversity is an enriching and valued goal. Yet fulfilling intentions about diversity can be difficult for a variety of reasons—the term *diversity* can take on many meanings, it can be difficult to recruit and retain diverse staff, or staff may be clustered in some parts of the organization and absent in others. Asamoah (1995) suggests that organizations conduct "diversity audits" to evaluate their strengths and weaknesses in building a multicultural workforce.

This exercise gives you a chance to formally examine aspects of diversity in your field agency, workplace, or college or university and to use this data to draw some impressions about the organization's pluralism and your place in it.

Instructions

Consider the following grid a tool in gathering data about the demographics of persons who make up your agency (or whatever organization you have chosen to examine). Talk to your field instructor and/or task supervisor before attempting to gather this information. What are their impressions and recommended strategies for gathering this information? What data may be most easily and comfortably obtained through casual observation? Through agency documents or records? Which of the items below are the most sensitive or taboo at your agency?

After you have the sanction to proceed, attempt to capture the makeup of your agency using the grid. Determine the total number of employees in the program or organization and the proportion represented in different groups. Record your findings in each cell of the grid.

Following this research, address the analysis questions and be prepared to discuss your observations with your classmates.

EXERCISE 18

Agency Analysis

Characteristics	Myself	Co-Workers	Management	Clientele
Gender				
Age				
Social Class				
Religion				
Ethnicity				
Race				
Dis/Ability				
Partner/Marital Status				
Education/Credentials				
Other (what's important to you?)				

Analysis Questions

1. What kinds of information were immediately available to you, and what things were hidden?

_____

_____

_____

_____

_____

_____

_____

_____

_____

_____

_____

2. What patterns do you find in looking at the grid? Are there any gaps in the data or areas that seem out of proportion with others?

_____

_____

_____

_____

_____

_____

_____

_____

_____

_____

3. How do you think the clients or service recipients perceive the agency?

_____

_____

_____

_____

_____

_____

_____

_____

_____

_____

4. Where do you fit into the organization? Are you more like or unlike the others who share your professional status? What are the main areas of similarity and difference between yourself and your co-workers? Between your co-workers and management? (What does the grid help you learn about yourself, your co-workers, administrators, and constituents?)

_____

_____

_____

_____

_____

_____

_____

_____

_____

_____

5. How does diversity (or lack of it) affect organizational effectiveness?

_____

_____

_____

_____

_____

_____

_____

_____

6. Based on your experience in gathering these data and based on your analysis of the grid, what changes might be needed at your agency with respect to diversity? Do they reflect isolated or systemic problems? How might this information or this exercise be helpful to you in a professional organizing or administrative position?

_____

_____

_____

_____

_____

_____

_____

_____

_____

Reference

Asamoah, Y. (1995). Managing the new multicultural workplace. In L. Ginsberg & P. R. Keys (Eds.), *New management in human services* (2nd ed., pp. 115-127). Washington, DC: NASW Press.

EXERCISE 19 *Framing Organizational Issues for Assessment and Change: Trouble at HighRisk Hospital*

Marcia B. Cohen and David Wagner

Purpose

1. To help you assess organizational issues for agency change.
2. To familiarize you with the skills and strategies employed by social workers in the role of change agent.

Background

Organizational change skills are essential to effective social work practice. The direct practitioner has a responsibility to identify organizational problems that negatively affect clients and to attempt to do something about them. Work with organizations entails specific practice skills, tactics, and strategies. Potential obstacles must be identified and alliances with influential actors need to be forged. Organizational assessment and intervention can be highly effective in making a human service agency more responsive to the needs of clients.

Instructions

Your instructor will divide the class into small discussion groups. Read the case material on HighRisk Hospital and discuss the situation, using the "Questions to Ponder and Discuss" that follow the case material. Each group will choose a recorder who will take notes on the group discussion and report back to the class.

Case Material

Cast of Characters

> *Emmanuel Power,* a social worker at HighRisk Hospital
> *Dr. Ree M. Burse,* an attending physician at HighRisk
> *Mrs. Burden,* an elderly hospital patient

Lotta Empathy, a social work supervisor

Dr. Will Collaborate, an attending physician at HighRisk

Ova Committed, a head nurse at HighRisk

Bea Ready, hospital utilization review coordinator

Bott Tomline, the new hospital administrator

Soshel Lee Conscious, former chief of medicine at HighRisk

Rea Firm, director of social work at HighRisk

The Case

Emmanuel Power ("Em" to his friends) is a social worker at HighRisk Hospital. He works in the hospital's geriatric unit. Many of the elderly patients on the unit have experienced severe social problems that compound their illnesses, such as inadequate incomes, lack of family and community supports, and a lack of home care resources for discharged patients. The department of social work has a consistent record of advocating for patients to remain in the hospital until a viable discharge plan can be put into place. In the climate of increased cost control and managed care, Em and the other members of his department often find themselves at odds with the doctors and administrators. These actors seem overly concerned with compliance with the federal Diagnosis Related Groups (DRGs) and other cost containment measures that led the hospital to lose money when patients stay more than the average length of time associated with their diagnoses.

One day, Em has a big argument with Dr. Ree M. Burse, who is upset that Em hasn't moved quickly enough to get Mrs. Burden out of the hospital and back home. Mrs. Burden is an elderly patient with diabetes, a fractured hip, and a chronic heart problem. She is frequently in the hospital, particularly in the winter and at holiday times. Mrs. Burden lives alone and refuses to consider nursing home or other institutional placements. Dr. Burse informs Em that it is ridiculous that Mrs. Burden has already been in the hospital for 14 days. He points out that the hospital is losing money on her. He says that he is tired of hearing that social service is waiting for home health care arrangements for the patient. He states, "She is ready for discharge. She needs to leave and if she can't go home, forms should be completed for a nursing home placement."

Em's run-in with Dr. Burse gets him support from his supervisor, Lotta Empathy, who has had this kind of argument with Burse many times before. Lotta notes there have been continued problems with Dr. Burse. "If Mrs. Burden was being treated by Dr. Will Collaborate, we wouldn't have this problem, Will works with social service," Lotta points out. Another problem is that the nurses on the floor, who are usually supportive of patients' needs and social workers' recommendations, can't stand

Mrs. Burden. "She is a pain in the neck and drives everyone crazy," says head nurse Ova Committed, "she should get out of here already!"

Although social workers note clearly in patient charts when there are social problems preventing discharge, the attitude toward continued stays varies with the personality of the doctors, the support of other personnel such as nursing, and the attitude of hospital administrators. After Em's altercation with Dr. Burse, he calms his anger long enough to think about how some sort of change could come to HighRisk. Perhaps there needs to be a systematic way in which all professionals could be apprised of patients' social conditions, a way in which social work's recommendations would get greater attention and respect. Ms. Empathy thinks this is an interesting idea. She sees the root problem as the lack of respect for social workers at the hospital as well as the attitudes of some doctors and administrators.

She notes that her friend, utilization administrator Bea Ready, has been conducting a review of HighRisk's 1997 cases, and mentioned that there was some evidence of possible premature discharges by certain physicians. Ms. Ready is concerned with the potential for lawsuits from patients and family members, and the resulting bad publicity.

Em visits Ms. Ready on the pretense of asking her a question. He tells her about his recent argument and she is sympathetic; she had a tussle with Dr. Burse about a patient last year. Em wonders whether there are many cases in the hospital that result in these kinds of problems. Ms. Ready says definitely yes, this always goes on, but it has been getting worse since the financial statement came out last year and new chief administrator, Bott Tomline, gave a speech to the attending physicians, residents, and interns that the hospital had better "get with the 1990s" and sharpen its business practices or go out of business. He urged the doctors to demonstrate more concern about use of hospital beds. Ms. Ready was a little surprised at the tone of his comments, because Mr. Tomline didn't even mention the usual caveat about patient care coming first. She also felt he was exaggerating the hospital's financial situation.

Ready informs Em that up until a year ago, there was a good hospital-wide committee composed of herself, social workers, doctors, and nurses who met weekly and gave systematic input about patients. The system worked very well. The social workers were able to communicate their concerns with a great deal of legitimacy through the committee, which was chaired by the chief of medicine (Soshel Lee Conscious). Unfortunately, Conscious left her position last year for a new job, and while the position was vacant the committee fell into disuse.

Ready thinks reviving the committee might be a good idea, but it will depend on who is assigned to it and what kind of power it has. She is not sure whether Tomline would endorse this new committee. Ready wonders whether Em has spoken with his own director, Rea Firm, about these issues. Rea had a big blowout with Tomline about patients' length of stays several months ago. Ready suggests that Em talk to Rea about the possibility of reviving the hospital-wide committee. While he was thinking all of this over, Em ran into Dr. Will Collaborate in the hall. After some small talk, Will suggests that Em and he chat sometime soon as he has several patients that need assistance from social work. He has been talking with some of the other doctors who also feel there should be more contact between disciplines for better discharge planning. He wonders why there is so little of this at HighRisk.

Em returns to his office to ponder the following questions.

1. What potential allies (individuals or groups) exist for Em Power as a social worker in the hospital, in view of his concerns about hospital discharges? What possible adversaries exist? Who might be neutral?

2. Identify some ways that the discharge issue at HighRisk can be framed or described, depending on the perspective of the person doing the framing. In other words, *what is the issue,* for social workers, nurses, doctors, patients, families, and hospital administrators?

3. How can Em frame the issue to create the most effective strategy for change?

4. Should Em move forward to develop a hospital-wide system of discharge planning? What questions might he want to ask before he did that?

5. Are there any alternative ways you can think of going about influencing hospital administration and policies besides reviving the hospital-wide committee? What are the pros and cons?

5 SETTING GOALS

EXERCISE 20 *Generating and Prioritizing Ideas Using Nominal Group Technique*

James Reinardy and Megan Morrissey

Purpose

1. To acquaint you with the nominal group technique (NGT): a group process for identifying and assigning priority to problems and issues.
2. To learn how NGT can enhance the work of task groups.

Background

Social workers function in task groups, such as committees, in virtually every professional setting. Some task groups may focus on agency or organization change, whereas others address the delivery of services. Task groups are particularly common in host settings, where the social worker is often part of a treatment team. Most social workers receive training in working in treatment groups but less attention is devoted to working in task groups. Nevertheless, this essential professional role is vital to the effective delivery of social services, to organizational response to client needs, and to agency functioning.

Professional social workers frequently work in task groups and teams as part of their professional roles. Task groups differ from treatment groups in that the goal of a task group is to produce a product, such as a policy, a plan, or an event. Relationships between group members are based on a division of labor and the talents or expertise needed to complete the product. In comparison to treatment groups, communication in task groups focuses on the discussion of the task, and it would be expected that self-disclosure would be low. The roles in task groups develop through interaction or are assigned formally, for example, "chairperson," "secretary," or "team leader."

Nominal group technique (NGT) is a process for identifying and assigning priority to problems and issues. It is one of a number of processes social workers employ to move groups through decision-making processes. These techniques are often used in macropractice settings and are sometimes used when social workers are members of task groups. In this exercise you'll select an issue and use NGT to generate options and priorities for action in response to that issue.

Instructions

Step 1: Independent Work

You or your instructor will select a question around which this exercise will be conducted. Typical questions might address an issue of importance locally that is receiving a lot of attention, or an issue being experienced in one of your field agencies. Some examples of questions you may use are listed below:

1. A family service agency has received a grant of $100,000 to provide services to older adults. What services are important for this agency to deliver to this community?
2. A neighborhood organization is concerned about steadily increasing vandalism, crime, and violence in the neighborhood. What actions can be taken to improve the safety of the neighborhood?
3. The Social Work Department is seeking student input on ways to improve the department and the curriculum. What specific actions could the department take to support students in social work?
4. Your agency wants to increase the use of volunteers to supplement its services. What strategies should the organization use to attract and maintain a volunteer workforce?
5. The local school system is concerned about the level of drug and alcohol use by students. What recommendations would you make to the school about steps they can take to decrease the use of substances?
6. You are assigned to a group project with classmates or colleagues. To work well as a team, what behaviors should be expected from each member?

Once the question has been presented, list it in the space provided and take 10 minutes to write down all of the ideas or answers that come to mind when you hear the question. Use a word or two, or a very brief phrase, in listing each idea. You should work silently and independently.

Step 2: Round Robin

Go around the group with each person taking a turn to state one of the ideas he or she had listed in the individual work phase. Your facilitator/instructor will record each idea on a flip chart. Continue going around the group until all of the ideas are exhausted. Some members may have more ideas than others. Some may drop out early but are welcome to return and contribute another idea at their next turn (even if they haven't written that idea down).

There is no discussion of ideas at this time. The group concentrates on getting all of the ideas down on the flip chart as efficiently as possible.

Step 3: Serial Discussion

The group goes through the list of items, discussing each one in turn. The major task here is to clarify and understand each of the ideas, not to argue the value of one idea versus the other. Ideas should be restated if they aren't clear to the participants. Similar ideas may be combined into one—but only if each contributor agrees that the end result captures his or her meaning.

Step 4: Preliminary Vote on Item Importance

Each participant votes independently on the items he or she thinks are most important.

Reflection on the Process

This is not part of the NGT process, but is a helpful step in learning how the process worked and how you can use it in your practice as a social worker. Address the debriefing questions at the end of this exercise in writing or as part of a group discussion.

EXERCISE 20

NGT—Independent Responses

1. List the question to be addressed:

_____

_____

_____

2. List your ideas and responses:

_____

_____

_____

_____

_____

_____

_____

_____

_____

_____

_____

_____

_____

_____

Debriefing Questions

. What were the strengths of using nominal group technique?

_____

_____

_____

_____

_____

_____

_____

. What limitations did you experience?

_____

_____

_____

_____

_____

_____

. Give some examples of situations in which you might want to use this technique in your work.

_____

_____

_____

_____

_____

_____

_____

EXERCISE 21 *Gladys: Working With a Client Over Time*

Kim Strom-Gottfried

Purpose

1. To practice skills in assessment in life-threatening situations.
2. To practice goal setting with an ongoing, voluntary client.
3. To practice a preliminary family interview.

Background

Social workers frequently have long-term, ongoing relationships with clients. These may occur in institutional settings such as nursing homes or residential facilities or when the social worker is providing case management or supportive services. Even when the focus of the working relationship is on sustaining the client or maintaining his or her functioning, crises and life events may alter the focus of work.

This exercise presents three vignettes from an ongoing case that require the social worker to reassess the client's condition, intervene with members of the client's network, and reestablish goals for work.

Instructions

Review materials in your text(s) on assessment in life-threatening situations. What are the key things to look for and questions to ask when determining whether a person is suicidal or self-destructive?

Next, your instructor will divide you into roles for each scenario. Anyone not assigned a role should be part of one of the "teams" helping to prepare the role players with their roles. Teams can help fellow students envision their role, develop questions, coach on behaviors to exhibit or look for, and so on. Read and prepare for only *one* scenario at a time.

Debrief after each scenario, with the role players going first. Questions for debriefing are included at the end of the exercise.

Scenario 1   The worker is a case manager serving low-income clients living in an elders-only high-rise apartment building. He or she and the public health nurse alternate visits with Gladys on 2-week intervals to make sure her medical and social service needs are met. Gladys is homebound, due mainly to her excessive weight, high blood pressure, and a diabetes-related leg amputation. She is 89, was widowed 20 years ago, and has a grandson who lives in the suburbs nearby with his family, although she rarely sees him.

The worker is shocked on arriving for this appointment to find her small, cluttered apartment to be unusually dirty and Gladys herself unkempt. She greets the worker from her recliner, but is uncharacteristically despondent and uncommunicative.

1. For the people playing Gladys or the family members, how did you experience the interview? What questions, statements, or actions helped you to feel heard? Which did not?

2. For the people playing the social worker, what did you feel were the strengths and weaknesses of the interview? What parts did you struggle with? How would you do things differently in the future?

3. For observers/team members, what strengths and weaknesses did you observe? Were difficult issues, such as depression, the suicide, and family conflict, adequately dealt with? Were there family members or parties in the role play that you particularly identified with? How might such identification affect your work in similar cases? Overall, what suggestions do you have for strengthening the interview in the future?

Scenario 2   Following the interview in Scenario 1, Gladys attempted suicide by taking a variety of prescription and over-the-counter medications, but was found by a fellow resident and taken to the hospital. The worker is now meeting with Gladys's 45-year-old grandson, Don, and his family to discuss her impending discharge from the hospital. Don has asked for assistance because he would like Gladys to stay with his family, rather than return to the Braden Arms high rise. Don's wife, Glennis, is vehemently opposed to the idea, feeling the responsibility for "entertaining" and caring for Gladys will fall to her, that Gladys has never liked her, and that the couple's children will lose out because of the diminished attention from their parents and the need to convert one of their rooms into space for Gladys. The children, Alisha, age 16, and Sondra, age 11, will attend the meeting. The social worker does not know how the siblings get along or their views on the matter.

1. For the people playing Gladys or the family members, how did you experience the interview? What questions, statements, or actions helped you to feel heard? Which did not?

2. For the people playing the social worker, what did you feel were the strengths and weaknesses of the interview? What parts did you struggle with? How would you do things differently in the future?

3. For observers/team members, what strengths and weaknesses did you observe? Were difficult issues, such as depression, the suicide, and family conflict, adequately dealt with? Were there family members or parties in the role play that you particularly identified with? How might such identification affect your work in similar cases? Overall, what suggestions do you have for strengthening the interview in the future?

Scenario 3   Plans to move in with Don and his family did not materialize. The Braden Arms reluctantly agrees to take Gladys back, but is concerned about her deteriorating health and potential for future suicidal behavior. In a follow-up meeting with Gladys, the social worker must develop new treatment goals—continuing former goals and/or adjusting them for changed circumstances.

In the session with Gladys, the social worker should review his or her assessment of the situation and develop a mutual contract for work. Recognize that Gladys and the social worker may not agree on what areas constitute a problem for work.

1. For the people playing Gladys or the family members, how did you experience the interview? What questions, statements, or actions helped you to feel heard? Which did not?

2. For the people playing the social worker, what did you feel were the strengths and weaknesses of the interview? What parts did you struggle with? How would you do things differently in the future?

3. For observers/team members, what strengths and weaknesses did you observe? Were difficult issues, such as depression, the suicide, and family conflict, adequately dealt with? Were there family members or parties in the role play that you particularly identified with? How might such identification affect your work in similar cases? Overall, what suggestions do you have for strengthening the interview in the future?

EXERCISE 22 *Contracting With an Involuntary Client: A Teenager in Foster Care*

Marcia B. Cohen

Purpose

1. To become familiar with the contracting process with an involuntary client.
2. To explore the impact of agency context, degree of client choice, and issues of diversity (such as age or race) on the contracting process.

Background

Contracting in social work refers to the process by which the client and worker come to a shared definition of the problem and a mutual agreement about goals, roles, tasks, and terms of work. Mutuality is essential in negotiating sound contracts with clients. Contracting should embody the social work values of client self-determination and empowerment and serve to reduce some of the inevitable power discrepancy between client and worker. For contracts to be mutual, the worker and client must jointly define the problem for work, explore the relevant data, and assess the client situation and available resources. Understood in this fashion, contracting is an explicitly client-centered activity.

The degree of client choice affects the contracting process. Negotiating agreements with involuntary clients can be particularly difficult. The challenge of contracting with an involuntary client calls for clarity on the part of the worker in distinguishing between the conditions of service that are imposed on the client and those that can be negotiated. For example, a child protection unit might mandate that parents meet with a worker on a weekly basis but not stipulate where the meetings will take place or how the meeting time will be spent. It is critical that the worker openly acknowledge the involuntary nature of the transaction. If common ground can be found between the involuntary client's felt needs and the services offered, a mutually agreed on contract may be negotiated even under these less than ideal circumstances.

Instructions

Your class will be divided into pairs with one person in each pair taking the role of the worker and the other, the client. You should read the case material carefully and think about how each of the characters is feeling about the upcoming meeting. The purpose of the meeting is to set some preliminary goals for work.

Each pair will role-play the first 15 minutes of the interview, switch roles, and role-play for another 15 minutes. List the preliminary contract resulting from the role play on the attached workbook page and be prepared to discuss it with the class.

After the role plays, your instructor will lead a class discussion on the contracting experience, using the discussion questions at the end of this exercise.

Case Material

Setting

The interview takes place in the social worker's office at the State Social Services building. This is the second meeting between the worker and client.

Roles

Tina: Tina is a multiracial 15-year-old girl from a single-parent family. Her biological mother is black and Tina also identifies as African American. Tina knows little about her father, whom she has never met. Tina has been in foster care for 3 years since the state child protective services had her removed from her mother's home where she had been sexually abused by her older brother Mike. Tina is angry that her mother allowed her to be placed instead of throwing her brother out of the house. She feels abandoned, rejected, and blamed for her brother's behavior. Tina does not get along well with the white foster family with which she is placed. The situation has gotten worse in the past 6 months. She has been fighting almost daily with her foster mother, Mrs. Teichen, over such issues as her school attendance, curfew, and how much makeup she wears. She has tried to get along and follow the Teichens' rules, but they are very strict. Tina finds her foster family unsympathetic and uncaring. She feels that no one understands her and that because everyone seems to think she is bad, she might as well prove them right. Child protective services policies require that Tina meet with a social worker twice a month. Her previous worker, a young white woman named Agnes, was transferred to another state office last month. Now she is assigned to Pat, an older black woman, whom she has only met with once before.

Pat: Pat is a black woman in her 40s with many years of experience as a social worker with child protective services. She was impressed by Tina's strength when she reviewed her record and met with her 2 weeks ago.

During this meeting, Pat explored Tina's foster care and family history. She also clarified her role as a child protection social worker, ascertained that Tina understood the mandated nature of their meetings, and indicated that while child protective services required that they meet, how they used their time together was pretty much up to Tina. Pat's objectives for this second meeting are to explore with Tina the current situation in the foster home and begin the contracting process. She suspects she will also need to repeat her offer of service to Tina, who proved hard to engage during their first meeting.

EXERCISE 22

Draft—Goals for Work With Tina M.

_____

_____

_____

_____

_____

_____

_____

_____

_____

_____

_____

_____

_____

_____

_____

_____

_____

Discussion Questions

1. As the client, what were your concerns about this new worker? How did you feel about working with her? Did these feelings change during the role play?

2. As the social worker, what were the obstacles to contracting?

3. Did the fact that services were mandated impede the contracting process? Was it possible to find common ground?

4. Did the issue of race explicitly or implicitly affect the contracting process? If so, how?

5. Did the issue of age explicitly or implicitly affect the contracting process? If so, how?

6. How were obstacles to contracting overcome? What might the worker have done differently?

EXERCISE 23   *The Smith Family: Multiple Perspectives on Service Goals*

Ronald H. Rooney and Anthony Bibus

Purpose

1. To experience how a family's difficulties can be perceived in a variety of different ways depending on the role that the observer is in.
2. To understand issues in contracting with families who have not applied for service.
3. To help you use this knowledge to critique a sample contract.
4. To develop skills in collaborative contracting.
5. To help you understand the role of authority in social worker-client interactions.
6. To develop an appreciation of the complexities in developing a contract when competing goals exist.

Background

Social workers and other helping professionals often interact with clients who have not applied for service. Guided by self-determination, social workers sometimes are confused about how to proceed when there are legal, health, or safety issues that conflict with the client's wishes. This exercise brings these dilemmas to life through the examination of a case and the critique of a sample contract.

Practice decisions often have to be made quickly with limited information. Our professional role has a strong, often limiting influence on our perspective and on how we interpret what we observe. We must develop conceptual frameworks and skills in critical thinking and practice that fill in the picture and lead to decisions and service contracts that are based on a balanced consideration of the facts, including strengths and resources as well as threats to the safety and well-being of clients. Contracts set up solely to address the professional's concerns can end up alienating the client and inhibiting successful, collaborative work.

This exercise involves a family situation that is based on an actual case and illustrates the tensions and dilemmas that arise in mandated child protection interventions. It will also provide you with chances to identify the approaches and skills necessary for effective, ethnically sensitive, and ethical social work practice with nonvoluntary clients. It is intended to provoke analysis of how the same behaviors can be interpreted in various and sometimes conflicting ways and to help you distinguish between facts and interpretations.

You will have chance to view the case from various positions within the child protection system and from the perspective of a family whose cultural background, worldview, or values may be different from your own. The complex dynamics of child protection, the tensions between parents' responsibilities, children's well-being, communities' and societies' obligations, and social work's helping and social control roles will come to life.

This exercise is designed to illustrate the challenges social workers may experience in finding a common purpose with family members and creating a plan when services may be fragmented and work at cross-purposes. Reaching for motivational congruence, that is, some basis for agreement between family members and practitioners on definition of the problem and solutions or goals, is critical.

Instructions

This exercise has four parts. First, you will review the case and make recommendations for services based on your perspective on the case. This will be followed by a discussion about these various viewpoints and how they may shape a social worker-client contract. Third, you will critique a contract that was developed for the case. Finally, you will have the chance to role-play a contracting session with Mr. and Mrs. Smith.

Case Review

Review materials in your text on setting goals collaboratively with clients. For ideas and resources for working with clients who are mandated or pressured to have contact with a social worker (in other words, "involuntary clients"), see Rooney (1992), Rooney and Bibus (1996), and Hepworth, Rooney, and Larsen (1997b).

Your instructor will invite 4-6 students to play roles as Smith family members—two parents and two to four children. Others will be invited or assigned to one of six groups—a group each of law enforcement officials, child protection staff, educators, counselors from the XYZ Chemical Dependency Treatment Center, family-based services providers, and community leaders.

Read "Intake Information Concerning the Smith Family" and the role associated with the group you have been assigned. Then, while your instructor meets with the family, meet with your group to prepare recommendations for the protective services social worker, who will be seeking your advice regarding services for the Smiths.

Discussion

When your instructor indicates, reflect on the discussion questions, based on your experience in the previous simulation.

Contract

Address the questions about creating a viable contract with the Smiths, then review the sample contract provided. Use the questions to critique the strengths and weaknesses of the contract.

Role Play

At the end of the exercise, your instructor will assign you to role-play one of three roles: Mr. Smith, Mrs. Smith, or the social worker. Read the roles and break into triads to role-play a contracting session. Debrief within your group about the successes and stumbling blocks of the role-played session.

Intake Information Concerning the Smith Family

Firefighters were called late last night when smoke was seen billowing out of the home. When unable to rouse anyone, they battered the door down. They found that the family had been leaving the oven open for heat, and something had caught fire. The adults in the household were inebriated and not easily aroused. The Smiths, who are in their 30s and Native American, have four children: two of them, ages 4 and 6, were at home. The parents were not sure where the other two, ages 8 and 10, were staying. When investigators checked the house further, they found basic foodstuffs lacking in the home and found mattresses on the floor.

School records indicate that the children are doing marginally, and are shy and reserved. Background inquiries suggest that Mr. Smith came to this community for a job after receiving training for a skilled position. He got the job and there were no problems with his effort, although he sometimes missed work, presumably because of alcoholism. He had earlier completed in-patient treatment at XYZ Chemical Dependency Center. Recently, he lost his job due to company shutdowns. His drinking appears to have increased.

Neighbors report that there appear to be a number of unknown people, perhaps relatives, who visit the home. The police have reports about "carousing" when these persons are around. The children have relatives in the community and apparently are accustomed to staying with them, sometimes without parental knowledge or permission. Many previous reports have been received about the condition of the Smith property and home; some may be generated by a county commissioner who lives nearby.

Role Instructions for the Smith Family

You are members of the Smith family. Each member of the group should take a particular family member role and read the intake information from the point of view of that member.

Family Members

> *Mr. Smith*
> *Mrs. Smith*
> *A 10-year-old*
> *An 8-year-old*
> *A 6-year-old*

1. Assess the family situation as a group from the point of view of your roles.
   a. What would the family want and need to do?
   b. What resources and strengths do you have?
   c. What resources or help do you want?

2. After a brief introductory meeting with you in your role as the Smith family, your instructor or another student in the role of the child protective services social worker assigned to your case will turn to each of six groups of professionals and community members who have worked with or known you in some capacity and ask for recommendations from their points of view. Listen to each group's recommendations and prepare to describe how you would respond, as the Smiths, to the recommendations. You will have an opportunity to propose alternative steps that are more congruent with your views of the problem and your goals as individuals and as a family.

Role Instructions for Groups

Law Enforcement Officials

You are investigating the fire at the Smith home and may present the case to the county attorney to charge the Smiths with criminal neglect for endangering their children. Your chief concerns are public safety and protecting the vulnerable from abuse or exploitation of others. You are compiling evidence on whether Mr. or Mrs. Smith has violated the law. Taking the role of law enforcement, what are your recommendations to the child protection worker assigned to the Smith family? What would you want the social worker to say to the family? What would you say?

Child Protection Staff

You are staffing a maltreatment report that the Smith children are neglected. Your paramount concerns are for the safety of the children and what living arrangements would be in their best interests. You know that children's ties to their family are crucial, but you will consider placing children into substitute care, at least until the parents stabilize the home situation. Taking the role of child protective services, what would you recommend to your colleague assigned to work with the Smiths? What should their social worker say to the family? What should be their next step?

Educators

You are the faculty and staff of the school where the Smith children attend. You have called the county child protection intake worker frequently in the past weeks expressing your concerns about the Smith children. You have noted that the children appear exhausted in class; do not interact with other children or with teachers; are thin, unkempt, and withdrawn; and often absent. Your chief concern, though, is that when you call their parents, they do not seem interested in the children's education, in their physical condition, or in the absences from school. In fact, the parents do not come to conferences at school when invited and have not cooperated with your attempts to meet with them in the home. You are frustrated because each time you have called with your concerns, the intake worker has explained that you have not identified a condition considered high enough risk for a child protective services assessment to be initiated. The intake worker suggested other referrals and asked you to keep observing whether the children are in danger or show more aggravated signs of abuse or neglect. You hear that the Smith family home burned down last night and the children are again missing school. Ironically, the child protection worker assigned to the Smiths will now be contacting you and asking for your recommendations. Taking the role of educator, what would you want the social worker to say to the family? What should be the family's next step? What would you say to the parents?

Counselors From the XYZ Chemical Dependency Treatment Center

Your treatment program for men who abuse alcohol or are chemically dependent has been asked by the Smiths' child protection worker to make a recommendation concerning Mr. Smith's difficulties with drinking. The Smiths have given you permission to release information about them. Because Mr. Smith had completed your in-patient treatment earlier, you want to consider whether he has relapsed, whether another course of in-patient treatment is called for, or whether you would advise alternative measures. You understand that relapse after treatment is quite common, but you are sensitive to the potential financial and emotional costs for clients faced with repeating treatment over and over again. Your program is based on the belief that alcoholism is an incurable disease and that abstinence from alcohol is the only way to keep it under control. Taking the role of counselors at the Treatment Center, what do you recommend for Mr. Smith and what do you want the child protection worker assigned to the family to say to them?

Family-Based Services Providers

You are staffing a referral to your unit to provide family-centered placement prevention and family preservation services to the Smiths. You believe in treating families as partners with strengths. You know from experience that children are safest and most likely to receive nurturing care if their parents have access to supports when their own resources are stretched. Difficulties in family life arise when family members' skills and resources in the community are not sufficient to meet their needs. Your role is to engage the Smiths in skill-building activities or supports they can use to grow from their strengths, raise their children, and maintain their family life. How should the child protection social worker assigned to the Smiths present your services? What would you recommend the social worker say to the family? In the role of family-based services provider, what would you say should be the family's next step?

Community Leaders

You are a group of elders and respected members of the Smith family's community. You understand the importance of extended family contacts and other cultural or ethnic connections for the Smiths, so when you hear about their situation, you feel an obligation to intervene on their behalf. Based on the historical oppression of members of your community by the dominant culture, you also distrust that authorities will be successful in their efforts, however well intentioned, to help the Smiths; in fact, they usually make things worse, breaking up families and placing the children out of the community. Taking the role of community leader, what would you say to the family? What do you recommend the child protection worker assigned to the Smiths say to the family? What should be their next step?

EXERCISE 23

Case Review: Recommendations

(Use this space for notes on recommendations, based on your group's role as law enforcement officials, child protection staff, educators, counselors from the XYZ Chemical Dependency Treatment Center, family-based services providers, or community leaders.)

_____

_____

_____

_____

_____

_____

_____

Discussion Questions

1. What are the key things you learned about multiple systems, after participating in the simulation?

_____

_____

_____

_____

_____

_____

_____

2. What are the key things you learned about work with involuntary clients?

_____

_____

_____

_____

_____

_____

3. Is empowerment and a strengths perspective inconsistent with work with involuntary clients?

_____

_____

_____

_____

_____

_____

4. Where is there potential for motivational congruence or agreement between the Smith family and the agency on the problem and its solutions?

_____

_____

_____

_____

_____

_____

5. What needs to happen to integrate roles and include family members as partners?

_____

_____

_____

_____

_____

_____

_____

6. How can the child protective services social worker address the divergent views of others who are also working with the Smith family?

_____

_____

_____

_____

_____

_____

_____

Contract Questions

1. Based on your readings and experiences, what should a good social worker-client contract contain?

_____

_____

_____

_____

_____

_____

_____

2. In regard to the Smith case, what elements of a contract are essential to assure the children's safety? Make a list—these will be the nonnegotiable parts of the contract.

_____

_____

_____

_____

_____

_____

3. What were the Smith family members' goals? Make a list—these will be potential areas for negotiation and mutual contracting.

_____

_____

_____

_____

_____

_____

4. How would services from other agencies be addressed in the contract?

_____

_____

_____

_____

_____

_____

5. Now compare the sample contract in this case with the lists generated in the previous questions. What would you keep? What is not essential or even could interfere with meeting needs of children and family?

_____

_____

_____

_____

_____

_____

_____

Sample Contract With the Smith Family

The following is a set of conditions and expectations regarding the care of the Smith children. This agreement is between Mr. and Mrs. Smith and the Department of Human Services (DHS) staff. The purpose of this agreement is to clarify and reinforce the importance and necessity of said conditions to ensure protection, training, and discipline of the children consistent with parental rights and responsibilities.

1. There shall be no consumption of alcohol or use of any other illicit drugs in the Smith home by anybody.

2. The only occupants of the home shall be Mr. and Mrs. Smith and the children unless the parents notify DHS first and obtain written permission. Further, Mr. and Mrs. Smith shall not allow any overnight guest or entertaining past midnight.

3. Mr. and Mrs. Smith shall follow a regular bedtime ritual with the children to include provision of adequate bedroom furniture including beds with frames, dressers, adequate sheets and other bedding, and making sure children brush teeth, wash face, hands, have pajamas on, and are in beds at a reasonable hour.

4. Parents' and children's clothes shall be organized in drawers and on hangers such that the older children can find their own clothes.

5. Mr. and Mrs. Smith shall ensure that the living quarters are maintained in a sanitary fashion and that all dishes are washed daily.

6. Mr. and Mrs. Smith shall ensure that there is food in the residence for the children at all times to include milk, bread, fruit, vegetables, and meat.

7. The children shall be supervised by Mr. and Mrs. Smith or another responsible adult at all times (this means a sober, safe individual with whom the children are familiar).

8. Mr. and Mrs. Smith shall allow unannounced visits by DHS staff.

9. Mr. Smith shall make all reasonable efforts to maintain a stable residence for the children and also maintain suitable and stable employment.

10. DHS shall assist the parties in achieving compliance with this contract.

Role Play

(Assume there has been a finding that maltreatment has occurred and protective services are needed. The children are with relatives pending the outcome of initial work with Mr. and Mrs. Smith.)

Social Worker

You will want to explore family members' points of view, but also explain how services are offered or required. You will need to explain any restrictions on services (eligibility, cost, length, etc.), the agency's expectations about what the parents are to do, your role, what is required, what is negotiable, and where there are choices. The Smiths may be of a cultural, racial, or ethnic background that you are not familiar with, so be prepared to be a learner. You may anticipate that the Smiths have had some negative experiences with the child welfare system in the past. Try to come to some agreement on what the agency (you) and the family can work on together and on some beginning tasks for you and for family members.

Mr. Smith

You are suspicious and fearful of working with social workers. You know that child protection takes children away. You are most concerned about lack of heat in the winter and having a fire hazard, and you are upset about not having the job you trained for (or any job) at the present time. You have been through alcoholism treatment and don't want to have to repeat it. When you are out of a job, depressed, and around family members and friends who drink, it has been very hard to avoid drinking. You usually know where your children are at night but did not on the night of the fire.

Mrs. Smith

It is embarrassing for you to work with social services. You would prefer to take care of problems in the family or consult with religious leaders. You know that drinking has gotten more dangerous as your husband is out of work and around other drinkers. You do not want the children or the family to be endangered by the risk of fire and too little heat. The lack of a job has created a lot of stress. You have just heard that a program offering families like yours housing and energy assistance has been cut due to welfare reform.

References

Hepworth, D., Rooney, R. H., & Larsen, J. (1997b). *Direct social work practice: Theory and skills* (5th ed.). Pacific Grove, CA: Brooks/Cole.

Rooney, R. H. (1992). *Strategies for work with involuntary clients.* New York: Columbia University Press.

Rooney, R. H., & Bibus, A. A. (1996). Multiple lenses: Ethnically sensitive practice with involuntary clients who are having difficulties with drugs or alcohol. *Journal of Multicultural Social Work, 4*(2), 59-73.

6 CREATING CHANGE: INTERVENTIONS

EXERCISE 24 *What You Look for Determines What You See*

Lynn Bye

Purpose

1. To understand that there are many different ways to view any given situation.
2. To heighten awareness about how the social worker's theoretical perspective influences the problems identified and interventions used in a given case.

Background

There are many different theories (e.g., ecological, cognitive, behavioral, general systems, psychoanalytic, and social learning) that can be applied when attempting to help people improve the quality of their life. Theories have been defined as "myths, expectations, guesses, and conjectures about what may be true" (Gambrill, 1997, p. 95). The framework provided by any given theory or combination of theories provides a lens that shapes what we think and what we say to our clients. It is important to be consciously aware of the theories used when working with clients so that we can critically evaluate our assumptions and search for alternative views (Gambrill, 1997). A single theory cannot possibly provide the "best guess" for what is happening with all clients. Clients also have a right to be informed about the logic and thinking behind any diagnosis and recommendations. This can happen only when social workers are able to clearly articulate the theoretical framework used in their work with clients.

This exercise gives you the opportunity to examine a case through a particular theoretical lens and compare your conclusions with those of your classmates using other theories.

Phase 1

Instructions

The entire class will read the case of the Shore family (Dorfman, 1988). Your instructor will have you number off from 1 to 6. You will be asked to remember the people who are in your group when you numbered off from 1 to 6 because you will be joining them later for part of the class. Your instructor will then divide you into groups where all the 1s are together, all the 2s are together, all the 3s are together, and so on.

Each group will be asked to select a recorder and review the Shore case using a specific theory. Each group will be assigned a different theory. For example, the group of 1s will be assigned to review the Shore case in terms of ecological-life model theory. The group of 2s will be assigned to review the Shore case in terms of cognitive theory, and so on. Using the theoretical perspective assigned, each group will need to decide the following four things:

1. The key assumptions of the assigned theoretical perspective.
2. The main problems in the family.
3. The most appropriate interventions.
4. In what ways the theory was useful (or not useful) in working with this family.

The Case
by Rachelle A. Dorfman

The Family

The problems of the Shore family are common ones. Among them are unemployment, illness, and the worrisome behavior of the children. What is uncommon is that despite the frequent help from various social services, the problems never get resolved and the family members never seem to function free from symptoms. Individually and collectively, their lives are marked by crisis and emotional distress.

Nancy is 43; her husband, Charley, is 51. The children are Rena, 18, who was adopted as a baby, and Michael, 12. Until recently, the entire family lived in the two-unit duplex they own. Nancy, Charley, and Michael still live in the second-floor apartment. Rena, who had occupied the first-floor apartment by herself since she was 13, has moved out; she lives nearby and is "on her own." Charley has been chronically unemployed for 4 years; the family survives largely on the disability checks Nancy has received every month for the past 10 years.

Nancy is a large woman. She calls herself "grossly obese" and makes frequent apologies about her appearance. Her hair is graying and her figure is decidedly matronly, but her flawless skin and the gap between her front teeth give her a youthful quality. The only reservation she has about being interviewed is, "After it's done, I will probably run from social worker to social worker trying to do everything suggested."

For most of her 23-year marriage to Charley, "trying to get everything fixed" has been her full-time job. She is at her best during family crises:

NOTE: From R. A. Dorfman. (Ed.). (1988). *Paradigms of clinical social work* (pp. 25-37). New York: Brunner/Mazel. Reprinted with permission of Brunner/Mazel.

"Then," she says, "I take control. I no longer dread the terrible things that might happen because they have already happened. It is the waiting for the crisis to occur that makes me worry." Her anxiety often turns into panic. She becomes nearly immobilized. Unable to leave the house, she chain-smokes and imagines the worst of all possible outcomes. Anxiety attacks occur daily.

There is no shortage of crises. Recurring flare-ups of a back injury that Nancy suffered as a young nurse incapacitate her without warning, confining her to bed for weeks or months. The flare-ups are not the only crises. Three times, doctors predicted that Michael, asthmatic since early infancy, would not survive until morning. Twice Rena ran away from home and was missing for several days.

The small apartment reverberates with the sounds of their crises. One typical scenario began with an argument. Rena, then 16, lunged forward to hit her mother. Charley, in frustration and fury, pulled Rena away from Nancy and beat her, bruising her face badly. It was on that evening, 2 years ago, that Nancy and Charley told Rena she would have to leave when she turned 18.

A new problem with a potential for crisis is emerging. The downstairs apartment, which is now vacant, has never been occupied by strangers. (Before Rena, Nancy's elderly grandparents lived there.) Because they need the money, Nancy and Charley have decided to rent it to a young couple. Nancy is anxious about being a landlord. She is trying to train Charley and Michael to keep their voices down and their steps light. She wishes that her family lived downstairs and the tenants lived upstairs, and says, "I'd rather they walk on me than we walk on them." Again, she fears the crises that are certain to erupt.

Rena has been in her own apartment a few blocks away for 3 months. Nancy worries about that, too. She feels that as an adopted child, Rena is especially sensitive to being "put out." Nonetheless, she still argues with Rena about her "laziness" and failure to finish anything, but there is less explosiveness now that she is on her own.

Despite some relief in the tension at home since Rena left, Nancy is still anxious and often depressed. She has gained 15 pounds, sleeps poorly, cannot concentrate, and is forgetful. Most of the time, she stays inside. Outside, she feels that people make disparaging remarks about her; only at home does she feel safe. Her days are filled with baseball games on TV, soap operas, needlepoint, and worrying about what will happen next.

Charley is blond, tall, and broad-shouldered. It is not difficult to imagine that he was once quite an appealing young man. When he was 27, his dreams and schemes interested and excited Nancy. Occasionally, he still talks of outlandish inventions and "get-rich-quick" schemes. The difference is that his wife no longer believes in him or his dreams. To her, they are annoying at best and embarrassing at worst.

Charley says, "All I ever wanted was to be somebody. I just want to be known for something, to have someone walk by my house and say, 'That's Mr. Shore's house.'" He boasts about the time he went to California "to become a movie star" and of all the rich and famous people he knew and still knows. He speaks wistfully of "just-missed" opportunities for stardom and of inventions that no one took seriously. He likes being interviewed, saying, "It's exciting." Nancy reminds him that the interview is for a clinical book, not a Broadway play.

Five years ago, Charley performed on amateur night at a downtown comedy club. Nearly every Thursday night since then, he has performed for free in front of a live audience, using the name Joe Penn. His pride is unbounded when he is recognized in public as Joe Penn. Occasionally, someone will even ask for his autograph.

His wife supports this activity because it makes him happy, but her perspective on his act is somewhat different from Charley's. The show embarrasses her. She says that although it is true that the audience laughs, they laugh at Charley, not at his jokes: "He is not funny," she maintains. Charley's defense is that probably Nancy's favorite comedian's wife doesn't think her husband is funny either.

Over the years, Charley has had scores of jobs. He was a salesman, a janitor, a self-employed carpet cleaner. Even though he lost jobs regularly, he had little difficulty finding a new one. Four years ago that situation changed. He began to experience long periods of unemployment. Several times in the past 3 months, Charley has mentioned suicide, always in response to a suggestion that he, like Nancy, should get on disability because of his "condition." Charley says that he would rather die first. Although he seems serious about this statement, he has no plan or means in mind.

The "condition" is bipolar depression that was diagnosed 2 years ago at the time of his first and only psychotic break and consequent 4-week hospitalization: "I always got depressed," he recalls, "but that was different. That time I really went off." Remembering his grandiosity and manic behavior, he says, "I guess you do those things when you are sick." He is maintained on lithium.

A "firing" precipitated his break. He had completed an expensive cooking course and was determined to prove he could "make it" in his first cooking job. He says he hit the chef when he could no longer tolerate the man's calling him names. (His bosses had complained that Charley was too slow and talked too much.)

Since his illness, he has had fewer grand ideas; he just wants a job he can hold. When he does allow himself to dream, mostly he dreams the way he did when he was a child, quietly and by himself. He liked to daydream while he works, which affects his performance. He was fired from his last janitorial job for forgetting to lock all the doors and for not cleaning thoroughly.

Presently, Charley attends a vocational rehabilitation program where he receives minimum wages for training in janitorial services, a job he says he already knows how to do. The program's goals are to develop the work skills and interpersonal skills needed for employment and to place him successfully in a job. Nancy is pessimistic about the outcome. She is angry because no one will tell her the results of his psychological testing. She says that if she knew for certain that Charley wasn't capable of holding a job, perhaps she wouldn't be so angry with him.

About Nancy, Charley says, "She is the best wife in the world, the same as my mother. She even worries like my mother, but I don't always like that because I don't feel like a man." The duplex they own was given to them by Nancy's Aunt Flo. Although Charley appreciates the generosity, he says, "*I* wanted to do that. *I* wanted to buy the house."

Nancy agrees that she is parental. She prefers to handle important matters herself, not trusting Charley's competence with dollars, documents, or decisions. She complains that when she sends Charley to the store for two items, he invariably comes home with one of them wrong. But most of all, she complains about not having enough money to pay the bills: "I worry and he doesn't give a damn." Charley says privately, "I worry, too, but I act like I don't because there is nothing I can do."

The couple frequently fights about Charley's compulsive lying. He tells Nancy what he believes she wants to hear, claiming he doesn't want to upset her with the truth. He says he would like to stop but he doesn't seem able to.

Charley usually stiffens as soon as he approaches the front door of his house: "Will there be a problem? Will Nancy complain about bills? Will Michael come home from school beaten up? They will want me to solve the problems. But I can't."

Being a father has been especially difficult. Charley and his son bicker and fight like small boys. Nancy finds herself storming in, breaking them up, and scolding them both. She says that each one fights for her attention, trying to outdo the other.

Because father and son tend to relate to each other like siblings, therapists who worked with the family in the past attempted to restructure the relationship by suggesting that Charley teach Michael how to fish and play miniature golf. Charley and Michael always return home from such outings angrily blaming each other for ruining the day. Nancy says, "The whole time they are out, I am in a knot worrying that they are going to come up the steps screaming. I am never disappointed." She wants Charley to act more like a father. Charley wants that, too. "But," he says, "sometime you just don't think about what you're doing when you do it."

Twelve-year-old Michael is tall and gangly. When he speaks, one can hear the phlegm rattle in his chest. It seems as though his voice is echoing through the mucus. His habitually knitted brow and his glasses make

Michael appear to be very intense. He talks about "feeling funny" and "feeling bad." He feels bad because "asthma has taken away part of my life." His theory is that God gives everyone something he or she is terrific at. He says, "I haven't found mine yet—the asthma keeps me from it. I can't be a great athlete because I can't run fast. I can't have a puppy because I would wheeze. I just want to be good at something." According to his theory, God also puts a scar on everyone. People have to overcome their scars before they can find their special thing. Michael says asthma is his scar and his is waiting to outgrow it so that he can "find himself."

In the meantime, he is unhappy and lonely. Attempts to make friends are unsuccessful. He feels that even when he tries to behave himself, it is useless because his reputation prevents the other kids from relating to him in a new way. They still tease and pick on him. If someone hits him, he neither hits back nor runs away. He just "stays."

When he is not being "silly," he is more successful in relating to adults. Always attuned to the news, he usually knows what is current in world events, politics, and business. He sympathizes with underdogs and victims and talks about becoming a psychologist so that he can help them. He is fiercely patriotic and always truthful. When asked why he tells the truth when a lie would avoid trouble, he says, "I am a Boy Scout; I cannot tell a lie."

Scouting is a highlight of his life, but there is trouble there, too. Camping trips require a level of coordination, self-control, and social skills that he doesn't have. He gets reprimanded when he puts his tent up wrong or ties his neckerchief incorrectly. When this happens, he says, the other scouts laugh and he feels like a fool.

In junior high, Michael is in a learning disability class. Although learning disabilities and special classes are part of his history, the current placement was not made because of them; tests show that he has overcome or outgrown any learning disability he had. The problem that still lingers and prevents him from being "mainstreamed" is his poor social judgment. The same behaviors he calls "silly," his teachers have called "bizarre." These include touching others, making strange noises and motions, and laughing too loud or at the wrong time.

Last summer, Michael went to overnight camps. This spring, his parents received a disturbing letter from the camp. Michael was not invited back. The reason given was more than the typical foul language and mischief of 12-year-old boys. Counselors complained that at mealtimes he played with the utensils and plates, poured things into the pitchers and bowls, and threw food. He did not get along with the other campers and was seen as the instigator of most of the problems that occurred that summer. The staff felt that when he wanted to behave, he could, and that he willfully chose to misbehave.

Michael reports the situation differently. One moment he says that he acts "silly" because he falls under the influence of others. A moment later he suggests that he acts that way so that others will like him. Still later he says, "I don't really want to act like that. It's really kind of stupid. I don't know why I do it."

Michael is ambivalent about his sister's leaving. He agrees that it is more peaceful at home, but now his parents are fussing about him more than ever. Nancy estimates that she spends "80% of her worrying time" agonizing about what will become of Michael.

Rena, four blocks away in a basement efficiency apartment, has agonies of another sort. She is attractive, intelligent, and talented. Everyone, including Rena, always expected that she would be successful. But in the past few years, no matter how promising her beginnings, eventually she either quits or fails at everything she starts.

With 31 cents in her purse and no job, she is overdrawn at the bank and can't pay her bills. She has taken loans to pay for college courses she never completed. Rena feels old and tired.

Her parents used to call it laziness when she refused to go to school and stayed in bed until midafternoon. They thought she was lazy when she dropped out of high school, got a GED, and enrolled in pre-med—only to drop out of that. They believed that if they allowed her to remain at home, she would "vegetate" and do nothing at all.

Nancy pressures Rena to "go to therapy" because she has come to believe that there must be something more seriously wrong with Rena than "laziness." Rena has agreed to go for therapy, partly because one usually does what Nancy wants. "Mother," she explains, "has a way of making you feel so bad and guilty, you finally either do what she wants or are mad because she makes you feel so bad." She has also agreed to go because she is lonely and confused. Unfortunately, there is a waiting list for outpatient services at the community mental health clinic—and Rena's name is at the bottom of that list.

Nevertheless, it seems that the therapeutic process has already begun. Rena writes her thoughts in her journal every day, and spends hours wondering about why she is the way she is. She is happy to be interviewed because she says she needs to talk about "this stuff."

She remembers when she didn't want to talk about "this stuff" or even think about it. At 16, when the adoption agency, at her request, sent some information about her birth mother, she forced herself not to think about it. Now she intends to find out about herself, even if it means thinking about painful things.

Like Michael, Rena has some theories. The first one is that she is so accustomed to living with problems and crises that she must create them when they do not exist: "Just look at my life. It is the only way I know how to live. When things are going well, I can't stand it." As proof, she describes her brief college experience. Her attendance was excellent; the work was easy for her. Then she met a boy. Not long after that, she dropped out, blaming it on him. She claims she merely needed an excuse to "mess up" and he was a convenient one.

She calls her second theory "the adoption." Even if her adoption explanation is a "cop-out," she feels that it gives her a starting point from which to consider her life. She notes that she has patterned her life in much the same way as her birth mother did. Her birth mother didn't get along with her parents and was a high school dropout. Like Rena, she picked boyfriends who seemed worse off than herself.

Rejection is another thing Rena thinks about: "I push people so much with my demands that they eventually drop me like a hot potato. Then I can say, 'See what they did to me. They left me out in the cold.' " Sometimes generous to a fault, but more often selfish and demanding, she offers her relationship with her adoptive parents as proof of how she forces her own abandonment.

The most recent project Rena has started is the search for her birth mother: "I want to know her, see what she looks like, talk to her. I would like to sing for my mother." Rena wonders about her birth mother's approval: "She didn't like me before. Will she like me now?"

An attorney is helping Rena through the morass of conflicting state and agency policies that keep her from finding her birth mother. Meanwhile, she attends meetings of adoptees, birth mothers, and adoptive mothers, at which members share information and discuss feelings. Rena is usually found in the hallways asking questions of birth mothers. She asks, "Do you ever think of your kid? How could you do it? Didn't you care?"

Family History

Nancy

Cute and precocious, Nancy was the cherished only child, only grandchild, and only niece of doting adults. She remembers those early years, the years before age 11, as golden. Although her mother, an exceptionally beautiful and somewhat self-centered woman, was often away socializing with a large circle of friends, there were always Aunt Flo and Gram to shower her with attention, affection, and gifts.

Little Nan was seldom childish, so the adults took her with them to the theater, the ballet, and fancy restaurants. Her manners were beyond reproach. To the delight of the grown-ups, she always cleaned her plate. She remembers, "They thought it was so cute because I ate everything and, at that age, never got fat."

Her earliest memory is of when she was 5: "I remember going to a store and getting a fried egg sandwich. I had to go a different way because I wasn't allowed to cross streets. Nobody was with me. A dog chased me home and tried to take my sandwich. I remember the smell of the sandwich and the dog chasing me. I was worried more about the dog biting my sandwich than biting me! That must have been the first clue to what food was going to be in my life."

Another memory is from the same period: "My father was a waiter. It was a big deal waiting for him to come home at night. He would bring food from the restaurant and we would all be together to eat it."

Her father was a shadowy figure. Between his job and his gambling, he was rarely home. Still, she felt closer to him than to her mother. One night, when she was 11, her parents told her that her father was leaving. It was difficult to understand—her parents never argued. Years later, she learned that the leaving was precipitated by gambling debts to "the mob." Her mother was either unable or unwilling to go.

Although Aunt Flo and Gram still bought her beautiful clothes and knit her angora sweaters, the golden years were over. Mother had to work now, so she was away more than ever, which seemed "just fine" with Mother. Nancy is convinced that her mother never wanted her, which her mother denies. They moved several times in the next few years; Nancy remembers each place in great detail.

The first two summers after the marriage broke up, Nancy's father drove a thousand miles to get her and take her back with him for a visit. Her most vivid memory is from the second visit, when she was 12. She wanted to buy something at the pool, so she went to the hotel room to ask her father for money: "My father was lying in bed undressed and his 'wife-to-be' was ironing, with nothing on from the waist up. That is when I realized he was sleeping with her. Before then, I didn't know anything about that."

After that summer, her father stopped coming for her and stopped calling. He remarried and had more children, but Nancy did not find that out until later. She remembers wondering why he didn't love her. She confided only to Aunt Flo's dog. The poodle would lie by her side as she alternately wept and fantasized about her father's return. Finally, when Nancy was 14, a relative had a chance meeting with her father and reported his whereabouts. She called him immediately.

Nancy feels that if she had not initiated that contact, she would never have heard from him again. Today, when he visits Nancy (about once a year), he talks about his three wonderful children, especially his eldest daughter, Sandy. Nancy cringes every time. Her father has *four* children—*she* is the eldest. She is bitter and resentful.

When Nancy was 15, her family moved into the duplex she still lives in. Gram lived downstairs with Grandfather, and Mother and Nancy lived in the upstairs apartment. The arrangement worked well. Nancy continued to spend a good deal of time with her beloved Gram. She made friends in the new school and began to date.

By high school, Nancy was overweight. Mother, however, was still "movie star" beautiful. Nancy says, "Boys would come over to see me, but they soon liked my mother better." She felt like an ugly duckling next to her seductive mother clad in tight sweaters.

After high school, Nancy went to nursing school on a full academic scholarship. For the first time, she lived away from home. "All I wanted," she recalls, "was to take care of people." She learned how to do that in the exciting atmosphere of the hospital, where she developed lifelong friendships with other nurses and doctors. Some of those doctors are involved now with Michael's treatment.

She calls the nursing years "the best years": "I felt so good about myself, totally in control. I was a damn good nurse. I was capable of handling anything that happened."

The only nursing she has done since injuring her back was part-time, "under-the-table" work in an old-age home. During that 18-month period, she retained none of her old confidence. She feared that at any moment a situation would arise that she could not handle. But, as usual, when emergencies did occur, she handled them quite well. Back pain and the threat of losing her disability payments because she was working "illegally" forced her to quit.

Following every flare-up of her injury, Nancy repeats the same pattern. Once the pain subsides, she feels a welling of desire to return to school for an advanced degree in nursing and to ultimately return to her profession. She calls nursing schools and fills out applications; twice she made appointments with admissions counselors.

Eventually, a pall of gloom comes over her because she again realizes the full extent of her physical limitations. The flare-ups are unpredictable and keep her off her feet for months. Even between acute phases, she is unable to sit for more than short periods without pain. The possibility of completing a graduate degree, much less maintaining a career, appears remote. When Nancy realizes this, she relinquishes her dream and returns to "earth" and to the family's problems.

Charley

Charley's childhood lacked the comforts of Nancy's. He had few possessions and his clothes were never "right." He felt loved by his mother, but he was hardly the center of anyone's attention. His father, a one-time amateur boxer, was a "tough little guy." He dealt with Charley the same way he dealt with problems on the street—with his fists.

Charley's mother and father fought constantly. Although Father never hit his wife, Mother was known to have taken more than a few swings at Father. Charley remembers one night when he was 5 years old. His father came home drunk, having gambled away his money. "Mom knocked him out cold." The scariest scene from his childhood was the night that his father got out his gun to "kill" his boss, whom he accused of cheating him. Charley doesn't remember the outcome; he only remembers the gray shiny gun.

By contrast, most memories of his mother are pleasant ones: "One day when I was about 6, I was watching Mother scrub the floor. There was an awful smell of ammonia. She stopped working, turned on the radio, and put her feet up. She said her feet were hurting. I rubbed her feet."

Another memory from the same period was from the first grade: "Whenever my friend and I would see each other, we would fall on the floor and wrestle. I remember my first-grade teacher, Miss Brown. She used to stick her long nails in our backs when she grabbed us. We had this cloakroom; there were little hooks on the walls. This one time, my friend and I were wrestling in the cloakroom. Miss Brown grabbed us both and hung us up on those little hooks."

When Charley was 6, his sister Pat was born. Two years later his sister Louise was born. Charley says he was a lousy brother to his cute kid sisters, always hitting them. He recalls a stunt he pulled on Pat, when he was 17 and she was 11. She was with a group of friends and he was with a group of boys. Unexpectedly, they met on the subway. Always playing the clown, Charley took his shoes and socks off, saying that they were on backward. His companions roared; Pat was red-faced.

Like Michael, Charley was teased daily by the other kids. He got beaten up regularly, until he managed to trade a prized toy for protection from a gang of four brothers. At 18, miserable and fed up with the fighting at home and on the streets, he enlisted in the Air Force. He proudly reports that he held that job for 4 years, the longest of any job. He still talks about the Air Force shows he performed in and drops names of the famous people he met during his enlistment.

After his discharge, he went to California. Charley paints the service years and the California period with a flourish. However, when he speaks of his Hollywood adventures and the starlets he dated, the details seem vague and much less compelling than the other details of his life.

Courtship and Marriage

Nancy and Charley's first date was at a picnic in the park arranged by mutual friends. They did not expect to be alone, but before they realized it, their friends had left for another picnic. Nancy will never forget those first few hours together. "He was so funny and handsome. He was different from anyone I had ever experienced. He told me he had been in the movies in Hollywood. He had ideas, inventions, and plans to have his own business. I believed everything he told me." Although he was only a delivery man for a florist shop, Nancy recalls, "he explained that he was learning the business to open his own shop."

Nancy promised to marry Charley in spite of her mother's and Aunt Flo's prediction that he would never make a decent living. Nancy wanted to prove them wrong. Two years after the picnic, they were married.

Charley's mother was struck and killed by a car shortly before the wedding. His father eventually remarried; he died of a heart attack several years ago.

The early years of the marriage were relatively free from the problems that currently plague them. Although Charley went from job to job, it didn't worry them. Nancy was more than willing to support the family by working at what she loved most—nursing.

They originally had a rich social life. Over the years, however, they lost many of their friends. Nancy feels that their friends left because, as they matured, they had less and less in common with Charley, who remained a "kid."

The couple's first problem was that Nancy could not become pregnant. Because of Charley's low sperm count and Nancy's irregular ovulation, pregnancy was nearly impossible. After 4 years, doctors suggested adoption. They had been married 5 years when they adopted 6-week-old Rena. Six years later, Michael was conceived.

Rena

Gram called her "the angel from heaven." Once again there was an only child, an only grandchild, and now an only *great*-grandchild as well. It was easy for the adults to dote on her; she was an exceptionally pleasant baby. At 5 months, Rena was standing. At 11 months, she could name the artist of each painting and print on Gram's walls.

Rena's early memories all include family members. She recalls playing a game with her father when she was just a toddler. She would sit on a special chair while he would go away and come back again. She recalls beckoning him to reappear. She also recalls a family vacation when she collected "teeny tiny" shells of different colors by the water's edge. When the vacation was over, she put them in a jar and took them home with her. She can still hear her mother screaming from the bathroom where Rena kept her "shells" in a jar of water, "Charley, Charley, these shells are moving!" Her father flushed what turned out to be snails down the toilet. Rena says she was very upset for a very long time.

Charley and Nancy knew that she was bright, but at first they did not realize the extent of her giftedness. At age 5, she bypassed the regular kindergarten program and entered a "mentally gifted" first grade. At a very young age, Rena began to "belt" out songs like a nightclub performer. Her parents remember other parents asking her for her autograph after an elementary school pageant. Everyone was impressed by her talent and was certain that she would have a future in show business.

She also displayed an unusual artistic talent, wrote poetry and short stories, and had an extraordinary mechanical ability. The latter annoyed Charley, because she was able to "fix anything" and he was not.

Birthdays, a happy time for most children, were unhappy for Rena. She moped about, looking sad and distracted. Eventually, she revealed that she always thought about her birth mother on that day, and wondered if her mother thought about her, too.

In grade school, there was some foreshadowing of her "not finishing anything." Then, however, when she dropped activities before completion, she always replaced them with others that were more challenging. Now she drops them in failure and despair.

The calm of her grade school years gave way to a turbulent preadolescence and adolescence. Rena says of herself at 12, "I was a different person. I was good in school and never got into trouble. All the elders loved me. I was very intelligent and could talk to anyone about anything. But, like Michael, the kids didn't like me." She spent most of her time downstairs with Gram and Great-Grandfather or with Aunt Flo.

Things were not going too well at home, either. Nancy had undergone one back operation and was facing a second. After that second operation, it was clear that she would never be able to stand the rigors of nursing again. Charley had to be the breadwinner. Michael was sick very often at that point, but the most difficult problem of all was Gram's death.

Rena's relationship with her great-grandmother had been unusually close. She spent more time in Gram's apartment than in her own family's. When Rena got yelled at, Gram would scream upstairs, "Don't touch that angel from heaven!" Several times, Gram slipped child abuse literature under the door. Rena said Gram was the only one in the whole world who ever loved her.

Shortly after Gram's funeral, Rena—who had been sharing a room with Michael—moved downstairs with her great-grandfather. It seemed a logical and convenient solution to the lack of space and privacy for a developing young girl. A year later, Great-Grandfather died, and Rena stayed downstairs alone, sleeping in Gram's bed. Her parents now regret the arrangement. They point to the deterioration in her behavior that followed.

At first things went exceedingly well. Rena, on a whim, auditioned for a role on a proposed TV series and was one of six finalists chosen for a national search. All the finalists were invited to New York for a screen test with a major television network. Charley was beside himself with aspirations to manage Rena and make her a star. The entire family was given the "star treatment." Unfortunately, Rena was told she was "too cute" for the part.

Shortly after that experience, Rena won the leading role in the school play. As Dorothy in *The Wizard of Oz*, she sang and danced and won the admiration of the entire school.

When the excitement of those two events passed and life returned to normal, Rena began to cut school. Then the fighting began in earnest. She refused to go to school or to keep the downstairs apartment clean. Charley and Nancy threatened, pleaded, punished, and hit. Twice Rena ran away. When she returned, she always promised to do better.

When she was 15, she got a part in a local dinner theater. Charley and Nancy allowed her to do the weekend performances if she attended school. When she was caught cutting again, her parents had her withdrawn from the company. They feel that she has never forgiven them for that.

Eventually Rena quit school. Now a few years older, she speaks of her shame and once more resolves to "do better."

Michael

Michael has been hospitalized 14 times and has spent hundreds of hours in hospital emergency rooms for asthmatic status, a type of asthma that gets out of control. (Sufferers are often near death as doctors struggle to bring it under control.) When Michael has an asthma attack, Nancy works closely by phone with the pediatrician monitoring his condition; she injects him with Adrenalin and helps him to breathe with a nebulizer. Michael's earliest memory is of not being able to breathe, crying, "Gimme air, gimme air." He says, "Once, an ugly lady came in and gave me a shot instead. I wanted to hit her and tell her I didn't need the shot. I am perfectly fine."

Nancy claims Michael was born unlucky. When he was only 8 days old, he hemorrhaged from a circumcision wound. Asthma first appeared when he was 6 months old, and he was sickly and prone to fevers throughout infancy. Nancy worried that he might not grow up at all. Now she worries about what his life will be like. Despite frequent illnesses, he was a happy baby. He walked, talked, and reached all the developmental milestones on schedule.

His worrisome health continued through the toddler stage. At 2 ½, he has his first grand mal seizure and has been on seizure medication ever since. Doctors hold the medication responsible for at least a portion of his behavior problems, specifically the hyperactivity, but no one is quite certain just how much of his problem can be attributed to adverse side effects.

His behavior was first identified as problematic in kindergarten. After 2 months of first grade, he was transferred from the regular classroom to an LD classroom. Teachers said he could not follow instructions and seemed "lost" and confused. The report from the school psychologist stated that he had fine and gross motor coordination problems.

At 12, Michael feels that he is different from the rest of the kids. However, he refuses to accept his very real physical limitations; despite constant failure and rejection, he continues to try out for the track and softball teams. On the other hand, he acknowledges his difference and alienation and says, "Sometimes I feel that I should be in another country or in another time zone. I wish I could start my life over again." He likes the idea of having his story in a book because people "pity the underdog."

The Shores (1936–1987)

Year	No. years married	Nancy	Charley	Rena	Michael
1936			Born		
1944		Born			
1954			Joins Air Force		
1955		Father leaves			
1958			Discharged from Air Force (age 22)		
1959		Moves to present house (age 15)			
1962			Nancy and Charley meet		
		(age 18)	(age 26)		
1964			Mother dies in accident shortly before wedding		
			Nancy and Charley marry		
		(age 20)	(age 28)		
1968	4	Decide to adopt a child			
1969				Adopted (6 weeks old)	
1974				Begins kindergarten ("gifted" program)	
1975	11	Michael conceived			Born
					Circumcision hemorrhages (8 days old)
1976					Develops asthma (6 months old)
1977		Receives first disability check			
1980					Begins kindergarten
1981	17	Second back operation (age 37)	Expected to be breadwinner (age 45)	Moves downstairs (age 12)	Placed in learning disability class
		"Gram" dies			

(continued)

Year	No. years married	Nancy	Charley	Rena	Michael
1982		Grandfather dies	Begins to perform in comedy club	Lives downstairs alone (age 13)	
1983			Chronic unemployment begins		
1984				Acts in dinner theater	
1985			Hits boss; is fired	Runs away twice	
			Psychotic break (bipolar depression)	Becomes interested in finding birth mother	
				Beaten by Charley (after fight with parents)	
				Drops out of high school	
1986			Enters chef school	Drops out of college	
1987	23		Attends vocational rehab program	Moves to apartment	

Figure 24.1. Time Line for Shore Family
SOURCE: Dorfman (1988). Reprinted with permission of Brunner/Mazel.
NOTE: The idea for constructing a time line about the Shore family came from Jay Lappin, M.S.W.

EXERCISE 24

Group 1

Ecological Theory-Life Model

The perspective of "person in environment" has been used in the social work field for many years. Ecological theory focuses on the fit between people and their environment. The goodness of fit changes over time and problems are thought to arise when there is no longer a good match between people and their environment (Kelly, 1968). The life model is a hybrid of ecological theory and suggests that human problems "fall into three interrelated areas: 1) life transitions involving developmental changes, status role changes, crisis events; 2) the unresponsiveness of social and physical environments; and 3) communication and relationship difficulties in families and other primary groups" (Germain & Gitterman, 1980, p. 13). The ecological-life model perspective divides the environment into systems of increasing complexity. Zastrow and Kirst-Ashman (1997) have identified four levels of systems: the microsystem, consisting of the family; the mesosystem, consisting of extended family, friends, colleagues at churches or temples, schools, and work; the ecosystem, consisting of local government; and the macrosystem, consisting of social institutions and processes.

Questions

1. Describe the assumptions of the ecological-life model perspective.

_____

_____

_____

_____

_____

_____

2. Using the ecological-life model perspective, identify the problems the Shore family is experiencing.

_____

_____

_____

_____

_____

_____

3. Using the ecological-life model perspective, describe the interventions you would suggest and state how they relate to the ecological-life model perspective.

_____

_____

_____

_____

_____

4. In what ways was this a helpful or not so helpful theory to use when working with this family?

_____

_____

_____

_____

_____

_____

Group 2

Cognitive Theory

Cognitive theorists maintain that human thoughts shape emotion and behavior. People are seen as "information-processing organisms" who are able to alter their thinking (Schuyler, 1991, p. 34). Problems are thought to be caused by faulty reasoning. To change behavior it is necessary to help the client become more rational and think about problems in a new way. The focus is on the client's belief systems and expectations (Okun, 1997).

Cognitive theorists do not deal with unconscious processes or developmental stages. The emphasis is on current problems, not resolution of things that happened in the past. Interventions are short term and aimed at solving the problem at hand. Clients are taught to identify and change dysfunctional thoughts (Beck, 1995), for example, generalizations such as "I *have to be* perfect" or "I can *never* do anything right." Rigid and unrealistic thoughts are believed to cause much emotional anguish and maladaptive behavior.

Questions

1. Describe the assumptions of the cognitive perspective.

_____

_____

_____

_____

_____

2. Using the cognitive perspective, identify the problems the Shore family is experiencing.

_____

_____

_____

_____

_____

_____

_____

_____

_____

_____

3. Using the cognitive perspective, describe the interventions you would suggest and state how they relate to the cognitive perspective.

_____

_____

_____

_____

_____

_____

_____

_____

_____

4. In what ways was this a helpful or not so helpful theory to use when working with this family?

_____

_____

_____

_____

_____

_____

_____

_____

_____

Group 3

Behavior Theory

Behavioral theorists believe that "behavior is affected by the events that follow it" (Wielkiewicz, 1995, p. 16) such as *positive reinforcement,* which is thought to increase behavior, and *punishment,* which is thought to decrease behavior. Human behavior is thought to be a matter of conditioned response. *Antecedents,* which are the events occurring immediately prior to a behavior, are also thought to be important in shaping behavior because they elicit certain responses. Behavioral theorists maintain that behaviors are eliminated (extinguished) when they are no longer rewarded.

Behavioral theorists look toward the identification of a stimulus or cues that trigger behavioral responses and examine the behaviors that receive reinforcement. Behaviorists also focus on the circumstances where a behavior occurs and assess the consequences of the behavior. Contingency contracting, where rewards and consequences are worked out in a contract, is one strategy for changing behavior (Arias, 1992).

Questions

1. Describe the assumptions of the behavioral perspective.

_____

_____

_____

_____

_____

_____

2. Using the behavioral perspective, identify the problems the Shore family is experiencing.

_____

_____

_____

_____

_____

_____

_____

3. Using the behavioral perspective, describe the interventions you would suggest and state how they relate to the behavioral perspective.

_____

_____

_____

_____

_____

_____

_____

_____

4. In what ways was this a helpful or not so helpful theory to use when working with this family?

_____

_____

_____

_____

_____

_____

_____

_____

Group 4

Systems Theory

Systems theory maintains that everything in a system is connected and that change in one part of the system creates change in all other parts of the system. As described in Exercise 2 in this workbook, families are examples of systems. Systems are ordered or organized in some way and have patterned behavior that recurs over time. Systems have boundaries that can be closed or open to people outside the system to varying degrees. Systems resist change because of the desire to maintain a state of balance, referred to as homeostasis. Each person in the system occupies a role or roles that prescribe behavior and his or her place in the hierarchy of power. All living systems must have input (taking things in) and output (disposing of things). Systems theorists believe in equifinality, meaning there are many ways to accomplish the same outcome (Zastrow & Kirst-Ashman, 1997).

Questions

. Describe the assumptions of the systems theory perspective.

_____

_____

_____

_____

_____

_____

. Using the systems perspective, identify the problems the Shore family is experiencing.

_____

_____

_____

_____

_____

_____

_____

_____

3. Using the systems perspective, describe the interventions you would suggest and state how they relate to the systems perspective.

_____

_____

_____

_____

_____

_____

_____

_____

4. In what ways was this a helpful or not so helpful theory to use when working with this family?

_____

_____

_____

_____

_____

_____

_____

_____

Group 5

Psychoanalytic Theory

Psychoanalytic theorists believe that our social-emotional functioning is largely shaped by previous psychological experiences. The unconscious is thought to have a significant influence over thoughts, feelings, and behavior. The psychoanalytic perspective suggests that humans progress through the oral, anal, phallic, latency, and genital stages of development. The human mental apparatus is thought to be divided into three realms: id, superego, and ego. The id has "no collective will, but only a striving to bring about the satisfaction of the instinctual needs subject to the observance of the pleasure principle" (Freud, 1965a, p. 73). The superego provides the "functions of self-observation, of conscience and of (maintaining) the ideal" (Freud, 1965a, p. 66). The ego is the rational region and mediates between the impulses of the id and the moral dictates of the superego. In the psychoanalytic perspective, anxiety "is the reproduction of an old event which brought a threat of danger; anxiety serves the purposes of self-preservation and is a signal of new danger . . . it arises during the process of repression; it is replaced by the formation of a symptom" (Freud, 1965b, pp. 84-85).

Questions

Describe the assumptions of the psychoanalytic perspective.

_____

_____

_____

_____

_____

_____

Using the psychoanalytic perspective, identify the problems the Shore family is experiencing.

_____

_____

_____

_____

_____

_____

_____

_____

_____

3. Using the psychoanalytic perspective, describe the interventions you would suggest and state how they relate to the psychoanalytic perspective.

_____

_____

_____

_____

_____

_____

_____

_____

4. In what ways was this a helpful or not so helpful theory to use when working with this family?

_____

_____

_____

_____

_____

_____

_____

_____

Group 6

Social Learning Theory

Social learning theorists maintain that people learn behavior by watching the behavior modeled by others. It is thought that humans learn by watching what others are rewarded or punished for. To learn new behavior by watching others, one must pay attention to the information being presented, retain this information in memory, practice the new behavior, and be sufficiently motivated to perform the new behavior. Defensive and aggressive behavior are thought to be frequently learned through observation rather than direct experience. To change behavior, "people need corrective learning experiences" and a belief in their efficacy. The expectation of efficacy "is the conviction that one can successfully execute the behavior required to produce the outcomes" (Bandura, 1977, p. 79).

Questions

1. Describe the assumptions of social learning theory.

_____

_____

_____

_____

_____

_____

_____

2. Using social learning theory, identify the problems the Shore family is experiencing.

_____

_____

_____

_____

_____

_____

_____

_____

3. Using social learning theory, describe the interventions you would suggest and state how they relate to social learning theory.

_____

_____

_____

_____

_____

_____

_____

_____

4. In what ways was this a helpful or not so helpful theory to use when working with this family?

_____

_____

_____

_____

_____

_____

_____

_____

Phase 2

Your instructor will have each group report its summary regarding the assumptions of its theory, the problems identified using the theory, the interventions suggested based on the theory assigned and their assessment of how useful their theory was when working with the Shore family.

Your instructor will ask you to get back into your original group with whom you numbered off from 1 to 6. This new configuration will result in a mix of people with one representative from each of the previous six theory groups.

In these new groups, you will need to again appoint a recorder and then combine all the perspectives from the previous groups. The groups will now need to identify the assumptions of the combined thinking because they will likely be different from the individual theories. The groups will also need to identify the problems of the Shore family using the combined theoretical approach. Finally, the groups will each need to suggest interventions based on the combined theoretical approach. When each group has had time to do this, you will be asked to share with the rest of the class the nature of your discussion and what you recorded on your worksheets using the combined approach.

The class will then discuss the ways that the theoretical approach influenced which problems were identified and the interventions suggested. The class will also discuss the advantages and disadvantages of using single or combined theoretical approaches.

Questions

1. Describe the assumptions of the combined theoretical approach.

_____

_____

_____

_____

_____

_____

_____

_____

_____

_____

_____

2. Using the combined theoretical approach, identify the problems the Shore family is experiencing.

_____

_____

_____

_____

_____

_____

_____

_____

_____

_____

_____

_____

_____

_____

_____

_____

_____

_____

3. Using the combined theoretical approach, describe the interventions you would suggest and state how they relate to the combined theoretical approach.

_____

_____

_____

_____

_____

_____

_____

_____

_____

_____

_____

_____

_____

_____

_____

_____

_____

_____

How similar or different were the views from the different combined theoretical groups?

_____

_____

_____

_____

_____

_____

_____

_____

_____

_____

_____

_____

_____

_____

_____

_____

_____

_____

_____

What have you learned about applying theories to real-life situations?

_____

_____

_____

_____

_____

_____

_____

_____

_____

_____

_____

_____

_____

_____

_____

_____

_____

_____

References

Arias, I. (1992). Behavioral marital therapy. In S. M. Turner, K. S. Calhoun, & H. Adams (Eds.), *Handbook of clinical behavior therapy* (2nd ed., pp. 437-455). New York: Wiley.

Bandura, A. (1977). *Social learning theory.* Englewood Cliffs, NJ: Prentice Hall.

Beck, J. (1995). *Cognitive therapy: Basics and beyond.* New York: Guilford.

Dorfman, R. A. (1988). The case. In R. A. Dorfman (Ed.), *Paradigms of clinical social work.* New York: Brunner/Mazel.

Freud, S. (1965a). The dissection of the psychial personality. In J. Strachey (Ed.), *New introductory lectures on psychoanalysis* (pp. 57-80). New York: Norton.

Freud, S. (1965b). Anxiety and instinctual life. In J. Strachey (Ed.), *New introductory lectures on psychoanalysis* (pp. 81-111). New York: Norton.

Gambrill, E. (1997). *Social work practice: A critical thinker's guide.* New York: Oxford University Press.

Germain, C. B., & Gitterman, A. (1980). *The life model of social work practice.* New York: Columbia University Press.

Kelly, J. (1968). Toward an ecological conception of preventive interventions. In J. Carter (Ed.), *Research contributions from psychology to community mental health* (pp. 75-99). New York: Behavioral Publications.

Okun, B. F. (1997). *Effective helping: Interviewing and counseling techniques* (5th ed.). Pacific Grove, CA: Brooks/Cole.

Schuyler, D. (1991). *A practical guide to cognitive therapy.* New York: Norton.

Wielkiewicz, R. M. (1995). *Behavior management in the schools: Principles and procedures* (2nd ed.). Boston: Allyn & Bacon.

Zastrow, C., & Kirst-Ashman, K. K. (1997). *Understanding human behavior and the social environment* (4th ed.). Chicago: Nelson-Hall.

EXERCISE 25 *Social Work Practice With Lesbian and Gay Families*

Linda E. Jones

Purpose

1. To examine personal and professional values related to gay and lesbian clients and families.
2. To determine various ethical principles of social work practice that serve to guide practice in complex family situations.
3. To recognize the multiple systems involved in client situations and to determine various roles social workers can play in addressing clients' concerns.
4. To illuminate multiple ways in which "family" can be defined and composed.

Background

In all fields of practice, social workers will inevitably work with gay men, lesbians, and their families. Families with gay and lesbian members experience the range of problems, concerns, and challenges that face any family. They also bring their own family dynamics to their interactions with each other and with those outside the family. However, the issues and challenges that confront gay men, lesbians, and their families always have to be considered within the social context of homophobia and heterosexism in which we all live, that are as much a part of the fabric of our society as are racism, sexism, ageism, and other systems of oppression. It is extremely important that social workers be conscientious in examining their own attitudes, beliefs, and values about gay and lesbian people and their families, in light of professional values and ethical principles that call on social workers to act to end systems of oppression and to oppose discriminatory practices based on sexual orientation.

Instructions

Your instructor will assign you (either individually or in small groups) one of the following cases involving a gay or lesbian family. Carefully read the case, think about it, and respond to the questions that follow. Be prepared to discuss your responses to the questions with your class.

EXERCISE 25

Case 1A

You are a school social worker in an elementary school. A fourth-grade teacher comes to you to discuss Sally, a 9-year-old girl who is not doing well in class. The teacher perceives the child to be increasingly withdrawn and states that she is not progressing academically as well as she should. While talking with you, the teacher says it has "crossed her mind" that the child may have been (or is still being) sexually abused. The teacher goes on to say that the child "comes from a very mixed-up home," but she does not elaborate.

When you look into the child's home situation, you discover that her parents are divorced and have joint legal custody. The child primarily lives with her mother, who is a lesbian, and with her mother's partner of 3 years. However, the child frequently visits her father and her new stepmother who live in the same town.

You must respond to the teacher's concerns about Sally.

Questions

1. What are the issues that need to be addressed? What areas/issues require special sensitivity?

_____

_____

_____

_____

_____

_____

_____

_____

_____

_____

_____

2. Is there other information that is important to gather before you proceed? From whom would you gather this information?

_____

_____

_____

_____

_____

_____

_____

_____

_____

3. Generate options for working with this family. What actions could you take?

_____

_____

_____

_____

_____

_____

_____

_____

_____

_____

4. Who would you try to involve in resolving this situation? Who would you include in a family conference? Why did you make these choices?

_____

_____

_____

_____

_____

_____

_____

_____

_____

_____

5. To what other resources might you refer various members of this family? Are there community resources that might be helpful to some or all of the people involved?

_____

_____

_____

_____

_____

_____

_____

_____

_____

_____

_____

6. In addition to microlevel interventions to address the immediate situation, are there other actions this case might prompt you to take, considering your various roles as a social worker?

_____

_____

_____

_____

_____

_____

_____

_____

_____

7. Are you aware of ways in which you thought about and/or responded to this case differently than you might have if there had been no one involved who is gay or lesbian? If so, why do you think this occurred? If not, why not?

_____

_____

_____

_____

_____

_____

_____

_____

_____

8. Were there things about this situation that made you feel *personally* uncomfortable? Did you find yourself making any assumptions, having particular feelings, or asking types of questions that might stem from a personal prejudice or stereotype?

_____

_____

_____

_____

_____

_____

_____

_____

_____

_____

9. Which social work values are particularly evident in this case situation? How are they evident?

_____

_____

_____

_____

_____

_____

_____

_____

_____

_____

10. Which ethical principles of social work guide you in your work with this family? Be sure to also consider ethical principles related to actions you might take in addition to microlevel interventions with this family (refer to Question 6).

_____

_____

_____

_____

_____

_____

_____

_____

_____

_____

_____

_____

Case 2A

You are a family court counselor working with a couple who is divorcing. The couple has agreed that the mother will have primary physical custody of the children (an 11-year-old boy and an 8-year-old girl), but they cannot agree on visitation issues.

The mother is trying to restrict the father's visitation because he is gay and lives with his partner of 4 years. She does not want the children to go to their father's house or to spend the night with him there. In addition, she does not want the father's partner to be allowed to interact with the children at all.

The father is not willing to agree to these stipulations, and he is threatening to reopen the entire custody agreement if the issues around visitation are not resolved to his satisfaction soon. He wants the children to visit in his house once a week for dinner and to spend every other weekend with him and his partner. Furthermore, he sees his partner as a coparent and wants and expects him to be involved with the children in a "stepparent" role.

As the resolution to the visitation conflict becomes more difficult and complicated, the children are becoming increasingly upset and are beginning to have difficulties in school.

Questions

1. What are the issues that need to be addressed? What areas/issues require special sensitivity?

_____

_____

_____

_____

_____

_____

_____

_____

_____

2. Is there other information that is important to gather before you proceed? From whom would you gather this information?

_____

_____

_____

_____

_____

_____

_____

_____

_____

_____

3. Generate options for working with this family. What actions could you take?

_____

_____

_____

_____

_____

_____

_____

_____

_____

_____

4. Who would you try to involve in resolving this situation? Who would you include in a family conference? Why did you make these choices?

_____

_____

_____

_____

_____

_____

_____

_____

_____

_____

_____

5. To what other resources might you refer various members of this family? Are there community resources that might be helpful to some or all of the people involved?

_____

_____

_____

_____

_____

_____

_____

_____

_____

6. In addition to microlevel interventions to address the immediate situation, are there other actions this case might prompt you to take, considering your various roles as a social worker?

_____

_____

_____

_____

_____

_____

_____

_____

_____

7. Are you aware of ways in which you thought about and/or responded to this case differently than you might have if there had been no one involved who is gay or lesbian? If so, why do you think this occurred? If not, why not?

_____

_____

_____

_____

_____

_____

_____

_____

8. Were there things about this situation that made you feel *personally* uncomfortable? Did you find yourself making any assumptions, having particular feelings, or asking types of questions that might stem from a personal prejudice or stereotype?

_____

_____

_____

_____

_____

_____

_____

_____

_____

_____

9. Which social work values are particularly evident in this case situation? How are they evident?

_____

_____

_____

_____

_____

_____

_____

_____

_____

10. Which ethical principles of social work guide you in your work with this family? Be sure to also consider ethical principles related to actions you might take in addition to microlevel interventions with this family (refer to Question 6).

_____

_____

_____

_____

_____

_____

_____

_____

_____

Case 3A

You are a social worker assigned to the oncology service of a large metropolitan hospital, and you receive a physician referral to visit Grace, a patient with late-stage melanoma who is experiencing unusual family stress. The doctor believes this high level of family stress is seriously affecting his patient's well-being, as well as decisions about her care. When you meet with 65-year-old Grace, she tells you she is a lesbian and has been in a committed relationship with Harriet for 15 years. Grace also has three adult children who are 37, 39, and 40 years of age.

Grace explains that she has not had a close relationship with her children, who live in other parts of the country, since she and their father were divorced about 20 years ago. Until this hospitalization and the children's arrival in town to be with her, they did not know the nature of the relationship between Grace and Harriet. The children are shocked by this news, and Grace is upset that her children now have this information at such a difficult time.

Harriet and Grace have discussed her rapidly worsening illness at length and have an agreement about the type of treatment and care that Grace wants. The children strongly disagree with what their mother and her partner have decided (to terminate treatment and receive medication and care that will minimize pain and discomfort in Grace's final days) and believe that their mother is not thinking clearly. The children have also discovered that their mother has not completed written medical directives about her wishes under these circumstances, and she has not legally designated Harriet as the person to make medical decisions on her behalf, should she become unable to do so.

The children have now told Harriet not to visit their mother in the hospital and to stop influencing their mother's thinking about her medical care. Grace is extremely upset and asks for your help with this situation.

Questions

1. What are the issues that need to be addressed? What areas/issues require special sensitivity?

_____

_____

_____

_____

_____

_____

_____

_____

_____

_____

2. Is there other information that is important to gather before you proceed? From whom would you gather this information?

_____

_____

_____

_____

_____

_____

_____

_____

_____

3. Generate options for working with this family. What actions could you take?

_____

_____

_____

_____

_____

_____

_____

_____

_____

4. Who would you try to involve in resolving this situation? Who would you include in a family conference? Why did you make these choices?

_____

_____

_____

_____

_____

_____

_____

_____

_____

_____

5. To what other resources might you refer various members of this family? Are there community resources that might be helpful to some or all of the people involved?

_____

_____

_____

_____

_____

_____

_____

_____

_____

_____

6. In addition to microlevel interventions to address the immediate situation, are there other actions this case might prompt you to take, considering your various roles as a social worker?

_____

_____

_____

_____

_____

_____

_____

_____

_____

7. Are you aware of ways in which you thought about and/or responded to this case differently than you might have if there had been no one involved who is gay or lesbian? If so, why do you think this occurred? If not, why not?

_____

_____

_____

_____

_____

_____

_____

_____

_____

_____

8. Were there things about this situation that made you feel *personally* uncomfortable? Did you find yourself making any assumptions, having particular feelings, or asking types of questions that might stem from a personal prejudice or stereotype?

_____

_____

_____

_____

_____

_____

_____

_____

_____

9. Which social work values are particularly evident in this case situation? How are they evident?

_____

_____

_____

_____

_____

_____

_____

_____

_____

_____

10. Which ethical principles of social work guide you in your work with this family? Be sure to also consider ethical principles related to actions you might take in addition to microlevel interventions with this family (refer to Question 6).

_____

_____

_____

_____

_____

_____

_____

_____

_____

_____

_____

_____

_____

Case 1B

You are a school social worker in an elementary school. A fourth-grade teacher comes to you to discuss Sam, a 9-year-old boy who is not doing well in class. The teacher perceives the child to be increasingly withdrawn and states that he is not progressing academically as well as he should. While talking with you, the teacher says it has "crossed her mind" that the child may have been (or is still being) sexually abused. The teacher goes on to say that the child "comes from a very mixed-up home," but she does not elaborate.

When you look into the child's home situation, you discover that his parents are divorced and have joint legal custody. The child primarily lives with his father, who is gay, and with his father's partner of 3 years. The child frequently visits his mother and his new stepfather who live in the same town.

You must respond to the teacher's concerns about Sam.

Questions

1. What are the issues that need to be addressed? What areas/issues require special sensitivity?

_____

_____

_____

_____

_____

_____

_____

_____

_____

2. Is there other information that is important to gather before you proceed? From whom would you gather this information?

_____

_____

_____

_____

_____

_____

_____

_____

_____

_____

3. Generate options for working with this family. What actions could you take?

_____

_____

_____

_____

_____

_____

_____

_____

_____

_____

_____

4. Who would you try to involve in resolving this situation? Who would you include in a family conference? Why did you make these choices?

_____

_____

_____

_____

_____

_____

_____

_____

_____

_____

_____

5. To what other resources might you refer various members of this family? Are there community resources that might be helpful to some or all of the people involved?

_____

_____

_____

_____

_____

_____

_____

_____

_____

_____

6. In addition to microlevel interventions to address the immediate situation, are there other actions this case might prompt you to take, considering your various roles as a social worker?

_____

_____

_____

_____

_____

_____

_____

_____

_____

_____

_____

_____

7. Are you aware of ways in which you thought about and/or responded to this case differently than you might have if there had been no one involved who is gay or lesbian? If so, why do you think this occurred? If not, why not?

_____

_____

_____

_____

_____

_____

_____

_____

_____

8. Were there things about this situation that made you feel *personally* uncomfortable? Did you find yourself making any assumptions, having particular feelings, or asking types of questions that might stem from a personal prejudice or stereotype?

_____

_____

_____

_____

_____

_____

_____

_____

_____

9. Which social work values are particularly evident in this case situation? How are they evident?

_____

_____

_____

_____

_____

_____

_____

_____

_____

_____

10. Which ethical principles of social work guide you in your work with this family? Be sure to also consider ethical principles related to actions you might take in addition to microlevel interventions with this family (refer to Question 6).

_____

_____

_____

_____

_____

_____

_____

_____

_____

_____

_____

_____

Case 2B

You are a family court counselor working with a couple who is divorcing. The couple has agreed that the father will have primary physical custody of the children (an 11-year-old boy and an 8-year-old girl), but they cannot agree on visitation issues.

The father is trying to restrict the mother's visitation because she is a lesbian and lives with her partner of 4 years. He does not want the children to go to their mother's house or to spend the night with her there. In addition, he does not want the mother's partner to be allowed to interact with the children at all.

The mother is not willing to agree to these stipulations, and she is threatening to reopen the entire custody agreement if the issues around visitation are not resolved to her satisfaction soon. She wants the children to visit in her house once a week for dinner and to spend every other weekend with her and her partner. Furthermore, she sees her partner as a coparent and wants and expects her to be involved with the children in a "stepparent" role.

As the resolution to the visitation conflict becomes more difficult and complicated, the children are becoming increasingly upset and are beginning to have difficulties in school.

Questions

1. What are the issues that need to be addressed? What areas/issues require special sensitivity?

_____

_____

_____

_____

_____

_____

_____

_____

_____

_____

_____

_____

_____

_____

2. Is there other information that is important to gather before you proceed? From whom would you gather this information?

_____

_____

_____

_____

_____

_____

_____

_____

_____

_____

3. Generate options for working with this family. What actions could you take?

_____

_____

_____

_____

_____

_____

_____

_____

_____

_____

4. Who would you try to involve in resolving this situation? Who would you include in a family conference? Why did you make these choices?

_____

_____

_____

_____

_____

_____

_____

_____

_____

_____

5. To what other resources might you refer various members of this family? Are there community resources that might be helpful to some or all of the people involved?

_____

_____

_____

_____

_____

_____

_____

_____

_____

_____

6. In addition to microlevel interventions to address the immediate situation, are there other actions this case might prompt you to take, considering your various roles as a social worker?

_____

_____

_____

_____

_____

_____

_____

_____

_____

7. Are you aware of ways in which you thought about and/or responded to this case differently than you might have if there had been no one involved who is gay or lesbian? If so, why do you think this occurred? If not, why not?

_____

_____

_____

_____

_____

_____

_____

_____

_____

8. Were there things about this situation that made you feel *personally* uncomfortable? Did you find yourself making any assumptions, having particular feelings, or asking types of questions that might stem from a personal prejudice or stereotype?

_____

_____

_____

_____

_____

_____

_____

_____

_____

9. Which social work values are particularly evident in this case situation? How are they evident?

_____

_____

_____

_____

_____

_____

_____

_____

_____

_____

_____

10. Which ethical principles of social work guide you in your work with this family? Be sure to also consider ethical principles related to actions you might take in addition to microlevel interventions with this family (refer to Question 6).

_____

_____

_____

_____

_____

_____

_____

_____

_____

_____

Case 3B

You are a social worker assigned to the oncology service of a large metropolitan hospital, and you receive a physician referral to visit George, a patient with late-stage melanoma who is experiencing unusual family stress. The doctor believes this high level of family stress is seriously affecting his patient's well-being, as well as decisions about his care. When you meet with 65-year-old George, he tells you he is gay and has been in a committed relationship with Harry for 15 years. George also has three adult children who are 37, 39, and 40 years of age.

George explains that he has not had a close relationship with his children, who live in other parts of the country, since he and their mother were divorced about 20 years ago. Until this hospitalization and the children's arrival in town to be with him, they did not know the nature of the relationship between George and Harry. The children are shocked by this news, and George is upset that his children now have this information at such a difficult time.

Harry and George have discussed his rapidly worsening illness at length and have an agreement about the type of treatment and care that George wants. The children strongly disagree with what their father and his partner have decided (to terminate treatment and receive medication and care that will minimize pain and discomfort in George's final days) and believe that their father is not thinking clearly. The children have also discovered that their father has not completed written medical directives about his wishes under these circumstances, and he has not legally designated Harry as the person to make medical decisions on his behalf, should he become unable to do so.

The children have now told Harry not to visit their father in the hospital and to stop influencing their father's thinking about his medical care. George is extremely upset and asks for your help with this situation.

Questions

1. What are the issues that need to be addressed? What areas/issues require special sensitivity?

_____

_____

_____

_____

_____

_____

_____

_____

2. Is there other information that is important to gather before you proceed? From whom would you gather this information?

_____

_____

_____

_____

_____

_____

_____

_____

_____

3. Generate options for working with this family. What actions could you take?

_____

_____

_____

_____

_____

_____

_____

_____

_____

_____

4. Who would you try to involve in resolving this situation? Who would you include in a family conference? Why did you make these choices?

_____

_____

_____

_____

_____

_____

_____

_____

_____

_____

5. To what other resources might you refer various members of this family? Are there community resources that might be helpful to some or all of the people involved?

_____

_____

_____

_____

_____

_____

_____

_____

6. In addition to microlevel interventions to address the immediate situation, are there other actions this case might prompt you to take, considering your various roles as a social worker?

_____

_____

_____

_____

_____

_____

_____

_____

_____

_____

7. Are you aware of ways in which you thought about and/or responded to this case differently than you might have if there had been no one involved who is gay or lesbian? If so, why do you think this occurred? If not, why not?

_____

_____

_____

_____

_____

_____

_____

_____

8. Were there things about this situation that made you feel *personally* uncomfortable? Did you find yourself making any assumptions, having particular feelings, or asking types of questions that might stem from a personal prejudice or stereotype?

_____

_____

_____

_____

_____

_____

_____

_____

9. Which social work values are particularly evident in this case situation? How are they evident?

_____

_____

_____

_____

_____

_____

_____

_____

_____

10. Which ethical principles of social work guide you in your work with this family? Be sure to also consider ethical principles related to actions you might take in addition to microlevel interventions with this family (refer to Question 6).

_____

_____

_____

_____

_____

_____

_____

_____

_____

_____

_____

EXERCISE 26 *Constructively Engaging Professionals in Complex Organizations*

Freda J. Herrington

Purpose

1. To practice constructively mediating the interaction between an individual client and a formal organization.
2. To practice the skills of empathy with a representative of the system.
3. To increase conscious awareness of feelings toward formal organizations and their personnel.
4. To explore the implications of the social worker's emotions for professional action.

Background

Social workers easily identify with the plight of a client approaching a complex institution or organization to obtain services and benefits or to resolve a problem in communicating with the organization's personnel. The professional's personal experiences resonate easily with many of the familiar difficulties that may surface in the person-system interaction. Locating the appropriate office or person, completing the necessary forms, and learning the system's unique language may all prove daunting for the unsuspecting individual. The temptation to immediately prepare for an aggressive confrontation with a system's representative may be very hard to resist. However, this is exactly what the social worker must try to do. Stereotyping system personnel as irredeemably uncaring bureaucrats or blaming them for the client's difficulties will be fruitless paths for the social worker and the client.

Starting with the tactics of confrontation and pressure may result in some immediate gains for a client. However, the potential for ongoing difficulty between the client and the formal organization requires thoughtful attention. If the social worker, motivated by anger and rescue fantasies, charges in to save the client from an insensitive bureaucracy, he or she may fail to build on the client's and the system's positive efforts. The social worker may miss an opportunity to help the client and the organization find their own ways of resolving problems. Additionally, the social worker and the worker's agency may receive their own negative stereotypes, therefore hampering future work between the agency and the organization.

The social worker's task is to implement skills that foster open communication instead of closed defensiveness. He or she must find ways to communicate an accurate understanding of the system's working arrangements and requirements as well as the client's concerns and goals. Lawrence Shulman (1992) has identified the skill of empathy for systems' representatives as an essential tool in beginning to establish a more constructive and productive connection between the client and a formal organization.

EXERCISE 26

Part 1

Instructions

Carefully read Norah Holmgren's (1990) short story "Social Security." On the sheet that follows, jot down some brief notes of your reactions to events and characters in the story. In your notes, try to distinguish between your emotional reactions and your thoughts and analytic responses to the story.

Social Security
by Norah Holmgren

My mother and I were sitting in the Social Security office. It was on the eighteenth floor of an old building in the heart of the city, but I could still hear the *swish swish* of cars passing on the freeway below. I stood up I could see them—long ribbons of them.

I don't live in the city anymore. The sight of ten thousand cars a day began to get me down. Where I live now, out in the country, I can distinguish each of my neighbors' cars by sound alone. In the evening when I come home from work, the children can hear me coming closer and closer. In the morning when I hear the rattles and explosions of the Ford truck next door, I know it's time to get up.

My mother had asked me to come with her to Social Security. She wanted me to speak for her and hear for her. She speaks English perfectly and her hearing is unimpaired. She simply can't believe what is being said. If I came with her, she said, we could talk things over later and try to make sense of them. It would be too late then, but it's better to try to understand anyway, isn't it?

In the waiting room we were among the Mexican families, the slim, young Chinese girls, the Filipino men, the gray old German men, and the old Swedish ladies like my mother who had been cooks and maids and seamstresses and bakery clerks. The music of these languages rose and fell. The clerks had to shout over the din. When it got too noisy, an armed guard would parade by us once or twice. We all had something in common: we were waiting for our names to be called.

The procedure was this: when we entered, a woman at the door questioned us about our business. If she couldn't turn us away, she gave us a number from 1 to 50. When that number was called, we turned it in and got a number from 51 to 99. When that number was called, our name was entered on a list. When our name was called, we could be shown in. We were told to expect to wait two or three hours for these transitions.

We sat side by side, not talking, observing the people in the room as they observed us.

When my mother's name was called, we stood up and were shown through a doorway into a vast room with rows and rows of desks. Our clerk beckoned to us. He was young, freckled, and dressed in a short-sleeved white shirt open at the neck and chest to reveal a spotless white undershirt. We sat down. I was going to do all the talking.

"I'm Mr. Sisk," he said.

"Ssss?" said my mother.

"Sisk."

"Yes," she said.

NOTE: From Holmgren, N. (1990). Social Security. In J. Mukand, *Vital lines: Contemporary fiction about medicine.* New York: Ballantine. Used with permission.

His last customer was still hanging around, though he had clearly been dismissed. He was a good-looking, tall old man who was standing very straight. He ignored us. It was Mr. Sisk he wanted.

"Why can't you be reasonable?" he said. "I'm an alcoholic. You know me. I never should have told you I haven't been drinking lately. It makes no difference at all. You know that."

"No, that's what I don't know," said Mr. Sisk.

We watched unashamed.

"You don't want to know."

"You aren't drinking now. Maybe you don't need a treatment program."

"I can't hang on much longer without help."

"The rules are clear. The key words are *currently* and *presently* and *at this time.*"

"Bend the rules a little. If I take a drink I'll be gone for months. Lost, lost, lost."

"Don't ask me to bend the rules."

My mother stood up. "The rules must be stupid and cruel," she shouted.

"Who are they for?"

Mr. Sisk looked at her. He didn't speak, but his eyes were blinking rapidly.

He stood up and led the man away.

"I couldn't help it," my mother said. "Do you think it will ruin our chances?"

"I don't think we have any chances to be ruined."

Mr. Sisk returned. He had buttoned up his shirt and put his jacket on. My mother handed him the letter she had gotten from Social Security. He looked it over and said, "What's the problem?"

I said, "What does it mean?"

"It means we paid her too much money, and now we have to get it back. We are going to suspend her payments until the money is made up. It will take nine months."

"Is there no alternative?" I said. "It isn't her fault you gave her too much money."

Mr. Sisk drew himself up in his chair. "We don't use the word *fault* here. She can fill out a hardship report, stating that she cannot live without her Social Security allowance." He found the form in his desk and handed it to me. I looked it over. Declare all your valuables. Declare all current sources of income. Declare possible sources of income. State names and addresses of family members. An inquisition.

My mother had a few old valuables. Her husband, my stepfather, had a pension. They could live without her money. It was just that she thought of her Social Security check as her own money, money she had earned by forty years of labor, money she could spend on herself with a clear conscience, not that she ever did spend much money on herself.

I said to her, "We don't want to fill out this form. All of this is none of their business. It seems that they have the right to withhold your money unless you tell them how much your wedding ring is worth and everything else."

Mr. Sisk addressed my mother in a very loud voice. "Are you willing to fill out this form?"

"I'm not deaf," she shouted at him.

He shuffled his paper. There was a commotion at the next desk. A redheaded clerk was yelling at an old woman in black. "Come back when you're sober."

"I'm not drunk. I've just had a little drink," she said.

"Sit down, then," the clerk screamed.

"Something about this place makes you want to yell," my mother said.

"It's because they think we're all deaf."

"I get so mad," my mother said. "Sure, that woman had a little drink. Sometimes you get so mad, sometimes you get so fed up, you just take a drink."

We got up to leave. "If you get a check from us by mistake, be sure to send it to me," said Mr. Sisk.

"You're going to make more mistakes? What's wrong with you people?" my mother said.

I took her out to lunch. I tried to minimize the loss of her money.

She said, "Stop trying to cheer me up. You're making me feel terrible." We sat in silence then.

After a while she started to talk. "I've worked and worked," she said. I sat very still. I hoped she would tell me her story. She rarely spoke about her early life. I knew only the generalities: Dad was good. Mother was a martyr, times were hard, you wouldn't believe it.

"When I was eleven—that was during the war—not much food then, the whole family got the flu at one time. There were seven of us children. Dad and I were the only ones who didn't get sick. Oh, how we worked. We cooked, we cleaned, we did the chores. I was so tired at night, I fell asleep in my clothes. My youngest brother died of pneumonia and was buried before the doctor got to us. My mother cried for months and months about that. It was just me and my dad doing all the work. We made soup, we dug potatoes, we fed the chickens. Oh, how we worked."

I waited but she didn't go on.

"What made you think of that story?"

"Mr. Sisk. I'd like to show him what work is."

We got up to leave. "I'm lonely," my mother said. "I'd like to go see Alice. Will you drive me over?"

Alice was a friend of hers I didn't care for. "I'll drive you, I'll wait for you, but I don't want to come in and visit."

"I don't want you to. I want to talk about places you've never been, times before you were born. You'd just be in the way."

After I'd dropped her off, I went into a little park near Alice's house and sat down with a book. There was an unexpected number of people in the park. A large table stood under the trees with paper cups full of water on it. People were watching the path expectantly. Soon tired men and women came running into the park. As each one crossed a chalk line, the bystanders would applaud and cheer. Friends would come forward to hug the runners. The event repeated itself over and over. The applause and cheers didn't diminish; they increased.

My mother soon came limping up the path. Runners passed her on either side. She paid no attention to them. I wanted to stand and applaud her, whose every race had been run without applause, but she would have been angry.

"Why are you smiling?" she said. "Are you laughing at me?"

"No. I'm appreciating you."

"Alice didn't remember the flu of 1917, but she was glad to see me."

Later that evening when I was back in the country and the children were in bed, I wrote a little note to myself. I planned to read it every now and then. It said: "Develop a terrifying persona for when you are old and at the mercy of systems. Save your money so you can always be independent. Never look as though you could be hard of hearing."

This morning when I was cleaning out my desk, I found it. I laughed first, then I called my mother to say hello.

Reactions to "Social Security"

Gut reactions or emotions evoked:

_____

_____

_____

_____

_____

_____

_____

_____

Thoughts about the situation, organization, and characters presented:

_____

_____

_____

_____

_____

_____

_____

_____

_____

_____

Part 2

Instructions

Your instructor will assist you in forming small groups with 4-5 of your classmates. Your primary task within your small group is to develop a role play based on the characters and events in the story with the addition of a social worker from a community center. The members of your small group will dramatize the following parts:

A social worker from the Golden Age Community Center
Mr. Sisk (the employee at the Social Security office)
The elderly woman
The woman's daughter (optional)
Observer/recorder

Together with your group members, decide which part each of you will play. A group of four students should omit the part of the daughter.

After your group decides on the assignment of the roles, take a limited amount of time (about 8 minutes) to discuss how you want to approach the role play. Avoid writing a script or completely mapping out the role play. The descriptions provided below serve as an initial orientation for each role. Allow some room for the spontaneous elaboration of each part. Move into your group's role play as quickly as possible.

Allow about 10 to 15 minutes for the role play. You are most likely to gain more from this exercise by moving into a specific role fairly quickly. Avoid a lot of discussion about the role play situation. Get into the action.

After about 15 minutes the observer should call "time" to signal the end of the role play. Before discussing what happened, each group member should write down at least two events that were especially interesting and increased your understanding of the skills for helping clients to become more adept at dealing with complex organizations. What did you discover or become aware of by stepping into the particular role you had for this exercise?

Begin your group's summing-up discussion with feedback from the observer. Allow the observer enough time to thoroughly share his or her comments without discussion from other group members. Once the observer has completed his or her comments, the group can open its discussion. Each group member should comment on his or her experience of playing a specific role or acting as the observer. Each group should briefly summarize (aloud) their experiences and learning for the rest of the class.

Roles

Social Worker From the Community Center: Your task is to assist your client in addressing the problem of her terminated Social Security benefits. At some point in your role play, you must discuss the problem with Mr. Sisk. Decide, with ideas from your group members, if you will do this with your client present or individually with Mr. Sisk. Try to implement the skills of clearly explaining your purpose and role and communicating empathy for systems representatives. Try to keep focused on finding constructive/positive options.

Activate your imagination, and try to explore a variety of options.

Mr. Sisk: Your task is to take the perspective of the Social Security caseworker. As Mr. Sisk, you are trying to adhere to the policies of your agency *and* respond to the concerns of your clients. You wish people would take more care in learning about their benefits and monitoring their monthly checks. Your supervisor evaluates the effectiveness of your work primarily in terms of how quickly you resolve benefit problems in accord with agency regulations. You are deeply upset when you have to tell someone that benefits are being stopped. You believe it is totally unprofessional to show these feelings in any way.

Elderly Woman: You are astonished and angry that the Social Security Administration refuses to share any responsibility for the error in overpayment of your benefits. You are irritated that you had to wait so long to see Mr. Sisk. His manner of talking with you has convinced you that he cares more about the rules than the people he is supposed to help. You are worried about managing without your benefits. Gradually, you begin to acknowledge some of your own responsibility for the overpayment. You are adamant about not applying for "hardship benefits." You are deeply concerned that something be done to keep this from happening to others.

Daughter: You share your mother's amazement and anger. You believe the Social Security Administration is looking for ways to withhold benefits. You feel protective toward your mother and are worried about the stress all of this imposes on her. Sometimes you speak for her to help her with bureaucrats like Mr. Sisk. You're puzzled and a little annoyed that the social worker from the community center keeps confirming your comments with your mother to make sure she agrees.

Observer/Recorder: Your task is to listen and observe the social worker's interactions. Watch carefully for the social worker's efforts to form a working relationship with Mr. Sisk. Does the social worker listen to Mr. Sisk and explore his views of the situation? How does the social worker express empathy to Mr. Sisk? What does he or she do and say to encourage the consideration of options? Does the social worker try to coach or teach Mr. Sisk? Does the social worker get stuck during the role play? If so, what do you notice about how this is happening? Sketch some notes of your observations and use these to share specific feedback after the role play is concluded.

Question

(Use this space to list two interesting events that increased your understanding)

_____

_____

_____

_____

_____

_____

_____

_____

_____

_____

Reference

Shulman, L. (1992). *The skills of helping individuals and groups* (3rd ed.). Itasca, IL: F. E. Peacock.

EXERCISE 27   *Coleadership of the Parenting Group*

Victoria Van Slyke

Purpose

1. To develop facility in the application of fundamental social group work concepts and practice techniques.
2. To understand the ways in which group leadership influences group process dynamics, which in turn shape the group experience and outcomes

Background

Social group work builds on the value base of client self-determination, empowerment, and the intrinsic worth of all individuals. The mutual aid model for social group work is particularly well suited to develop a democratic alliance of individuals who need each other to work on certain common problems. Once a mutual aid system has been developed as a series of helping relationships, the purpose that brought the members together may be actualized. Mutual aid groups may be designed to enhance members' functioning in relation to selected psychosocial phenomena, such as aging, parenting, or socioeconomic status.

The mutual aid model emphasizes reciprocal assistance, mutual responsibility, belonging, and being heard, as well as freedom of choice and freedom to challenge authority (Glassman & Kates, 1990). Although the mutual aid model can be used very effectively in a range of clinically oriented groups, it also can be effective in self-help and community groups, for example. In contrast with most therapy groups, where the group leader retains far more power by design, the mutual aid model enables the planned transfer of power from the group facilitator(s) to the members. Hence, it is very compatible with empowerment-oriented practice, as well as promoting a strength-based mutual aid process.

Role-playing has been described as a realistic enactment of a social role in an imagined social situation (Shaw, 1980). It is frequently used in group work as an interventive technique, and it is also a powerful learning tool for social work students who wish to develop proficiency in group work. Simulating a multisession, ongoing mutual aid group provides an intensive and time-extended experiential "learning lab" for group work practice. Experiential learning provides an ideal medium for developing skills in group leadership, including cofacilitation of groups. Simulated group experience also provides opportunities for direct observation and analysis of group process dynamics and role behavior, as well as various interventive techniques used by group leaders. It also invites students to examine their own emotional and behavioral responses as evoked by the simulated group process to increase self-awareness and enhance professional use of self in this practice mode.

Instructions

Your instructor will assign you to a role in the simulation of a parenting support group. You will be assigned to a coleader, group member, or group observer role. Students who volunteer and are selected for either of the two group coleader roles may be eligible to earn extra credit, commensurate with the additional preparation time required before and after group sessions. The instructor will serve as consultant to the coleaders throughout the simulation. Group observers will form a second outer circle around the inner circle of the simulated group, in a "fishbowl" arrangement. Participants will maintain this spatial arrangement throughout the simulated group sessions and subsequent debriefings. Observers will provide the participants with feedback, which has been gathered on the forms below.

This group simulation exercise is designed in four experiential segments, or sessions. Each segment has accompanying observational tools that will be used to identify and analyze relevant elements of group process and social group work. These segments are summarized here; the actual forms you will use to record and analyze your observations are found after the group members' role descriptions. During the debriefing that follows each simulated group session, your instructor will lead a class discussion that critically examines specific elements of that group session and that draws on the divergent perspectives of group members, group leaders, and observers. Forms A-E, described below, will help provide a vehicle for debriefing various dimensions of group experience.

Segment 1/Week 1

Form A: Pre-Group Self-Assessment of Group Leader Strengths and Areas of Discomfort (to be completed independently by all members of the class, then shared in dyads, *prior to* the simulated Group Session 1)

Form B: Observational Record of Task-Oriented and Maintenance-Oriented Behaviors (to be completed independently by observers during the simulated Group Session 1, and serve as basis for giving feedback during discussion and debriefing of Group Session 1)

Parenting Support Group Session 1 (simulated 60-minute group, followed by 40 minutes of all-class discussion and debriefing)

Segment 2/Week 2

Form C: Assessing Coleader Compatibility and Complementarity (to be completed independently by all members of the class prior to simulated Group Session 2, then disclosed in a role play format between two prospective group coleaders. All class members will be paired in dyads for concurrent role plays between prospective group coleaders)

Form D: Group Process Log—Observational Analysis of Group Dynamics (to be completed independently by observers during simulated Session 2, and serve as basis for giving feedback during discussion and debriefing of Session 2)

Parenting Support Group Session 2 (simulated second meeting of Parent Support Group for 60 minutes, followed by 40 minutes of all-class discussion and debriefing)

Segment 3/Week 3

Form E: Observational Analysis of Group Leader Skills (to be completed independently by all observers during simulated Group Session 3, and by all other members of the class *after* the simulation, but *before* debriefing discussion begins)

Form D: Group Process Log—Observational Analysis of Group Dynamics (to be completed independently by observers during the group simulation, and by all other members of the class *after* the group simulation, and *before* debriefing discussion begins)

Parenting Support Group Session 3 (simulated third meeting of Parent Support Group for 60 minutes, followed by 40 minutes of all-class discussion and debriefing after all class members have completed Forms E and D)

Segment 4/Week 4

(Forms E and D: Use as in Week 3)

Parenting Support Group Session 4 (procedures as in Session 3)

Social Group Work Simulation: A Mutual Aid Model
Parenting Support Group for Caregivers of Children at Risk

Coleaders

You are cofacilitators of a 6-week group for persons who are parenting children at risk for neglect or maltreatment, as well as for parents who experience being overwhelmed by the demands of caregiving. The general purpose of the group is to increase self-awareness, obtain social support, and gain skills for stress management and more effective parenting. Although all members have agreed to participate in the group, some members are ambivalent about whether the group can truly be of help to them, and some feel ambivalent about disclosing their difficulties to others. You have met jointly with each member in a pre-group interview and have obtained the information summarized in the group member role descriptions provided below. Your plan for the first group session includes

1. Facilitating a get-acquainted process among the members
2. Encouraging members to share with each other the difficulties or concerns that brought them to the group, and to talk about their hopes, expectations, and reservations about the group
3. To review the purpose of the group and discuss the parameters (i.e., confidentiality, being on time and attending regularly, and norms such as treating one another with respect, offering support, etc.) for participation
4. To begin building a climate of mutual support and modeling positive communication, as well as facilitating the disclosure of information by members
5. Facilitate the process by which common ground may be identified to form the basis for collective and individual goal formulation relative to participation in the group, given common and individual problems and concerns of the respective members

During each group session, the coleaders help each other facilitate the work of the group. Between group sessions, the coleaders will discuss their perceptions and feelings about the group and their respective roles in it, as well as plan appropriately for the upcoming session. This collaboration can be helpful in allowing practitioners to share alternative frames of reference regarding the interactions that occur in the group and in more effective preparation for future group sessions. The instructor will be available to provide consultation to the coleaders that supports their leadership development.

Group Members

Member 1

You are a teenage (age 18) single parent of a 7-month-old daughter. You are enrolled in your senior year in high school in a special program for teen parents. Your daughter accompanies you there each school day. You are living with your parents but feel resentful at their attempts to "run your life" now that you've assumed the responsibilities of parenthood. You have had no contact with the baby's father since before her birth, and have no information about his whereabouts. You have felt overwhelmed at times by the baby's frequent crying and your inability to soothe her. With all the stress of studying and forfeiting your formerly active social life, your temper is often on a short fuse. Responsibility for your daughter sometimes feels like more than you can handle. You were referred to the group by the school social worker, and agreed to participate. You and your family are Hispanic.

Member 2

You are a 30-year-old mother of four (ages 3 months to 5 years) and full-time homemaker. Following the birth of your last child you have been receiving treatment for depression. The constant needs and demands of caring for four preschool-age children often feels overwhelming, and recently you have been spending more time in bed during the day, finding it harder and harder to respond to the children's basic needs for food, diapering, dressing, supervision, and nurturing. Your husband works long hours outside the home and appears to have little energy for parenting tasks when he is at home. You have been referred to this parenting support group by the psychotherapist treating you for depression. You and your family are Caucasian.

Member 3

You are a 42-year-old father of two teenage sons (14 and 16) who have both run away from home on at least two occasions in response to your harsh "discipline." You work nights at an automobile assembly plant and your wife works days in a food processing plant. You were referred to the group by your parish priest, from whom the boys sought assistance, and despite your serious misgivings about it, you have agreed to participate in the group. You have never been in such a group before and feel quite guarded, defensive, and embarrassed about being there. You are a third-generation Italian American; your spouse is Caucasian.

Member 4

You are a 23-year-old mother of 2-year-old twins. You are recovering from alcoholism and have not had a drink for 4 months. Your children endured serious neglect and lack of supervision in your drinking days and you feel anxious to "make it up to them." Your husband still drinks, sometimes heavily, but does not see any need for chemical dependency treatment, which he has refused to consider in the past. You also feel a real need for support—for parenting two toddlers entering the "No!" phase of development, and for maintaining your sobriety while residing with someone who occasionally abuses alcohol. Your AA sponsor encouraged you to seek support from other parents. You and your family are African American.

Member 5

You are a 62-year-old grandmother who is feeling overwhelmed by the demands of caring for your daughter's three school-age children following her sudden and unexpected death last year. Their father left the state after telling you he was "too broken up" over his wife's death to care for the children and they have had no contact with him for months. The children are having serious behavior problems since their mother's death and father's departure. These behaviors have stretched you to your wit's end. You hope that this group will help you parent your grandchildren through this highly stressful time. Your husband is retired and lives at home with you. He loves his grandchildren, but he, too, is at a loss about how to get through this difficult time. You and your family are Caucasian.

Member 6

You are a 35-year-old career middle manager who has worked outside the home throughout your daughter's life. She is now 12 years of age. Several years after the divorce from your daughter's father, when she was 6 years of age, you grappled with questions about your sexual identity, and you ultimately "came out" as a lesbian. Although you are not presently involved in a committed relationship with a woman, you do date occasionally, and your daughter is aware of your sexual orientation. Up until this point, she has appeared to be accepting of it; however, you have not ever heard her discuss it openly with friends or other family members. Recently, your daughter has openly refused to respect the 10:00 p.m. weekend curfew you have established for her. She has also challenged direct assertions of your parental authority in a manner you regard as belligerent. For example, she has refused on several occasions to clean up her room, help with laundry, or put away the groceries. Given the persistent demands of your fast-paced career, your daughter's non-compliant and challenging behaviors feel like the last straw—"I can't do battle on both fronts, work and home," you have explained. Your workplace Employee Assistance Program has recommended this parenting support group to you. You and your daughter are Caucasian.

Member 7

You are a 28-year-old mother of a 4-year-old who has been diagnosed with autism. Following her birth, you left a successful career in accounting to become a full-time mother and homemaker. Although your daughter's autism is regarded as mild by professionals with expertise in pervasive developmental disorder, your child's developmental impairments have caused you to question whether you were ever meant to be a mother, and whether it is possible to sustain a loving relationship with this child. Your daughter's ability to bond and express affection is somewhat limited, and she sometimes displays repetitions of certain movements, temper tantrums, and some rigidity in patterns of daily living (e.g., breakfast can be nothing except Cheerios and milk). You are missing an active social life and the rewards associated with your last job. You're not sure what "normal" means anymore, but you have avoided direct association with other parents of autistic children. The last time your child began to hit your leg when you attempted to redirect her away from a hazard in the living room, you found yourself hitting her back, and having a difficult time regaining control of yourself. You feel increasingly resentful of the incessant demands of caring for a developmentally disabled child day after day. Your husband travels frequently, but expresses devotion to both you and the child. Your family is African American. You have been referred to this parenting group by your local community help and referral line.

EXERCISE 27

Form A: Pre-Group Self-Assessment of
Group Leader Strengths and Areas of Discomfort

1. What do you perceive as your strengths and weaknesses as a group leader?

_____

_____

_____

_____

_____

_____

2. How comfortable are you being regarded as a model for appropriate interpersonal communication, interaction, and resolution of disputes? Why?

_____

_____

_____

_____

_____

_____

3. What kinds of groups members are likely to make you feel uncomfortable?

_____

_____

_____

_____

_____

_____

4. What situations or events during group sessions do/would you find especially challenging or stressful to deal with?

_____

_____

_____

_____

_____

_____

_____

_____

_____

_____

5. How comfortable are you in the group when there is conflict?

_____

6. How comfortable are you when there is silence?

_____

7. How comfortable are you when your leadership authority is questioned?

_____

8. How comfortable are you when members express strong anger or raw pain?

_____

9. How comfortable are you when you have to disclose your feelings to the group?

_____

10. How comfortable are you when members take responsibility for the group?

_____

11. How comfortable are you when you are evaluated by group members?

_____

Form B: Observational Record of Task-Oriented and Maintenance-Oriented Behaviors

Task-Oriented Behaviors

Individuals in the group who perform these functions very effectively

Initiating

    Surfacing a concern or issue _____

    Suggesting an approach to the group _____

    Proposing a specific action _____

Challenging

    Recalling the group to its purpose/task _____

    Pushing for action or decision _____

    Generating more activity _____

Clarifying

    Defining issues or terms _____

    Interpreting situations or concepts _____

    Assuring mutual understanding _____

Summarizing

    Restating ideas and suggestions _____

    Synthesizing related comments _____

    Proposing a consensual group position _____

Analyzing

    Systematically weighing a proposal _____

    Testing feasibility _____

    Volunteering related data _____

Informing

    Expressing an opinion _____

    Expressing feelings _____

    Giving or calling for factual information _____

Maintenance-Oriented Behaviors

Individuals in the group who perform these functions very effectively

Disclosing

    Sharing personal concerns or wishes

     _____

    Responding openly to others

     _____

    Revealing private information

     _____

Overseeing

    Seeking to make tacit norms explicit

     _____

    Comparing group's behavior against its accepted standards or norms

     _____

    Proposing new norms or standards

     _____

Gatekeeping

    Reflecting an interest in members and their contributions

     _____

    Suggesting approaches that help others

     _____

    Affirming others when their views or suggestions are not accepted or used

     _____

Processing

    Staying conscious of the way the group's work is being handled

     _____

    Sharing observations about the group's relational process

     _____

    Encouraging the group to reflect on how it is functioning and what it is doing

     _____

Harmonizing

    Searching for common ground

     _____

    Interpreting emotional content

     _____

    Encouraging careful listening

     _____

Compromising

    Changing a win-lose posture

     _____

    Allows facts and feelings to alter his/her position

     _____

    Trying to hear and satisfy concerns of group members with opposing views

     _____

Form C: Assessing Coleader Compatibility and Complementarity

The purpose of this assessment is to determine the feasibility of cofacilitating a group, given potential differences in style, theoretical orientation, and approach. This assessment will be completed by pairing all class members in dyads that will concurrently role-play an initial meeting between prospective group coleaders. You and your prospective coleader have been asked to consider cofacilitating a support group for women who have recently completed prison terms and are making the transition to life in the community. Participation in this group, which will be offered by a community-based agency serving women offenders and their families, is voluntary. Discuss the following issues with your prospective coleader to determine how compatible (i.e., harmonious) you would be as coleaders, and to what degree each one's strengths would tend to offset the other's weaknesses or limitations.

1. What are your beliefs about the human growth and change process?

2. What are your respective expectations regarding what this group can or should accomplish?

3. Discuss with each other your strengths and weaknesses as group leaders. Describe circumstances that cause you to feel uncomfortable (make use of Form A, which you completed previously).

4. Where, when, and how would you deal with conflict between the two of you?

5. How would you deal with conflict between either of you and members of the group?

6. How would you deal with intense expressions of emotion? crying? anger?

7. How will you respond to talkative or silent members? To scapegoating within the group?

8. What are your preferred ways of intervening in the group? Preferred use of group techniques? Do you tend to intervene quickly or slowly? Do you wait for members to engage in mutual aid?

9. What are areas of similarity and potential compatibility? Of potential conflict or disparity? Ways in which you would tend to complement each other?

Form D: Group Process Log—Observational Analysis of Group Dynamics

Group Session Number _____

1. Briefly describe interactional dynamics observed in the group related to the following group processes. This will help provide a basis for specific feedback during debriefing discussion.

_____

_____

_____

_____

_____

_____

_____

Note behavior and interactional context associated with:

Group cohesion/bonding

_____

Stages of group development (cues regarding current stage and transitions)

_____

Patterns of communication and interactional sequences

_____

Group decision making

_____

Group norms (tacit and explicit)

_____

Informal structure (subgroups and alliances)

_____

Conflict

_____

Form D: Group Process Log—Observational Analysis of Group Dynamics

Group Session Number _____

1. Briefly describe interactional dynamics observed in the group related to the following group processes. This will help provide a basis for specific feedback during debriefing discussion.

_____

_____

_____

_____

_____

_____

_____

Note behavior and interactional context associated with:

Group cohesion/bonding

_____

Stages of group development (cues regarding current stage and transitions)

_____

Patterns of communication and interactional sequences

_____

Group decision making

_____

Group norms (tacit and explicit)

_____

Informal structure (subgroups and alliances)

_____

Conflict

_____

Form D: Group Process Log—Observational Analysis of Group Dynamics

Group Session Number _____

1. Briefly describe interactional dynamics observed in the group related to the following group processes. This will help provide a basis for specific feedback during debriefing discussion.

_____

_____

_____

_____

_____

_____

_____

Note behavior and interactional context associated with:

Group cohesion/bonding

_____

Stages of group development (cues regarding current stage and transitions)

_____

Patterns of communication and interactional sequences

_____

Group decision making

_____

Group norms (tacit and explicit)

_____

Informal structure (subgroups and alliances)

_____

Conflict

_____

Form E: Observational Analysis of Group Leader Skills

A Functional Classification of Group Leadership Skills

Facilitating Group Processes	Data Gathering and Assessment	Action
1. Involving group members 2. Attending to others 3. Expressing self 4. Responding to others 5. Focusing group communication 6. Making group processes explicit 7. Clarifying content 8. Guiding group interactions	9. Identifying and describing 10. Requesting information, questioning, and probing 11. Summarizing and partializing information 12. Synthesizing thoughts, feelings, and action 13. Analyzing information	14. Supporting 15. Reframing and redefining 16. Linking members' communications 17. Directing 18. Giving advice, suggestions, or instructions 19. Providing resources 20. Modeling, role-playing, rehearsing, and coaching 21. Confronting 22. Resolving conflicts

NOTE: This conceptualization of group leadership skills is taken from Toseland and Rivas (1995).

Instructions: Using the list of group facilitator skills above, note those skills that you actually observed in use, or that *might have been* effectively used, in the simulated group session.

Skill	Situation/Context (note opportunity or actual application)	Significance (note implications for group process or actualization of group's purpose)

References

Glassman, U., & Kates, L. (1990). *Group work: A humanistic approach.* Thousand Oaks, CA: Sage.

Shaw, M. (1980). *Role-playing.* La Jolla, CA: University Associates.

Toseland, R. W., & Rivas, R. F. (1995). *An introduction to group work practice* (2nd ed.). Needham Heights, MA: Allyn & Bacon.

Form E: Observational Analysis of Group Leader Skills

A Functional Classification of Group Leadership Skills

Facilitating Group Processes	Data Gathering and Assessment	Action
1. Involving group members 2. Attending to others 3. Expressing self 4. Responding to others 5. Focusing group communication 6. Making group processes explicit 7. Clarifying content 8. Guiding group interactions	9. Identifying and describing 10. Requesting information, questioning, and probing 11. Summarizing and partializing information 12. Synthesizing thoughts, feelings, and action 13. Analyzing information	14. Supporting 15. Reframing and redefining 16. Linking members' communications 17. Directing 18. Giving advice, suggestions, or instructions 19. Providing resources 20. Modeling, role-playing, rehearsing, and coaching 21. Confronting 22. Resolving conflicts

NOTE: This conceptualization of group leadership skills is taken from Toseland and Rivas (1995).

Instructions: Using the list of group facilitator skills above, note those skills that you actually observed in use, or that *might have been* effectively used, in the simulated group session.

Skill	Situation/Context (note opportunity or actual application)	Significance (note implications for group process or actualization of group's purpose)

References

Glassman, U., & Kates, L. (1990). *Group work: A humanistic approach.* Thousand Oaks, CA: Sage.

Shaw, M. (1980). *Role-playing.* La Jolla, CA: University Associates.

Toseland, R. W., & Rivas, R. F. (1995). *An introduction to group work practice* (2nd ed.). Needham Heights, MA: Allyn & Bacon.

EXERCISE 28 *Choosing a Strategy for Community Intervention With R&M Properties*

Megan Morrissey and James Reinardy

Purpose

1. To select and develop a strategy of intervention for addressing a community-wide problem.
2. To review critically the role(s) of social workers in professional practice in relation to community-level interventions.
3. To understand and apply concepts, principles, and strategies of community organizing models in a specific case.
4. To engage in constructive controversy to understand this strategy as a method of group intervention.

Background

Social work claims as its unique professional niche the "person-in-environment" construction of personal problems. Nevertheless, interventions strategies often direct professional change efforts exclusively to one level: micro, mezzo, or macro. In agency settings, however, there are times when the social contributions to personal problems become obvious, raising the question of professional roles in addressing problems at a community-wide level of intervention. This exercise presents such a situation and requires that social workers in a role play situation decide on a course of action (or inaction) in response to a community-level problem that is influencing individual case work.

The role play also introduces a strategy of constructive controversy. This strategy can be employed to build consensus in group situations in which conflict threatens the cohesiveness of the group.

Instructions

Your instructor will assign you to a group with three other students, and will assign a position for your group to take in response to the case material presented. Each group will promote either a community development strategy or a social action strategy to address the problem presented in the case. After reading the case material, work with the other members of your group to develop a strategy using your community intervention model to respond to the problem presented. The questions accompanying the case may be helpful in determining your strategy. After outlining a strategy, your group should articulate three specific reasons for promoting your particular intervention model.

Your groups will then divide and merge with groups that had the opposite strategy, forming new groups. Following your instructor's directions, each "side" will in turn state its position, listen to the arguments of the other side, and repeat the arguments of the other side. The newly formed groups, now composed of persons taking opposite positions, then work toward consensus to develop a new strategy of intervention.

Choosing a Strategy With R&M Properties

Rampin County Family Service Center is a satellite social service office connected with County Social Services in a large, urban setting in the Midwest. Rampin County Social Services established the satellite office to provide more efficient service to residents on the southern edge of the city in an area poorly served by public transportation.

This public "one-stop" agency is situated in a racially diverse neighborhood (30% of the population is African American; 12% is Chicano/Latino; 4% is Asian American, primarily from countries of Southeast Asia; 3% are newly arriving immigrants with a large representation from Somalia; 1% is Native American; and the remaining 49% is Caucasian). The neighborhood's average income falls below the city's median, and a large proportion of the residents receive some type of financial assistance. Unemployment is high, with about 16% of the adult population out of work. Few residents own their own property. Much of the housing in the area consists of large apartment buildings that are owned and managed off-site by a large, privately owned company, R&M Properties, based in a wealthy outer-ring suburb of the city.

The Family Service Center provides a range of services used by local residents, including parenting education classes, social skills training for children and adolescents, employment readiness training and job referral, financial management workshops, and other support groups. A Home-Based Family Services Unit with six social workers, a case aide, and a supervisor is located at this satellite office. Each social worker in the Home-Based Unit carries a case load of approximately 18 families. This number of cases is higher than average for the county. In fact, the unit normally has eight social workers, but a 12-month hiring freeze at the county has meant that vacant positions have gone unfilled. Clients for home-based services are referred on a voluntary basis. Referring institutions include the courts, schools, hospitals and medical clinics, and churches. Clients also self-refer. Social workers in the Home-Based Unit provide case management and some in-home family counseling for clients. Since moving services out of a centralized downtown office, the center has been well received in the surrounding community, and the social workers in the Home-Based Unit in particular have a positive reputation in the surrounding community.

At a recent unit meeting of the Home-Based Unit, four of the six social workers mentioned problems they had encountered in visits to client homes. Clients had had the heat turned off in their apartments despite a city ordinance requiring heat through the month of April. Some workers noted that their clients often went for weeks with no hot water, whereas others said sometimes clients had no water at all—hot or cold. Still other clients were complaining that emergency exits were often blocked, safety lighting was not reliable, and in some buildings the security system did not work at all. Clients also complained that landlords and building managers were unresponsive to their complaints. Comparing notes at the unit meeting, the social workers quickly realized that all of the clients who had reported these problems with their housing lived in buildings owned by R&M Properties.

The neighborhood had long-standing problems and complaints against these and other absent property owners, and assisting clients in addressing housing-related problems had become a routine part of case management for social workers in this unit. This time the problem seems to be more widespread: All of the workers have had at least one negative experience with R&M Properties, and all agree that R&M does not provide decent or safe housing for tenants.

At the unit meeting several of the social workers raise the possibility of trying to address client housing concerns through collective action. Some of the workers urge a social-political action approach, targeting R&M Properties. Others agree that R&M represents a major financial drain with little reciprocal input for the neighborhood, but they feel that housing concerns are more widespread—any collective action should address the community as a whole, including those who do not rent from R&M. They oppose a social action approach and wish instead to pursue a community development response, involving clients in an organized approach.

EXERCISE 28

Community Development

You are a social worker in the Home-Based Services Unit at the Family Service Center. Your task is to work with other social workers in your unit to develop a strategy for a community development approach to working on the issue described in the case and to articulate three specific reasons for adopting a community development approach. The following questions might be helpful as you design your strategy.

1. How do you define the problem that is presented, and what aspects of the problem lend themselves to a community development approach for addressing the issue?

_____

_____

_____

_____

_____

_____

_____

2. What limitations, if any, exist to taking a community development approach? How can these obstacles be overcome/avoided in developing a strategy?

_____

_____

_____

_____

_____

_____

_____

3. What are the benefits of a community development approach?

_____

_____

_____

_____

_____

_____

4. What risks, if any, exist in adopting this approach—for the social workers, clients, and agency?

_____

_____

_____

_____

_____

_____

5. What role(s) should agency social workers and supervisors play in supporting and/or designing a community development approach?

_____

_____

_____

_____

_____

_____

Outline a strategy for a community development response, and articulate three specific reasons for adopting this approach for this problem.

_____

_____

_____

_____

_____

_____

_____

_____

Social Action

You are a social worker in the Home-Based Services Unit at the Family Service Center. Your task is to work with other social workers in your unit to develop a strategy for a social action approach to working on the issue described in the case and to articulate three specific reasons for adopting a social action approach. The following questions might be helpful as you design your strategy.

1. How do you define the problem that is presented in this case, and what aspects of the problem lend themselves to a social action approach for addressing the issue?

_____

_____

_____

_____

_____

_____

_____

_____

2. Is this campaign winnable? What do you want to win? What/who is the target? Why?

_____

_____

_____

_____

_____

_____

3. Who are your allies in a social action approach?

_____

_____

_____

_____

_____

_____

4. What risks, if any, exist in adopting this approach—for social workers, clients, and the agency?

_____

_____

_____

_____

_____

_____

5. What role(s) should agency social workers and supervisors play in supporting and/or designing a social action approach?

_____

_____

_____

_____

_____

_____

_____

_____

_____

Outline a strategy for a social action response, and articulate three specific reasons for adopting this approach for this problem.

_____

_____

_____

_____

_____

_____

_____

_____

_____

_____

EXERCISE 29 *Family Interventions During a Life Crisis*

Theora Evans

Purpose

1. To incorporate knowledge about assessments and goal-setting with intervention planning.
2. To apply this knowledge to a case where the needs of the family and individual members change over time.

Background

Families have a range of strengths and capacities that allow them to adapt to developmental changes and life events. Sometimes, though, challenges to the family can be overwhelming. Such crises test the coping abilities of the family and its individual members. This exercise introduces you to a family facing a life crisis. You will review data, form an assessment, determine goals for work, and develop an intervention plan that specifies how those goals might be reached. The assessment, goals, and intervention plan will then be reformulated as the family's circumstances change.

Instructions

1. Read the introductory information for the case, then write an assessment of Toirelle and her family, from the perspective of the outpatient social worker. Based on the information you have, what are the strengths of the family and the family members? What coping strategies and protective mechanisms are at play in the case? Where are areas of concern? What might be the problems for work? How does your understanding of the family's socioeconomic class and culture influence your assessment? What theoretical orientation supports your assessment? You may use an ecomap and genogram to supplement your narrative assessment. What additional information would you want to increase your understanding of the family or to support your assessment?
2. Develop five preliminary goals for work with the family at this point in time. Although goals are typically developed in conjunc-

tion with the client, you can think of the five you develop as constituting those areas you believe are the most crucial at this time.

3. Develop an intervention or treatment plan that you would recommend for addressing the needs (identified above) of the family and its members. How does the plan build on the family's strengths? Who else might need to be involved to successfully carry out the plan? Is the theoretical orientation that guides your assessment reflected in your plan? Are there areas for attention that were identified in the assessment that are *not* reflected in the goals and plan? If so, why?

4. Submit your assessment, goals, and plan to your instructor or to a fellow classmate for review.

5. Read the case update and revise your assessment based on changes in the family's situation.

6. What new goals are needed, based on changes in the case? What previous goals seem to have been met or seem unnecessary at this point in time?

7. Develop a treatment or intervention plan to address the new goals in place. Who should be involved? What skills and techniques will be crucial at this point? Does the intervention plan reflect changes in your assessment and the strengths of the family and family members?

8. Examine some of the challenges that the social worker might face in this case. Where are sources of support for you, as the worker? What would facilitate you in pursuing these resources or supports?

9. Prepare to discuss your findings in a discussion with your class.

| Introductory Information | You are the social worker at the outpatient psychiatric unit of a regional university hospital.

Toirelle Jackson recently graduated with a degree in sociology from a historically black university on the East Coast. She is a strikingly beautiful, young, African American woman, 21 years old, articulate and well dressed. Two weeks ago, she relocated, with some ambivalence, to this small, predominantly white, university-town where her mother resides.

Toirelle relates that she had been an average student with a full social life. She actively participated in cultural activities on and off campus, such as theater, charity fund-raisers, museum exhibits, art shows, and government events. She also volunteered on the pediatric unit of her alma mater's university-owned hospital. She dated a number of young men, with the intent of eventually marrying an intelligent, young professional with a secure financial future.

The Presenting Issues

This office visit was initiated by Toirelle's mother, Anita, who wanted her daughter to seek counseling as an adjunct to her medical treatment. A week ago Toirelle received a diagnosis of end-stage breast cancer. Toirelle reports finding the mass in her breast during a self-examination. She states that she had no previous health concerns prior to that discovery and there is neither maternal nor fraternal family history of the condition. Anita scheduled the visit with the social worker in reaction to statements made at the time of Toirelle's diagnosis. Both attending physicians, a surgeon and an oncologist, said that a positive emotional response on Toirelle's part would be a key indicator of a successful treatment outcome, though neither ordered a mental health referral.

When asked to share her immediate concerns with you, the client replied that she had only one. She wanted the answer to "Why me?" Toirelle states that she is a "spiritual person" who recently prayed that God cure her condition. Beyond wishing she were cured and wondering why she was afflicted, she later admitted other concerns: fear of loss of her hair as a result of chemotherapy, lack of access to her friends who are widely scattered across the continental United States, and her unhappiness regarding her sister Kary's impending arrival in town in response to Toirelle's diagnosis. She expanded on the latter statement by adding that she did not want to observe Kary's interactions in the community, that is, new friends and dating. Toirelle also added that she resents meeting and interacting with her mother's friends and colleagues. She says that she does not want to be pitied.

Family Dynamics

Toirelle and her siblings, one sister and two older brothers, grew up in a working-class neighborhood in a major Midwest urban city. Toirelle's brothers, Cortez and Dorian, were 7 and 6 years older, respectively, than she. The children were educated in parochial elementary and secondary schools and all attended college. Cortez drowned at age 19 while boating with relatives. Dorian, now 30 years of age, resides in the South and is a manager for a Fortune 500 company.

The client's parents divorced when she was 9 years old. She and her siblings lived with their mother during their formative years. Toirelle indicated that her childhood and youth were somewhat turbulent. Her parents' divorce and the trauma following the death of her brother were particularly hurtful. Although Cortez was older, he was always at home as she was growing up and was perceived as a caretaker. Toirelle states that she and Dorian were not very close when she was young: in addition to being 6 years her senior, he attended a seminary in another state during his high school years and he immediately went downstate to college upon graduation. She also briefly mentioned that her early and middle adolescence had been difficult. She said that she was a shy little girl and that it was hard to work through identity issues. At the time of Cortez' death, all the family members dealt with the grief in their own ways. In the years that followed, the family talked together about the loss, shared recollections about him, and honored his memory.

Both Claude—Toirelle's father—and Anita are professionals. They have an amicable relationship. Their interactions are limited to communication regarding the needs and concerns of their young adult children. Toirelle states that her father, age 48, has maintained a nurturing and supportive relationship with his children following his divorce from her mother. Claude remarried after the divorce, and Toirelle says that she liked her stepmother, Sarah, though the marriage between her father and stepmother ended within 5 years. The client and her stepmother have not kept in touch. Sarah moved to the West Coast and Claude still lives in their hometown.

Toirelle describes her mother, age 48, as a successful woman, who is respected by her peers. She says that her mother is aloof and that it is hard for her to read her mother's emotional side. Toirelle clarifies, stating that her mother is thoughtful, supportive, and accessible but that she does not share her feelings. Anita moved to this university-community, 4 years ago, after Toirelle and Kary were in college, relocating to take advantage of opportunities for further professional development.

Kary, Toirelle's younger sister, arrived in town 1 week ago from an adjacent state where she attended college and worked part-time. She will graduate from college in a month. Neither Toirelle nor Kary were residents in this community previously. They have historically shared a "love-hate relationship," competing with each other but enjoying each other as well.

Case Update: Five Months Later

Toirelle has completed chemotherapy and has undergone a radical mastectomy. She has reacted poorly to the high-dose chemotherapy and each treatment has been followed by a hospitalization. She was unable to either work or engage in volunteer activities during that 3-month period. In a few weeks, she will participate in a clinical trial, receiving an autologous bone marrow transplant followed by radiotherapy. Toirelle's treatment protocol is being managed by two premier health care facilities, an East Coast university-hospital and the regional university-hospital here in town. On her travels between these facilities, Toirelle sees friends and relatives, visits museums, and attends cultural activities. She decorates her bedroom with African artifacts purchased while on the East Coast. Anita accompanies Toirelle on each of these out-of-state trips.

Toirelle knows that her condition is life-threatening and that her prognosis is poor. She attends mass at the local Catholic Church when possible, prays regularly with friends by telephone, and reads her bible daily. Toirelle's brother and her father visit on alternating weekends, both when she is in the Midwest and on the East Coast. The client has been visited by her maternal grandmother and uncles. She has also allowed some very close friends to visit her at home. Toirelle is very sensitive about her physical appearance and discourages visits from her friends when she is not at her best. She has maintained her relationships with friends via telephone, correspondence, and in-person visits when she feels energetic. Frequently, nurses and other allied professionals also visit with the client when they are off-duty. Friends, family, and acquaintances have sustained her by bringing favorite meals to her at home or in the hospital.

The client is seldom alone. Either Anita or Kary is constantly with her. Kary secured employment shortly after she arrived in town. She and Anita have flexible schedules, which allows them to attend to Toirelle. Toirelle now speaks very fondly of them and wonders how she would have managed this ordeal without their love and support. The local American Cancer Society (ACS) has not been a resource for Toirelle, having been unable to locate a support person who was either age or culturally compatible.

Initially, you (the social worker) and Toirelle interacted on an infrequent basis, with Toirelle controlling the frequency of the sessions. She now calls and schedules her visits more frequently. Toirelle has completed a "living will" instructing health providers not to resuscitate. The family is simultaneously rallying to address Toirelle's needs and grieving what they suspect will be her imminent death.

7 EVALUATING EFFECTIVENESS

EXERCISE 30   *How Do We Know We're Helping?*

Kim Strom-Gottfried

Purpose

1. To help you understand the reasons for evaluating practice effectiveness.
2. To examine some of the shortcomings in subjective appraisals of effectiveness.
3. To examine alternative ways of assessing progress.

Background

Increasingly, the people who pay for social work services (whether insurance companies, government agencies, or the clients themselves) demand to see evidence that the intervention is making a difference. Some social workers feel these demands intrude on their practice and reject the use of evaluation instruments. Others acknowledge that evaluation is important, but prefer to use their instincts to tell them that their work is having an impact. Others believe that such methods are unreliable and suggest that tools such as goal attainment scaling, assessment instruments, and other methods should be used to more carefully track and document progress.

This exercise introduces you to two brief readings that offer different perspectives on evaluating effectiveness and asks you to critically examine the two viewpoints and develop your own position about how you'll "know that you're making a difference."

Instructions

1. On the following page, list all reasons for and against practice evaluation—Why is it important to do? Why is it not important? Your instructor may assign you to groups for brainstorming.
2. After a discussion of your results, read the following articles and address the questions at the end of the exercise.
3. Consider cases from your field placement. List some methods that are or could be used to evaluate the outcomes in cases and the effectiveness of the social workers in bringing about those outcomes. If you don't have access to field cases, address the question as it might apply to cases presented elsewhere in the workbook, for example, the Carr family in Exercise 8.

EXERCISE 30

Evaluating Practice Effectiveness

Why?   *Why not?*

_____   _____

_____   _____

_____   _____

_____   _____

_____   _____

_____   _____

_____   _____

_____   _____

_____   _____

_____   _____

_____   _____

_____   _____

_____   _____

_____   _____

_____   _____

_____   _____

_____   _____

Evaluating Effectiveness From the Practitioner Perspective
by Martin A. Elks and Karen E. Kirkhart

Although systematic evaluation has been conceptualized as a tool for improving human services programs, relatively little evidence exists that shows how evaluative information is used to enhance direct clinical practice. Quantitative studies of clinical use of evaluation have shed little light on the research-practice linkage. The authors report the results of a qualitative study of 17 social workers designed to develop a more complete understanding of how practitioners evaluate themselves in their day-to-day practice. Three main findings emerged from the interviews: (1) an acknowledged difficulty in really knowing one's effectiveness; (2) a perceived incompatibility between evaluation and practice; and (3) the presence of an implicit model of self-evaluation comprising five components: intuition and experience, personal and professional issues, client change, business aspects, and the therapist-client relationship. Several social work implications for the teaching of self-evaluation in schools of social work and for clinical practice are discussed.

Key Words: *effectiveness; evaluation; practice; self-evaluation model*

Systematic evaluation has been conceptualized as a tool for improving the quality and effectiveness of human services programs. Much systematic evaluation is conducted within the service system and for primarily formative reasons. Ideally, such self-evaluation provides growth and renewal for those who work within the service system. Yet even though evaluators are committed to this ideal, relatively little evidence exists that evaluative information is used to actually improve service.

The difficulty in identifying connections between empirical evidence and clinical practice is neither new nor unique to evaluation. The integration of research and practice has been a long-standing concern of the helping professions (Mullen, 1978; Thomlison, 1984). Historically, much has been written on the two communities of research and practice, citing differences in values, purpose, and methods (Andreozzi, 1985; Rodman & Kolodny, 1964). In the early 1970s, evaluation was heralded as a logical bridge between research and practice, and the development of new methodologies flourished. However, it soon became apparent that evaluation and practice were also difficult to link effectively. Many evaluative methods did little to facilitate practice integration. For example, single-system designs that focus on the clinical perspective address many of the practical and methodological limitations of group designs, but they fail to address many other requisites to evaluation-practice integration (Barlow & Hersen, 1984). Most evaluation methods that do address themselves to direct practice (Barlow, Hayes, & Nelson, 1984; Bloom & Fischer, 1982; Jayaratne & Levy, 1979) are still only a theoretical ideal, and the debate continues regarding the fit between the methods of empirical evaluation and the exigencies of actual clinical practice (Blythe, 1992; Witkin, 1992).

Evaluation from clinical and administrative perspectives has developed out of different research traditions with relatively little exchange, and research on use has followed suit (Kirkhart, 1986). Empirical research on the use of evaluative information has focused primarily on administrative or program levels (Cousins & Leithwood, 1986). Use of evaluative information by clinicians or direct practitioners is less understood. Typically, studies with clinicians have approached evaluation with a theoretical model of use clearly in mind and have found that the clinician's view of evaluation did not conform to the model being tested (Eldridge, 1983). This research tradition has contributed to an understanding of what the evaluation-practice linkage is not, but it has yielded little insight into what it is. An alternative research model is needed, one that is exploratory rather than confirmatory, building a model of evaluation from the practitioner's own accounts rather than superimposing an ideal model and testing for conformity (Scott, 1990).

The overall goal of the authors' research was to develop a more complete understanding of the clinical use of evaluative data and its relationship to direct practice. Objectives include describing the use of evaluation by the practicing clinician, examining evaluative decisions made by clinicians regarding their own practice in a context relatively free from formal systems of accountability, and examining the relationship of evaluation use to improved clinical practice. The research questions included the following: How do clinicians evaluate their performance and practice? How do they know they are doing a good job with each client? What information is used and how?

Methods

Sample

Private practitioners were selected for this study for the following reasons:

- Private practitioners represent a significant section of social work practice.
- Self-evaluation is important to private practitioners because they are not formally responsible to agencies or supervisors for the quality of their work.
- Direct clinical practice may be examined relatively free from contextual influences such as agency policy and procedures.
- Private practice is seen as an ideal by many students and agency practitioners and therefore an important area for research.

The sample comprised 17 clinicians in private practice (11 women and 6 men). All were located in a metropolitan setting in the northeastern United States. Data were collected using semistructured interviews. Interviews were conducted in person, by appointment, at the home or office of the private practitioner and lasted 45 to 90 minutes. Interview topics corresponded to the research objectives and questions identified earlier. All interviews began with the following questions: How do you evaluate what you are doing? How do you know you are doing a good job? How do you know you are not doing a good job? The interviewer then asked open-ended questions to elicit the roles, if any, evaluation plays in the practitioners' work, the types and sources of information they use in their practice, and the manner in which they use the information.

Toward the end of the interview, and only if not already covered by the practitioners themselves, the interviewer asked about sources of evaluative information such as scales and questionnaires, reading, use of colleagues, and systematic notetaking tools that are seen in the current research literature as important for practice evaluation (e.g., Barlow et al., 1984; Bloom & Fischer, 1982).

Data Analysis

The interviews were tape-recorded and transcribed. The transcripts were then coded and analyzed for themes and patterns (Bogdan & Biklen, 1982; Corbin & Strauss, 1990). The aim of the analysis was to use a grounded theory approach (Glaser & Strauss, 1967) to develop an accurate description of how practitioners evaluate their practice using the words and concepts that they regard as important and significant (Blumer, 1969).

The authors used a grounded theory approach to inductively derive themes that are based ("grounded") in the data. In this study the data are transcripts of interviews of social work practitioners in private practice. Each concept or issue mentioned by the interviewee in regard to self-evaluation was given an identifying code. The codes were then sorted or grouped by hand and referenced by transcript page number. Gradually and over repeated interviews, key or frequently used codes began to emerge from the data. The codes were then grouped to represent higher-order themes or patterns. For example, the theme "client change" comprises four codes: symptom and problem alleviation, improved appearance and mood, decreased resistance, and increased skills. The final task of the analysis was to discern the relationships between the themes and codes and to describe an overall model of how practitioners use them in their actual practice evaluation.

Findings

Two findings emerged from the interviews: Practitioners acknowledged difficulty in really knowing their effectiveness, and they perceived incompatibility between the roles of evaluator and practitioner. Also, an implicit model of self-evaluation was found. (Numbers next to each extract refer to interviewee identification number and page of interview transcript.)

Difficulty in Really Knowing One's Effectiveness

Interviewees were keenly aware of the limitations they face in demonstrating that they are helpful to clients and that clients would not necessarily get better by themselves without the practitioner and his or her interventions.

17-4 It's hard to take credit in this sort of work for really helping people, because you don't really know how much what you're doing in your office is really helping to bring about the change in someone's life . . . so you are always questioning, Is it really something you are doing here, or might this have happened anyway? . . . So it's really complex.

9-7 See, I'm not even sure that anybody knows why psychotherapy works. One of my secret suspicions is that mostly people get better by themselves, and we're privileged to see it here and be with the people and collect the money.

6-6 I almost feel like I never really have any way of knowing. I'm sitting here and I'm telling you these parameters, but to really know . . . I'm not sure that I do.

However, the presence of doubts about knowing one's effectiveness appears to be more a philosophical concern than one that directly impinges on practice. As shown later, practitioners made many statements that they believed were very effective and indeed had a coherent model for evaluating their practice effectiveness.

Practitioner Role Versus Evaluator Role

Throughout the interview process, it was very clear that evaluation was equated by the practitioners with science, measurement, and research methodology and was not for them. Evaluation was seen as something researchers do involving measurement, follow-up studies, formal studies, questionnaires, and research methodology designed to prove effectiveness. As such, evaluation is alien to private practice, because few practitioners feel competent at research or with formal procedures.

Evaluation and judgments of effectiveness were regarded as not being a personal strength or not part of the job. Practitioners readily admitted they could not prove effectiveness to evaluators because "the people who write evaluation articles would not accept their methods of measuring themselves." Nevertheless, the practitioners appeared confident about their effectiveness and saw no need to change as long as they were achieving acceptable results.

15-11 It's not my job to evaluate somebody—it's my job to help them move on with their lives. . . . Don't ask me to evaluate people—that just clutters my mind . . . so I just stay away from it.

16-3 Well, I try not to focus [on my effectiveness]. . . . I feel like people give me money and for that they should get something useful to them, but I try not to obsess over [my effectiveness] because I could drive myself crazy worrying about it. I can't dismiss it, but it's not real important.

9-9 Other things . . . are more urgent. My system is that I have a rotating pile of papers, and whenever it's time for paperwork, I take the one on top and I either do something with it or put it on the bottom, and evaluation has been circulating for a while. Every time it comes up maybe I write a sentence or two . . . so I feel something's happening . . . .

Perhaps the incompatibility between the needs of practitioners and the requirements of formal evaluation can best be seen in their consistent attitudes toward research instruments and scales.

14-7 Instruments are not a part of the way I operate. I feel from myself and the feedback that I get from my patients that I am doing a very [emphatically] good job that I find to be very gratifying and therefore I don't feel the need for a lot else.

13-5 I don't hear evaluation as anything like how I quantify in any sense. On a practical level I wouldn't consider them [scales and instruments] to be quite honest. I'm really moving from one thing to the next and really I don't have the time. Seems to me to do something like that [administer instruments] would be an extreme luxury—and in some way a nice luxury if I had the time. . . .

Private practitioners seem to have little use for formal, quantifiable evaluation instruments. Such instruments are seen as luxuries, requiring too much time, and possibly more relevant to other helping professionals such as psychologists.

Ignorance may be another reason for role incompatibility.

12-3 The reason I don't use [evaluation measurements] is because I don't know of them—that is, in terms of keeping up with lots of other things, that's an area that I've not kept up with or learned about as it evolved, so ignorance is probably the reason.

11-1 I received a questionnaire once from a group therapy association but never used it because I was afraid it might show me to be no good. [The respondent freely admitted she was not very good with groups.]

However, several interviewees admitted to a willingness to use formal instruments, albeit rather ambivalently and not confidently.

Research instruments were used by two interviewees (both male) in specialized areas such as behavior modification with children, formal professional peer reviews, and smoking cessation and pain control. These are areas where behavior research has been prominent or where standardization and objectivity are important (as in peer reviews).

Specific criteria were spelled out by one interviewee who used a "pain questionnaire" as to why it (and presumably any other potential instrument) was chosen:

9-5 It was simple, it was quick, it appeared as if the client could do it in his own time, or if I had to do it, it would only take five minutes. . . . I was thinking that I could use it not only as an evaluation instrument, but [also] as a treatment tool.

Such criteria epitomize a pragmatic professionals' approach to research instruments: They are not central to practice, have doubtful utility, and are to be used only if they require little time and effort and are potentially beneficial to the client in themselves.

Pragmatic-Professional Model

No practitioner offered an explicit, well-articulated model for self-evaluation. It was nevertheless possible to perceive the existence of an underlying or implicit model of practice evaluation and to classify into a coherent framework the concepts and issues that practitioners as a whole thought were important to their practice and its evaluation. The authors have termed this model of self-evaluation the "pragmatic-professional model" to contrast it with others such as the "scientist-practitioner model" (Barlow et al., 1984; Jayaratne & Levy, 1979) or the "reflective-practitioner model" (Schon, 1983).

The pragmatic-professional model is characterized by its down-to-earthness, immediacy, and practical relevance. Practitioners needed no statistics, computers, or elaborate theory to use the model. These practitioners were comfortable with the way they were operating; saw themselves as at the peak, or approaching the peak, of their effectiveness and expertise; and regarded formal evaluation procedures as being irrelevant at best and intrusive at worst.

The model consists of five main components or sources of evaluative information: the intuition and experience of the social workers themselves, professional and personal values, client change, business aspects, and the practitioner-client relationship. All are used intuitively and refined with experience.

Intuition and Experience

When the practitioners were asked how they evaluated their practice, the response was overwhelmingly by intuition.

15-6 I've got to tell you it comes down to a great feeling.

14-2 I would say that in part it come simply from being sensitive to whether people are feeling good or bad. I evaluate what I do emotionally.

13-1 Some of it is thought out and some of it probably is intuitive. . . . I hate to admit this but it's a very intuitive process—I was going to say subjective, but I think intuitive is better because intuition is the blending of the thinking and the feeling. I know I'm not being very clear . . . what I'm trying to get at is that there is this whole thing in my head that tends to screen and evaluate all the time, but when you ask me how I do it it's hard for me to break it down and put it into words.

However, this intuition is not naive but is refined by years (up to 30) of experience. Practitioners were highly confident in their ability as therapists, counselors, and so forth. Their confidence has come from surviving and even flourishing in private practice and not from books on research.

17-9 I've done this for a long time. . . . I've done everything, I think I can do much of everything. . . . .

15-1 I think that when you do this year after year you notice these things. . . . Your experience with these things is the only teacher, there's no prescription for it. . . . Someone said to me, "You know, it takes about 10 years before you think you have some idea about what's going on."

11-1 After 30 years one has a sense of confidence that one is doing a good job.

4-4 I've been around this community for 30 years. . . . I've spent a lot of time and energy . . . developing what I do.

Statements about confidence in one's effectiveness appear to contradict earlier statements about not really knowing if one is effective. However, the issue seems to be that of not being absolutely certain of one's effectiveness and being unable to prove it to evaluators, while at the same time knowing enough to be confident one is doing something worthwhile for clients. Pragmatic professionals seem to be able to live with this ambiguity and uncertainty.

Professional and Personal Values

There are four sources of evaluative information that the social worker brings to the situation, has internalized, or is primarily responsible for: an internalized model of the ideal practitioner, personal life and circumstances, notetaking, and reading.

The Ideal Practitioner

Practitioners have internalized a series of rules of practice by which they measure their performance as therapists.

8-2 I have a set of internal standards that I've never articulated, so this will be a first, but I have some internal standards . . . fairly strict parameters . . . about my own behavior and how I will engage with a client that I think are probably a more reliable gauge of how I am doing than what the client says.

4-1 I use these standards as barometers, as ways to monitor myself and my ongoing practice.

The practitioners assume that the better they match their performance standards or rules, the more effective they will be. This assumption frees the practitioner from worrying too much about positive outcomes, because these are assumed to follow from the good practice of the ideal practitioner. Also, it is much easier to monitor one's own behavior than to engage in measuring outcomes or monitor the behavior of the client (especially outside the therapy situation).

These ideals also serve as a safeguard to relying entirely on client statements of change. For example, a practitioner's internal rules and orientation may lead him or her to distrust a particular client's statements. Ethically, too, practitioners regard these standards as the bottom line of practice—whatever else may happen, he or she should adhere to these standards.

What are these ideal rules of practice? The following general list is take from the interviews: maintaining a professional stance; not taking sides; maintaining distance between the client and his or her problems; keeping in touch with one's own physiological reactions (e.g., anxiety, fatigue, boredom, concentration); and working through one's own personal problems. Any indication that a practitioner is failing in any of these dimensions is a sign that something is wrong.

Personal Life and Circumstances

Practitioners evaluate themselves from the feedback of their spouse, friends, family, and colleagues (and in one instance, his golf game). Using friends and family for consultation is not surprising, because often practitioners are married to other helping professionals, have other members of the family in the same professions, and often have colleagues who are also personal and family friends. Thus, the distinction between a practitioner's professional and private life may be very blurred.

> *6-7 I don't really see that much separation between—and maybe some might think I'm crazy—my professional life and my personal life.*

Of the 11 interviewees who were married, nine (82 percent) were married to another clinical social worker, physician, psychologist, psychiatrist, or psychiatric nurse-hypnotherapist. A majority reported that they often used their spouses as a source of consultation and feedback for cases. This interrelatedness extends into the larger family as well. For example, one practitioner is one of three sisters, all of whom are social workers, and another, who is married to a psychiatrist, receives referrals from her father (a physician) and sees clients in a room in his office.

Private practitioners overwhelmingly relied on colleagues for support, feedback, and advice. Typically the use of colleagues for evaluative feedback is in the form of a peer group or reading group that meets regularly (e.g., biweekly or monthly). Similarly, practitioners reported a large overlap between their colleagues and their personal friends. One interviewee is a member of a sports team composed entirely of mental health professionals.

One result of the connectedness among mental health professionals on both levels is the presence of an informal network where professionals "get to know what's going on in town," which is another source of evaluative information.

Notetaking and Reading

Whether practitioners take minimal or copious notes, little use is made of them. Practitioners rarely read more than the notes of the last session with a client, and systematic review of notes is usually only done if the practitioner has a persistent problem with a client or if an insurance company requests a report on treatment progress. For some practitioners, the move to private practice carried with it the benefit of being free from the burden and requirements of paperwork in an agency setting.

The content of notes varies from significant events to the general topic of the session and whether the client paid the fee. Not surprisingly, notetaking is not seen as being of great relevance to practitioner effectiveness. Practitioners often remark that they have an excellent memory, especially for affective material, and hence do not need notes.

> *5-9 My practice has very, very little paperwork. I'm trying not to take notes after every session. I feel like a free woman. What I have decided to do is that if something significant happens I would note it.*

As with notetaking, reading was never volunteered as a source of self-evaluation. Once prompted, however, interviewees commented about the role of reading in their practice. For example, practitioners read from a very little (some acknowledged an aversion to it) to a considerable amount.

> *13-4 I read very little when it comes to the field as such. What I tend to do is scan.*

> *6-4 I read quite a bit. I go through periods of reading a lot and then not reading very much. . . . I just bought ten books, and [now] I'm in a period of reading quite a bit.*

> *15-8 The journals seem to pile up at the end of my desk, and I may read three articles a year, but I get all the journals. I will read the cover of what's in them, and even if I did see one I might like I might not read it, but I make a note of it.*

Practice literature is overwhelmingly preferred to "research" literature, the latter being seen to be limited to teaching and not practice. Pragmatic professionals read not to evaluate themselves but to be of use to clients and to further improve their already considerable skills.

> 11-1 I don't read research because I'm not interested in it, and I don't feel I know how to read it anyway. . . . I read a lot of practice books.

> 7-7 I try to read journals, books . . . that are useful for my client.

Reading groups seem to be a popular way of keeping up with the literature, and those who belong to such groups seem to value them greatly.

> 8-5 I'm in two peer supervision and reading groups. Reading is crucial, it keeps me alive. Reading is what I do to keep me stimulated and attuned.

> 6-4 I think [reading groups] can be a big help, just in terms of the use of certain metaphors that one reads about and then uses in therapy that make sense to people.

Client Change

Practitioners gauge their effectiveness in relation to client change. For some practitioners, any change is assumed to be good, the assumption being that clients seek help because they are "stuck." Any movement from a stuck position is assumed by definition to be a positive change.

> 15-1 I assume that they come to me because they've got difficulty, so I'm looking to see change . . . usually in contrast from when I first met them.

> 10-2 A client who is changing will usually talk about experiencing a shift . . . they will either use the work "shift" or something equivalent to it.

> 3-6 I don't always look for resolution or closure, but [rather] for movement or satisfaction with where the person is at.

Six areas of change for the better include (1) symptom or problem alleviation; (2) improved quality of life; (3) development of an "internal orientation," or taking control of one's life; (4) increased skills, even to the point of imitation of the therapist; (5) decreased resistance to therapy and increased insight into problems; and (6) improved personal appearance and mood. The following excerpts from interviews illustrate each area of change:

Symptom or Problem Alleviation.

> 17-1 What conflicts, what symptoms brought them in initially, whether they feel that there has been a decrease in their level of depression, whether they are sleeping better, whether they are not battling as much with their husband or with their wife, or whether Johnny's academic performance is improved or not, whether he's gotten fewer in-school suspensions this semester than last semester.

15-1 When people get better and don't come back anymore. Someone might deal with a spouse in a totally new way and they'll recognize that, and that's a behavior that I'd never seen before or heard them talk about before. Or things change in their job scene, or they decide to move, or you see a change in patterns of behavior.

Improved Quality of Life.

13-2 How they report how things are going in their lives, which is a little bit beyond symptoms. They're beginning to talk about the quality of their life; for example, "I was able to take the risk to get out of this marriage and to get into a new one, or be single and feel OK about that." So if I begin to see them come alive, it makes me feel very good and gives me some sense that I'll be able to help them in the process.

8-3 I have one client who said, "I've had a lot of therapists but you're the only one who got me married"—I know exactly what we did together so that she was able to go for what she wanted in her life.

Development of an "Interior Orientation."

16-1 I guess the primary thing is an interior orientation—if the person can shift from making decisions about life in terms of external kinds of situations. . . . When people stop projecting onto others, when they stop blaming other people.

8-2 If a client really begins to get a grip and begins to take steps toward getting his life under his own control, then I think somehow we're doing a good job.

Increased Skills.

5-10 I'll tell you another way [I evaluate therapy]. I'm thinking of another person, a person who's been very, very depressed for a number of years due to loss, and she—and many of my people are doing this—adopted my technique. . . . So in a sense I have modeled for them, demonstrated, taught them a way of dealing with life's problems.

3-1 "You've helped us to talk, communicate"—it sounds so basic, but that's the kind of feedback that I get from clients. . . . They've found their old coping mechanisms or they've developed some new ones. . . . They come back and say, "I had a couple of days when I really felt down this week, but I handled it differently."

Decreased Resistance to Therapy and Increased Insight Into Problems.

17-1 Basically another tool is how much resistance I am getting in therapy. As I move close and identify underlying issues, is there more of a tendency to withhold, to cancel, to avoid, to move more to small talk?

5-1 Now after many months she's really willing to talk about [her problem]. When I confront her with some of his behavior [that] seems negative, she's able to hear it where before she would either get upset or would change the subject.

Improved Personal Appearance and Mood.

> *15-1 Also you can see a countenance change . . . it's vibes, it's a look in the eye, maybe even new hairstyle or new clothing, an aura or reflections.*

> *7-1 The way they look, how they present themselves, their mood, their affect, their thoughts, their general rapport.*

The Ideal Client

Thus, not only does the practitioner have a model of an ideal practitioner, he or she also appears to have a model of an ideal client in mind. An ideal client is growing and changing, has few problems that require counseling, reports a good quality of life, looks good, takes control of his or her life, and has good communication skills. Such an ideal allows for the evaluation of progress to the degree that the client moves toward the qualities of that ideal.

Lack of Change

Relatedly, lack of change is universally recognized as a negative indicator of treatment—unless the client is happy with no change.

> *15-5 I get very uncomfortable when therapy goes on for a long period of time, beyond three years, and I don't see any change . . . especially if it's a younger person . . . between 23 and 35.*

> *8-3 We feel stuck, there's no movement, and the client [and I] feel discouraged . . . the client will say "nothing seems to be changing."*

> *6-2 When I hear the same thing over and over every week, [it seems that] not much effort [has been] made to do anything to change their behavior or the things that they are complaining about.*

Business Aspects

Private practice forces practitioners to consider financial aspects of their work. Thus, two sources of self-evaluation are the same as for any business: Are the clients satisfied with the service, and is the business making a profit? Some practitioners refer to business concepts directly, such as referring to clients as "buyers" and considering whether they are getting their "money's worth." Others use concepts that have clear business overtones:

> *17-2 Well, if one considers or admits that part of being a therapist, or an aspect of being a therapist in private practice, is that you are also wearing a businessman's hat, then paying the rent and putting some money in the bank is an indication that I'm doing well.*

> *15-7 In other fields you consider yourself successful if the business works and earns you an income. I'm not so sure that should be overlooked.*

Thus, if the practitioner is making money, has a waiting list of clients, and has clients who express satisfaction with the services they have received, then the practitioner concludes that he or she is doing a good job. Should any of these indicators decline, then the practitioner can assume that he or she is not effective.

Furthermore, these business concepts are not antagonistic to the other sources of self-evaluation in the model. For example, a good relationship with the client may also be seen as good public relations with the consumer and is likely, through word of mouth, to generate new clients. Clients who make positive changes in their lives are also likely to be satisfied and pay their fees. Clients who wait to see a popular practitioner who charges a high fee may be more likely to expect positive outcomes and a good relationship with the practitioner.

Practitioner-Client Relationship

Therapy is seen as a two-way relationship between the client and practitioner. This relationship, referred to in terms of a "match," "alliance," "bond," and as that of "cosleuths," can be very close.

15-10 My treatment of my client is so much a part of me. . . . There's a piece of me that gets intermingled in [clients'] lives, and they become real. . . . I think that's an important part of the therapy. . . . This is a real relationship, . . . a very unique phenomenon.

14-2 When you see someone over an extended period of time you become as acquainted with the facial expression of the patient as you do with the facial expression of your own family members.

It is not surprising, then, that the relationship that exists between the therapist and client is an indicator of how well the therapy is going or is likely to proceed. It is assumed that a good relationship will facilitate positive change for the client and that a good relationship in the counseling situation will generalize to other settings outside counseling. It is also assumed that the counseling relationship mirrors relationships the client is having with people outside of counseling and, hence, that the benefits of the therapeutic relationship will transfer to other relationships.

1-4 I would look at how the person relates to me in the interview and assume that . . . whatever they do with me they do with other significant people in their lives.

Indicators of a good relationship include keeping the next appointment, cooperating, and being honest.

17-1 If they [clients] keep their next appointment, if they continue to maintain the therapy contact, that at least tells me that I'm doing something right, that they are at least finding it comfortable to come in and continue to talk and continue to explore what brought them in.

9-4 I think what's necessary in therapy is to have a therapeutic alliance, so that it's me and the client joined against the disorder, . . . if there's harmony and cooperation and treatment compliance.

6-3 There's a sense of straight talk between me and the client—the communication is direct and straightforward, it's not obstructed. That's when I feel I'm doing a good job.

Indicators of a poor relationship include disharmony, anger, and dislike of the client.

9-4 There's disharmony, argumentativeness, little honest inquiry or honestly asking questions with an open mind, defensiveness, even outright anger.

4-5 I decided I wouldn't be good for her because I was too reactive to her. . . . She wasn't really willing to hear anything else, and I really didn't want to be a part of that.

3-2 There are other times where I think my button gets pushed and I'm not really able to help them.

Discussion and Conclusions

Practitioners evaluate themselves using a number of indicators of both broad and narrow focus, and it is possible to construct an implicit model of self-evaluation used by social work practitioners that reflects their concerns. Such a model appears to be far removed from the textbook prescriptions of objective scientific and systematic methods of evaluating practice, but it is a valid and useful model from the perspective of the practitioners and seems to service their requirements well.

This research is nevertheless limited in that we used practitioner self-report as the only source of data. Further research that uses observational data or data of actual therapy sessions with comments by practitioners and clients would enable researchers to study specific instances of evaluative judgments as they occur. Such data could further elaborate the model and suggest new areas to pursue.

A number of questions may be asked about the pragmatic-professional approach to self-evaluation. For example, is the model valid from the client's perspective? Should the model be taught to students and recommended within the profession? Should the nature of private practice change to incorporate more scientific methods of evaluation, or should evaluation research do more to reflect actual practice?

The social work profession would be enhanced by further research using qualitative methods. Such research could help bring the roles of evaluator and practitioner close together and explore areas for their mutual enrichment. For example, the seeming contradiction between practitioners' doubts about really knowing if they are being effective and other statements about their confidence in their effectiveness needs to be explored. Perhaps some practitioner-oriented evaluation researcher could help devise ways in which some of these doubts could be alleviated.

References

Andreozzi, L. L. (1985). Why outcome research fails the family therapist. In L. L. Andreozzi (Ed.), *Integrating research and clinical practice* (pp. 1-9). Rockville, MD: Aspen.

Barlow, D. H., Hayes, S. C., & Nelson, R. O. (1984). *The scientist practitioner: Research and accountability in clinical and educational settings.* New York: Pergamon.

Barlow, D. H., & Hersen, M. (1984). *Single case experimental designs: Strategies of studying behavior change* (2nd ed.). New York: Pergamon.

Bloom, M., & Fischer, J. (1982). *Evaluating practice: Guidelines for the accountable professional.* Englewood Cliffs, NJ: Prentice Hall.

Blumer, H. (1969). *Symbolic interaction: Perspective and method.* Englewood Cliffs, NJ: Prentice Hall.

Blythe, B. (1992). Should undergraduate and graduate social work students be taught to conduct empirically based practice? Yes! *Journal of Social Work Education, 28,* 260-263.

Bogdan, R. C., & Biklen, S. K. (1982). *Qualitative research in education.* Boston: Allyn & Bacon.

Corbin, J., & Strauss, A. (1990). Grounded theory research: Procedures, canons, and evaluative criteria. *Qualitative Sociology, 13,* 3-21.

Cousins, J. B., & Leithwood, K. A. (1986). Current empirical research on evaluation utilization. *Review of Educational Research, 56,* 331-364.

Eldridge, W. D. (1983). Conceptualizing self-evaluation of clinical practice. *Social Work, 28,* 57-61.

Glaser, B. G., & Strauss, A. L. (1967). *The discovery of grounded theory: Strategies for qualitative research.* New York: Aldine.

Jayaratne, S., & Levy, R. L. (1979). *Empirical clinical practice.* New York: Columbia University Press.

Kirkhart, K. E. (1986, August). *Public service evaluation: Administrative and clinical perspectives.* Paper presented at the 94th annual convention of the American Psychological Association, Washington, DC.

Mullen, E. (1978). The construction of personal models for effective practice: A method for utilizing research findings to guide social intervention. *Social Service Research, 2,* 45-63.

Rodman, H., & Kolodny, R. (1964). Organizational strains in the researcher practitioner relationship. *Human Organization, 23,* 171-182.

Schon, D. A. (1983). *The reflective practitioner: How professionals think in action.* New York: Basic Books.

Scott, D. (1990). Practice wisdom: The neglected source of practice research. *Social Work, 35,* 564-568.

Thomlison, R. (1984). Something works: Evidence from practice effectiveness studies. *Social Work, 37,* 51-56.

Witkin, L. S. (1992). Should empirically based practice be taught in BSW and MSW programs? No! *Journal of Social Work Education, 28,* 265-268.

The View From the Other Chair
by Eric E. McCollum and Jim Beer

It was a hot August morning when Jim Beer picked me up at the office and we began the hour-long drive through Midwestern cornfields. The back of Jim's car was packed with equipment—video camera, tripod, tape recorder, extra tapes—and I felt like a *National Geographic* explorer heading out into the unknown. There was only one difference: *National Geographic* explorers aim their cameras at other people, and today, I was to be the object of study—at least one of them.

Jim turned off the main road, wound through elm-shaded streets, and finally stopped the car in front of Jerry and Cathy's house. While he unpacked his equipment, I stood for a moment, looking around. Kids' voices from a basketball game drifted across the vacant lot next door. Somewhere down the block, a screen door slammed, accompanied by a shout of, "I'm leaving, Mom." Neither the town nor the house were as I had imagined them from listening to Jerry and Cathy talk during our sessions. Their conflicts and concerns didn't seem to fit the neat corner house in this serene neighborhood. I'd imagined something less wholesome, I guess a house that mirrored the struggles going on within it—an unkempt lawn perhaps, or peeling paint. What strange images of our clients' lives we build based on 50-minute sessions, once a week.

I gave Jim a hand with the camera and tripod as he led the way to the front porch. He'd been here before, but this was my first visit. Cathy met us at the door, dressed in shorts and a sleeveless blouse, her fair hair pulled back with a headband. Although casually dressed, she still had a stylish flair, and I could see how she'd make a success out of her home cosmetics business. She directed Jim to the front room while Jerry took me to the kitchen to show me the new drywall and window frames they'd put up—a remodeling job that had been a contentious issue between them in past sessions. Tall and with crew-cut hair, his hands showed the ravages of his job as a mechanic. After the tour, they offered us iced tea and cake and then, like teenagers on a first date, we sat for a moment wondering how to begin. Jim broke the ice.

"Shall we look at the tape?" he asked. We all nodded, and Jim pushed the play button on the VCR. An image of our most recent therapy session flashed on the screen.

NOTE: This article first appeared in the *Family Therapy Networker* and is copied here with permission.

"I'm curious to know what you all think of the session as we go along," Jim said, fast-forwarding the tape past the getting-settled stage, "and what question you'd like to ask each other about the work you've been doing together."

We all took a deep breath at that point, wondering what we'd gotten ourselves into.

That morning with Jerry and Cathy was a unique opportunity in my nearly 20 years as a therapist. While I'd occasionally looked at tapes of sessions with clients before, the focus had always been on *them*—their problems, what they were doing that got them in trouble, what they might do to change. Never before had I sat down with my clients to view a tape of a session and talk about the process—what was helpful, what wasn't, how they felt about what we'd done, how I felt about it. Never before had I made such a direct effort to cross the border that separated my clients' world and mine.

This journey started when Jim approached me about helping him with his Ph.D. dissertation. I assumed he wanted me to be on his committee and assured him that I would be. But that wasn't what he wanted. He was looking for a therapist to study, someone to help him examine a single case of marital therapy in depth to see how clients and therapists learn to work together. I was his candidate. He wanted to find a willing couple for me to see, observe each of our sessions, talk to us separately afterward to hear what we thought about what had happened, and then go over the videotapes with us, asking us to comment on what was going on. Jim called it an ethnographic study, but I saw it as a chance to finally hear what my clients thought of being in therapy with me. Although I hadn't any idea what they would say, I was curious to know.

Jim observed the first 10 of my sessions with Jerry and Cathy before he left for an internship. After the 10th session, we all met together to look at the tape. When Jim was gone, Jerry, Cathy and I met 11 more times. We continued to tape our meetings and sent the videos on to Jim, sometimes recording an addendum of our thoughts about the session. "Research without the researcher," we called it. The whole project was, by turns, exhilarating and sobering, and it brought me face-to-face with fundamental questions about our field: What does it really mean to collaborate with clients? What can be learned from the study of just one couple working with one therapist? What do I really think is important in therapy? One of Jim's questions proved consistently hard to answer: "What do you think Jerry and Cathy would say about the session today?" he asked after each therapy meeting. "How do you think they saw what happened?"

Most days, I was damned if I knew.

In the history of our profession, the views of clients have had little influence on the development of what we do. Psychoanalysis interpreted clients' criticisms of therapy as an expression of what was wrong with the client. Analyzing this phenomenon—resistance was the heart of treatment—and accepting clients' suggestions or complaints about therapy at face value didn't make sense when the conventional wisdom said those dissatisfactions reflected the clients' inner conflicts, not the shortcomings of psychoanalysis. While we've come a long way from traditional psychoanalysis, I think some vestiges of that approach remain. Even now, when we pride ourselves on being client-focused, co-constructive and conversational, in important ways we're not. Therapists still set the rules and rarely consult clients about how to make therapy more helpful to them. Is it always good to steer away from "problem talk" and ask about solutions? Does interrupting a sequence always help? Are there times when compliments annoy clients? Had Freud asked his clients what they thought would help them or what they wanted from therapy, we might have a very different profession today.

Jerry and Cathy came to see me after 14 years of marriage. They were struggling with a slow-growing marital malaise that had no specific focus. While they didn't like where they found themselves as a couple, they weren't sure where they wanted to be, either. And the stakes were high. Cathy was clear from the beginning that if therapy didn't help, divorce was the only other option. In our fourth session, I tried a technique I'd learned about from Australian therapist Michael White's work and externalized the disquiet they felt. If they joined forces to fight their dissatisfaction, I thought, maybe they could pull closer together.

"Are there ever times when you conquer this Pressure between the two of you?" I asked. "Are there times when you tell Pressure to back off and let you enjoy your marriage?"

When Jerry and Cathy could recount only a few recent good times, I suggested that they go home and try for a week to observe instances when they could keep Pressure from driving a wedge between them.

I left feeling it had been a good session, meeting many of my criteria for competent therapy—coherent, organized around a theme, using a theoretical model consistently. I found out months later, when therapy was done and I read their reactions in Jim's dissertation, that the couple felt the session was a flop. In a postsession interview with Jim, Cathy said the focus on exceptions was "corny" and was worried that I misunderstood her grave doubts about whether or not the marriage could survive. She felt it was fine to talk about good things, but not at the expense of discussing the "real problems." Jerry felt the session had had a "surface" feel to it.

I was chagrined when I read their comments. I'd been trying so hard to help them and had been so convinced of my success, that hearing their criticisms hurt. It helped to know that therapy was over and that Jerry and Cathy were satisfied with the outcome. My "Michael White session," Jim and I came to call it, hadn't been a fatal flaw, but we'd seen things so differently! Jerry and Cathy clearly didn't share my standards for "good therapy," and wanted something very different. Cathy told Jim, "To me, positive is not what we need to fix. It's the negative. What's the use of having wonderful bonding time if the night before was terrible? To me, Eric clearly didn't see the depth of the problem at that point."

"What's Eric thinking? What does he think of us?" Cathy and Jerry asked Jim time after time in their postsession interviews. The issue came up again when we all met together.

"It kills me sometimes to not know what you're thinking," Cathy said to me in her living room. "I'd give anything to know." Jerry nodded his agreement.

Their wish to know what I thought challenged what I'd been taught early in my career—that we must protect our clients from what we think of them, doling out our opinions only in scrupulously constructed interventions. There's a reason for this injunction, of course. The therapist's power in the therapeutic relationship may give an offhand remark more impact than we would ever guess. We need to be careful, but how careful? Jerry and Cathy said they would sacrifice a little caution for a better sense of my reactions.

"I respect your opinion," Cathy told me. "You've talked to lots of people about problems and have a lot of experience that I don't have."

What about the fear that I would unduly influence them?

"I may not agree with you," Cathy continued. "I'll still make up my own mind."

Cathy told me how dismayed she had been in the first session when Jerry brought up their two earlier experiences in therapy. My reassurance that I would try not to repeat what they had found unhelpful before (the counselors told Cathy she needed to accept that Jerry wouldn't change and "quit whining about it"), was, in fact, not reassuring at all. When we all met together, Cathy told me, "I don't want you to be afraid to say 'You're doing *this* wrong,' or 'You're looking at *this* out of perspective.' " Unfortunately, there was some accuracy in what she feared. I had found myself being careful with her, knowing how she'd been treated in therapy before. When I saw her ambivalence about Jerry—asking him to change something but still being dissatisfied when he did—I was reluctant to point it out, fearing it would sound like what she'd been told before. I saw my restraint as helpful. Cathy didn't. My efforts to protect her without knowing what protection, if any, she felt she needed, had backfired. And without Jim's research, I'd never have known about it.

As important to Cathy and Jerry as knowing what I thought about them was being sure that I understood them. Both rated our third session a "10" on the 1 to 10 scale Jim used with all of us. "One" meant the session had not been helpful, while "10" meant it had been extremely helpful. What made the third session a "10?" Cathy explained it to Jim this way: "I really felt Eric knows where I am today . . . I don't think he ever heard me before to where I really feel I am . . . until today." What had been so helpful to Cathy and Jerry that day wasn't some clever intervention. The difference was my ability to let them know I understood that their lives were on the line here, that their problems had tied them in knots they weren't sure could ever be untied. It wasn't so important that I help them do something about it just then, only that I grasp how serious it was.

To get away from the endless search for understanding that can stretch traditional therapy into a years-long venture, family therapists have taken the path of problem solving and action. We acknowledge the importance of empathy and the client-therapist relationship, but often relegate them to the murky land of "joining"—something to be gotten out of the way before real therapy can begin. For Cathy and Jerry, at least, this wasn't so. Feeling understood as they told their story was powerful. And healing.

"Were you embarrassed the day we brought up our sex problems?" Jerry asked me that morning in August. I thought for a moment, remembering the session several weeks before, trying to reconstruct what I'd been thinking.

"I wasn't embarrassed," I said, "but I felt pretty cautious, because I could tell it was a painful thing for both of you."

"I could see on your face that you were nervous," Jerry said.

Cathy chimed in, "I told Jerry in the car on the way home that I thought we'd embarrassed you. I could see you didn't know exactly what to say."

Her comment brought me up short. I *hadn't* known what to say, but should I tell them that? Talking about my indecision and uncertainty felt dangerous. Would it hurt them to know I sometimes didn't know what to do? Would it shake their confidence in our work together? And who would my silence protect—them or me? Despite the fear that I was breaking another therapy taboo, I struggled to match their candor with my own.

"I guess I really didn't know what to say. Would it have been better if I'd just told you that I felt like we were into something deep here, and that I needed your help in knowing exactly how far we could go?"

"It might have," Jerry said. "I felt bad about it later. I wondered if we'd done something wrong."

Cathy had a different view.

"I like it better when you're in charge," she said to me, "especially when it comes to the hard things. We're the ones who made a mess of our marriage, after all."

It was the kind of talk I've often wanted to have with my clients, the chance to step out of character and ask, "What is it you want from me, *really*? I know you're scared. Sometimes, so am I. Now, how can I help?" Later, Jim asked Jerry and Cathy why they hadn't shared some of their ideas with me during our sessions. "Eric's the professional," Jerry replied. "It just doesn't seem right. It's kind of like I wouldn't go to my doctor and tell him that I sure like those X-rays he took of me. I don't know anything about X-rays, so it isn't my place."

Hearing that comment, it dawned on me what different people Cathy and Jerry were in their own home. They responded to Jim's questions, offered their own views, and asked questions of me. In therapy, they were nothing like this. Many of our sessions had a tension and desperation you could feel. I'd picture them at home as a dispirited, humorless couple. Instead, I saw Cathy fondly needle Jim about his "famous 10-point scales," Jerry work to put this thoughts into words, and the two of them discuss easily and clearly their ongoing evaluation of therapy. The discrepancy left my head spinning. Had I been wrong about these two? Had I misjudged them and seen them defective when clearly they weren't?

The answer is more complicated than a simple personal failing. Jerry's comment about "his place" offered a clue. I hadn't misjudged them. I'd only seen what the therapy room let me see and had missed the parts of Cathy and Jerry that weren't in "therapy character." That's not to say that there was something duplicitous about what they said or did in our sessions. Rather, it is a testament to how limiting the therapy room is, how what happens there is organized to allow only a slim and circumscribed part of both the client and the therapist to appear. Clients' trouble and therapists' expertise come through the door easily, while clients' strengths, successes and playfulness, and therapists' doubts, confusion and uncertainty are rarely seen. That really doesn't diminish therapy or its usefulness. But we will always know only one small part of our clients. They are infinitely more complex than what emerges in therapy. For that matter, so are we.

Throughout therapy, my efforts to compliment Jerry and Cathy on the progress they made often left Cathy feeling unsettled.

"It scares me when you say we're doing a good job," she told me in our 10th session, as I once again tried to highlight progress. "I don't trust it. We've been here before and then slid back."

After watching herself say that again on tape in her living room, Cathy stopped the VCR.

"Right there, I just pushed Eric all the way back." She laughed. "He tried to say something nice and I just went 'Whooaa! Don't say that nice thing.'"

She got more serious and she turned to me.

"How did you feel, Eric, when I said that to you?"

It was a startling moment. Rarely had one of my clients asked me so straightforwardly how I felt about working with them. If they had, I'd turned the focus back to them, wondering if their curiosity indicated some insecurity about how they were coming across. Cathy's earnest question, however, and the openness of our conversation that morning, nudged me out of the protective shell of "therapist" by inviting a more personal response. I told her that I hadn't felt put off, that I realized she was scared. I didn't want to push her, but I didn't want to ignore good things, either. I reminded her that we'd made a little joke of it in the session as I changed from saying they'd made progress to saying, "You two are talking about some tiny, little differences in how you get along."

"It felt nice that I could joke with you about it," I said, "because when I first met you, I don't think I could have done that. I don't think you'd have known me well enough to know that when I was joking, I wasn't making fun of you."

Cathy agreed. "I was in a different place emotionally back then," she said.

Then Jim offered another thought: "I wonder if Eric can joke with you now, Cathy, because you've had enough interaction with him to know he understands."

"I do now," she replied.

It was a sweet moment, full of understanding and a kind of connection I'd never felt with a client before. We'd peeked through the scrim of "therapy" and caught a glimpse of each other as people.

In the three years since I last saw Jerry and Cathy, I've taken them with me, in my mind at least, to several professional meetings and workshops and as I read professional journals and articles I've been sent for review. They've followed along as I supervised, taught, and met with clients. Their presence has given me a new vantage point from which to access the work I do. Much of what I've noticed had been disturbing.

Amid all the talk of collaboration, equalizing professional hierarchies, and creating space for our clients' voices, I've yet to find an actual client participating in the debate. At conferences, presenters and panels opine about what clients need and want, but no client is there to speak for him- or herself. Our codes of ethics are formulated to protect clients. Have we ever asked them what kind of protections they need or want? As we move toward shorter, more focused therapy to "better serve our clients," why don't we ask if briefer approaches are helpful, or if they serve clients' needs? How many of our outcome studies include measures of client satisfaction with treatment? How many of our training programs use client input as part of students' evaluations? As we educate ourselves about gender, race, and class differences, does it occur to us to ask our clients if they find our knowledge of these things helpful?

Hearing our clients' voices doesn't mean we must blindly do anything they say. I honestly don't know, for example, if it's better for a couple to stay together or divorce, nor do I know who's right or who's wrong in most situations. When clients ask me to make such judgments, I have to decline. When I suggest that we listen to our clients' voices, what I have in mind is that we enter them into the larger conversations about therapy we are currently having as a field. We need such talk not to change *them* but to change *us*, to reshape our ideas of what therapy is, how it can help, what place it should occupy in society. And it's only fair, after all. Our clients hold a major stake in the outcome.

Cathy and Jerry left therapy after 21 sessions. Like so many therapy experiences, we ended not with a bang but with a gradual realization that they didn't need to come back. The time between sessions lengthened. We sometimes found ourselves with little to talk about. They'd made many changes during the months of our work together and were more settled than they had been in a long time. Cathy had come out from behind her emotional wall and felt the marriage would be livable for her, now. Jerry had learned to turn the TV off and listen to his wife.

We said goodbye in the same waiting room where we'd met. I found myself lingering with them, wondering if I had the courage to ask the questions I hadn't asked. They were the hardest ones, the most personal—Did I really help you? Do you think I'm a good therapist? Do you like me as much as I've come to like you? Crossing that last barrier, however, and acknowledging some of my own needs as a therapist, was more than I could do that day. Instead, I tried to put some closure to all that we'd done.

"You two have really given me something special," I said. "Therapists and clients don't usually get together and talk about therapy the way we did. You've taught me a lot."

It sounded lame to me, pale against the excitement of our experiment. But it was the best I could do.

What Cathy and Jerry taught me has woven its way into my life as a therapist, lying quietly below the surface for weeks at a time before emerging when I need it. Just last week, I watched one of my students try to compliment a single mother on what a good job she was doing with her son.

"But you don't understand," the client said plaintively. "I don't feel like I'm doing a good job. I don't feel like I'm doing anything right."

As the student was about to try again, I called in and interrupted, remembering Cathy's admonition that problems had to be understood before strengths would seem relevant.

"Listen to her," I said to my student over the phone. "Slow down. Explore it a little more. She knows what she needs to be talking about."

Discussion Questions—Readings on Evaluation

1. What are your initial reactions to the articles? What key points did you take away from them?

   Elks and Kirkhart article

   _____

   _____

   _____

   _____

   _____

   _____

   _____

   _____

   _____

   _____

McCollum and Beer article

_____

_____

_____

_____

_____

_____

_____

_____

_____

2. How would your list of pros and cons for evaluation change as a result of what you've read?

_____

_____

_____

_____

_____

_____

_____

_____

_____

_____

3. Elks and Kirkhart offer five categories that practitioners use in self-evaluation. Describe the strengths and weaknesses of using each approach to evaluate effectiveness.

Intuition and experience

_____

_____

_____

_____

_____

_____

_____

_____

_____

Personal and professional values

_____

_____

_____

_____

_____

_____

_____

_____

_____

Client change

_____

_____

_____

_____

_____

_____

_____

_____

_____

Business aspects

_____

_____

_____

_____

_____

_____

_____

_____

_____

Practitioner-client relationship

_____

_____

_____

_____

_____

_____

_____

_____

_____

_____

4. In what way(s) does the experience described by McCollum and Beer contrast with the techniques used by the therapists whom Elks and Kirkhart interviewed?

_____

_____

_____

_____

_____

_____

_____

_____

_____

_____

_____

5. Based on what you have read, what strategies do you recommend for evaluating our effectiveness as social workers?

_____

_____

_____

_____

_____

_____

_____

_____

_____

_____

6. How does your answer to Question 5 change if the "client" is a group, organization, or community?

_____

_____

_____

_____

_____

_____

_____

_____

_____

_____

7. What responsibilities for assessing practice effectiveness do the Code of Ethics, licensure boards, and funders place on social workers? Do any of those bodies offer guidelines for selecting measures for evaluating effectiveness?

_____

_____

_____

_____

_____

_____

_____

_____

_____

List of Methods to Evaluate Outcomes

_____

_____

_____

_____

_____

_____

_____

_____

_____

_____

EXERCISE 31 *Tracking Progress Through Single-Subject Design*

Raymond S. Kirk

Purpose

1. To lay the foundation for single-system designs and methods for evaluating case practice by developing skills in graphing and interpreting time-series data.

Background

The Council on Social Work Education (CSWE) accreditation standards require, among other things, the development of competencies in research and case practice evaluation. Among the most useful methods available to individual practitioners for evaluating their own interventions with individual clients or client *systems* (e.g., families, classrooms, neighborhoods) are the single-system methods.

Single-system (single-s) methods differ from classical research methods in that there are no control participants or clients who do not receive treatment, with which to compare to those who do receive treatment. Rather, in single-s evaluations each client or system is compared to itself over time; preferably, measurement data gathered during treatment are compared with the same type of measurement data gathered prior to treatment. The pretreatment period is frequently referred to as the *baseline* period. If baseline data are gathered for some reasonable period of time prior to intervention or treatment, then the changes that may occur in the measurement data during treatment are more likely to be able to be attributed to the intervention than if no baseline data are available. Measurement data can (and should) be gathered during treatment even if no baseline measures are available, so that the practitioner can track client progress during treatment, even if these data cannot be compared with pretreatment data.

Selecting measures for single-s applications requires that the data can be gathered repeatedly over the course of treatment, and thereafter, if circumstances permit follow-up contacts with the system. The practice of taking multiple measures over time results in a *time series* of data that can be plotted on a graph to give the practitioner a visual representation of how the system is progressing.

It is important to keep in mind that all measures obtained using single-s methods are time-dependent and that when you draw graphs of these data that "time" is always the x-axis. The scale may be in hours, days, weeks, sessions, or any other time-related interval, but it will always be "time." Each measure obtained along the time line is dependent on everything that has happened to the system during the time preceding the time you obtained your most recent measure. This is the meaning of time-dependent, and it is the basis of single-s methods.

Several good introductory texts are available (Bloom & Fischer, 1982; Blythe & Tripodi, 1989; Marlow, 1993; Tripodi, 1994) that explain issues of measurement in case practice evaluation. For example, measures employed should be reliable, and valid for the purpose intended; they should be fairly sensitive to change so that if the client improves or deteriorates the measurement data so inform the practitioner as early as possible; and there should be a fairly direct relationship between the measure and the clinical or social problem being addressed during the intervention. These and other "rules" of measurement will be more fully developed in courses on research methods that the typical social work student will take. The student will also learn a variety of statistical procedures to test the measurement data for statistical significance.

It is not the purpose of this exercise to address measurement selection or statistical procedures. Whatever measures are chosen in a particular intervention, and whatever statistical testing procedures are selected for significance testing, single-s measurement always provides the opportunity to "draw a picture" of client change or progress using time-series data. In fact, some of the statistical tests available require precisely drawn graphs to "count" occurrences of desired or undesired behavior that occur either above or below some clinical criterion or mathematically determined performance criterion.

The purpose of this exercise is to introduce you to the practice of drawing a picture of the clinical progress of the system that is the subject of the intervention. If you are comfortable with graphing time-series data, and with interpreting the clinical implications of the resulting "picture," then you will be better prepared to demonstrate your own practice effectiveness and learn more advanced research methods and analytic techniques.

Instructions

The examples that follow provide data sets that you are to plot on the graph paper provided.

Unless instructed otherwise, you should work alone. It should take 5 or 6 minutes to complete each graphing exercise. You will discuss your results as a group.

As you draw the graphs of the data, think about what the data mean and be prepared to discuss what the "picture" of the data appear to reveal about the client system or the intervention. There are some discussion questions associated with each graph, and space below each question to take notes or record your thoughts during the discussion sessions.

EXERCISE 31

Activity 1

You are a social worker employed by an economic services unit in a county department of social services. You are working with a population of single-female-headed households receiving Temporary Assistance to Needy Families (TANF). A large number of these families live in a large, subsidized housing project (the Billings Housing Project) in your county's largest city. Among the several hundred low-income families in the project are about 150 families receiving TANF benefits. Because of the large number of clients in that location your agency decides to offer several services on location at the Billings Project. Classrooms are set up, and child care is provided to TANF moms so that they can attend Adult Basic Education courses, GED courses, a variety of vocational courses, practice job interviewing skills, and so on.

In this case, the system is the housing project and the clients are the TANF recipients within the project. In addition to tracking progress on individual clients through their case records, you decide to measure the unemployment rate among households in the project as a broader indicator of the success of the overall intervention, not just the individual interventions developed for each client. The Department of Employment Security (DES) can provide you with very accurate data about the unemployment rate in the project using new geo-mapping techniques. There are several pros and cons to using the Billings Project unemployment rate as a measure for your department's multiservice intervention in the project. However, for purposes of this activity, the measure will suffice.

DES has given you quarterly unemployment rates for the past 3 years, on a quarterly basis. These data are presented in Table 31.1. Your first task is to plot the data on the graph provided, labeled Figure 31.1a.

Discussion Questions

Table 31.1   Unemployment Rates for Residents of the Billings Project for the Past 3 Years
(in percentages)

Qtr 1	Qtr 2	Qtr 3	Qtr 4	Qtr 5	Qtr 6	Qtr 7	Qtr 8	Qtr 9	Qtr 10	Qtr 11	Qtr 12
30	34	33	34	36	37	38	36	36	35	38	39

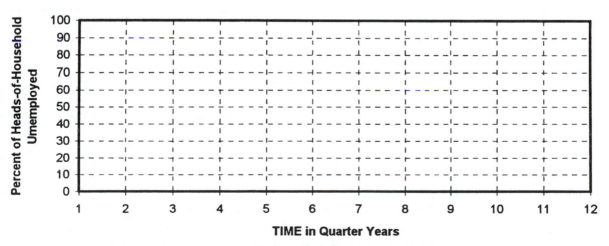

Figure 31.1a.   Unemployment Rates at Billings Project for the Past 3 Years

1. Does the trend line in this picture appear to be very dynamic (i.e., lots of movement up or down), or fairly stable over the 3-year period?

_____

_____

_____

_____

_____

_____

_____

_____

2. What might we do to make this graph more interesting or meaningful, or to draw our attention to the changes that may be occurring?

_____

_____

_____

_____

_____

_____

_____

_____

Your second task is to replot the same data (from Table 31.1) on the next graph, labeled Figure 31.1b, which has different y-axis values than Figure 31.1a.

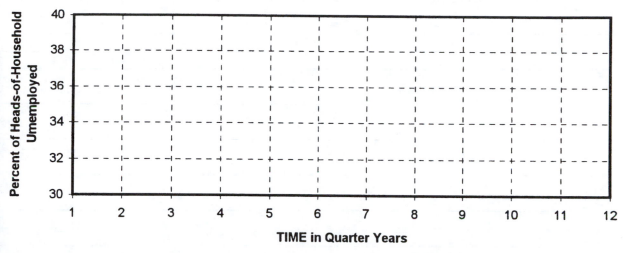

Figure 31.1b.   Unemployment Rates at Billings Project for the Past 3 Years

Discussion Questions

1. Now does the trend line in this picture appear dynamic; does there appear to be change over time?

_____

_____

_____

_____

_____

_____

_____

_____

_____

_____

_____

2. If your intervention were reasonably successful (i.e., if unemployment dropped by 2% or 3% per year starting two or three quarters after your intervention began), which figure (31.1a or 31.1b) would be most likely to draw your attention to the change?

_____

_____

_____

_____

_____

_____

_____

The data presented in Table 31.2 are hypothetical data from the first six quarters of your intervention. These would represent quarters 13 through 18 of the total time line of the project so far, including the 12 quarters of pretreatment baseline data that you obtained from DES.

Your next task is to draw a continuation of the data on the next graph, labeled Figure 31.2. You must replot the baseline data to get the full picture of how your intervention data compare to the baseline data, over time.

Table 31.2   Unemployment Rates at Billings Project During Six Quarters of Intervention
(in percentages)

Qtr 13	Qtr 14	Qtr 15	Qtr 16	Qtr 17	Qtr 18
40	40	38	36	35	36

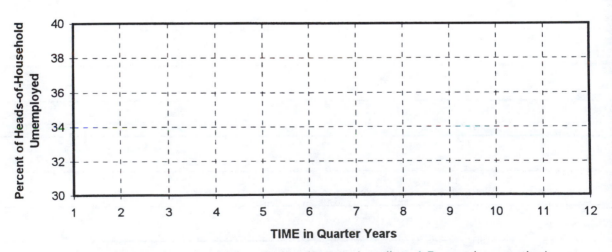

Figure 31.2. Unemployment Rates at Billings Project (3 years baseline; 1.5 years intervention)

Discussion Questions

1. Did the addition of the treatment data affect the appearance of the baseline data?

_____

_____

_____

_____

_____

_____

2. Does there appear to be a change in the pattern of unemployment in the Billings Project?

_____

_____

_____

_____

_____

_____

3. What, if anything can you say about the influence of your intervention on these data?

_____

_____

_____

_____

_____

_____

_____

4. What other things might we want to know, beyond what is on our graph, to help us explain these data?

_____

_____

_____

_____

_____

_____

_____

_____

_____

Activity 2

In this activity, you are a school social worker who has been asked by an elementary classroom teacher to help her with a child, Mickey, who frequently disrupts her class by hiding under his desk and making "animal noises," getting out of his seat during lesson periods and bothering other students, repeatedly yelling out questions unrelated to the topic being discussed or taught at the time, or displaying other disruptive kinds of behaviors. Your conversation with the teacher reveals a high level of frustration on her part, and she has already asked the principal to consider removing the child from her classroom. You are aware that Mickey is experiencing a great deal of family stress right now, and you believe that removing him from class would be damaging to him and would certainly not help the situation at home. You convince the teacher to work with you to reduce the number of disruptive acts and to try to keep Mickey in class.

For you to better understand the magnitude of Mickey's problem, you ask the teacher to keep a log of incidents for a week, noting the time of day that each occurs, what the class was doing at the time, whether the incident required physical intervention by the teacher, whether the incidents involved other children, and so on. This is your *assessment* period, but you are also collecting baseline data on the number of disruptive acts per day.

In this case, the system is an individual, Mickey. But depending on how the assessment and intervention unfold, the system might expand to include Mickey's family. You might consider "Mickey and the teacher" to be the system, depending on whether you consider the teacher only to be an "agent" in your intervention with Mickey or you focus some part of your intervention on the teacher. For example, you might teach the teacher some coping strategies of her own, so as not to let Mickey's behavior have such an impact on her. For purposes of this activity, we'll consider Mickey to be the system.

At the end of the following week, the teacher comes to your office with her log, and together you discuss Mickey's data. The number of disruptive behaviors are presented in Table 31.3.

Your first task is to plot the baseline data on the graph provided, labeled Figure 31.3.

Table 31.3   Number of Disruptive Behaviors by Mickey, Per Day

Monday	Tuesday	Wednesday	Thursday	Friday
5	6	4	2	4

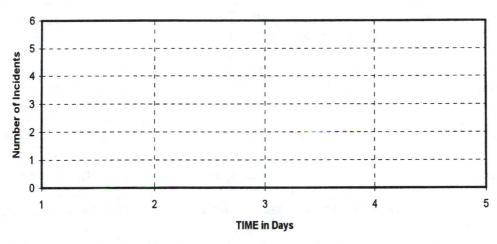

Figure 31.3. Number of Disruptive Behaviors Per Day

Discussion Question

1. Is the "0 through 6" scale selection for the y-axis appropriate?

_____

_____

_____

_____

_____

_____

_____

_____

_____

_____

_____

You show the graph to the teacher as an aid to the discussion about how to intervene. (Having a visual aid during clinical discussions or sessions is another good reason to gather and plot time-series data!) During your conversation about the week and Mickey's behavior, the teacher states that "Thursday was actually a pretty good day for Mickey. I didn't go home feeling strung out and exhausted the way I did most other days." Picking up on this statement, you discuss with the teacher what would be a reasonable expectation for Mickey; one that would allow him to stay in the class, but also one that recognizes that Mickey is still a troubled child who may be disruptive from time to time. Together you conclude that if Mickey's disruptions were reduced to two or fewer per day, the teacher could cope and Mickey could stay in the class.

What has happened is that you have used the graph and the teacher's feelings about the differing levels of disruptions to "negotiate" a criterion that defines the clinical success: two or fewer disruptions per day.

Using the other information in the log, you and the teacher construct a behavioral intervention that the teacher agrees to employ. For purposes of our discussion, we need not know the exact components of the intervention. However, if this were a real case, you would specify the components precisely, and measure them as well, so that you can build your case for "practical plausibility" if your intervention is successful.

Table 31.4 presents 3 weeks of treatment data gathered by Mickey's teacher after your intervention was implemented.

Draw these data on the graph provided, labeled Figure 31.4. Note that there is a horizontal line on this figure just above the "2" level on the y-axis, depicting the "clinical criterion" for success. There is also a vertical line between Days 5 and 6, depicting the beginning of treatment.

Table 31.4   Number of Disruptions During Treatment Period

M	Tu	W	Th	F	M	Tu	W	Th	F	M	Tu	W	Th	F
5	4	6	4	3	4	3	1	2	4	2	1	3	2	1

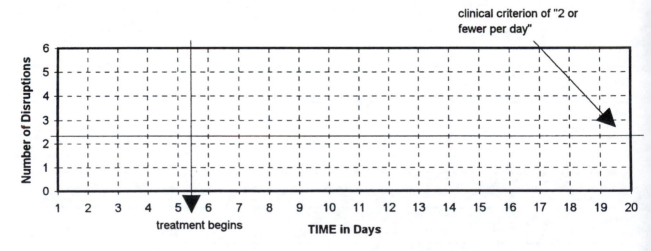

Figure 31.4. Number of Disruptive Behaviors Per Day, Baseline and Treatment

Discussion Questions

1. Does this picture imply that your intervention is working?

_____

_____

_____

_____

_____

_____

_____

_____

2. Are there features of the data in the "treatment curve" that support or weaken the "plausibility argument" for your intervention?

_____

_____

_____

_____

_____

_____

_____

_____

Additional Outside Activity

Read Collins, Kayser, and Platt (1994) and come back to class or the discussion group prepared to discuss how the authors tailored their single-s measures to evaluate and assist in a conjoint marital therapy intervention.

- How were measures tailored to the presenting problem?
- How were the data gathered between sessions used to guide the content of subsequent sessions?
- How did they use the act of measurement to engage the couple in the treatment process?
- How were data used to know when to "terminate," and how were they used to test the durability of the intervention during follow-up?

Reference

Collins, P. M., Kayser, K., & Platt, S. (1994, March). Conjoint marital therapy: A practitioners approach to single-system evaluation. *Families in Society: The Journal of Contemporary Human Services,* pp. 131-141.

Bibliography

Bloom, M., & Fischer, J. (1982). *Evaluating practice: Guidelines for the accountable professional.* Englewood Cliffs, NJ: Prentice Hall.

A comprehensive text. Excellent coverage of measurement issues, ways of obtaining data, selecting measures, single-s designs, and statistical procedures.

Blythe, B. J., & Tripodi, T. (1989). *Measurement in direct practice.* Newbury Park, CA: Sage.

Not as comprehensive as Bloom and Fischer, but a "quick read" on many of the same issues, particularly on integrating measurement into direct practice and beginning measurement during assessment and carrying it through to termination and follow-up with clients.

Marlow, C. (1993). *Research methods for generalist social work.* Pacific Grove, CA: Brooks/Cole.

Good discussion of single-s designs in generalist practice, as well as broader discussions such as developing research questions. Text is broader, topically, than others listed, but not as detailed. Includes sections on qualitative as well as quantitative data, writing research reports, and using research findings to evaluate practice.

Tripodi, T. (1994). *A primer on single-subject design for clinical social workers.* Washington, DC: NASW Press.

Focusing exclusively on single-s methods, this book offers a rich variety of examples and applications throughout the various stages of interventions. Also presents C-statistic and Z-statistic testing for data stability and difference testing, respectively.

EXERCISE 32 *Evaluating Communication Skills Through Process Recordings*

Julie S. Abramson

Purpose

1. To develop the capacity to evaluate communication patterns in a social work interview.
2. To learn skills in developing alternative interventions.

Background

Process recordings of students' interviews with their clients continue to be used as a teaching tool by field instructors and those teaching social work practice courses. This unique social work approach to professional skill development requires that you write as close to verbatim an account of your exchanges with the client as possible, annotated by commentary regarding your thoughts and feelings about the interaction.

From your efforts to reflect on and recount these interactions, you will learn to track themes in both the substance and process of the interview and thus to self-correct on the spot. From such a process, you will develop analytic capacities and an improved ability to evaluate your own practice. It is a more active method of learning than listening to tapes or reporting on work with clients verbally, although these methods may provide greater accuracy about the interaction. Finally, process recording provides a mechanism to assure that some time in supervision is devoted to examining specific social work interventions as the foundation for professional practice.

Instructions

The following exercise can used informally for self-evaluation or as part of a formal written assignment per your instructor's preference. It consists of three parts, in which you write a process recording, complete an in-depth assessment of the recording, then videotape and analyze a role-played interview.

EXERCISE 32

Part 1: Process Recording

Write a process recording (or use one that you've done for your field placement) in two columns following the format of the example below:

Narrative	Student Reactions
Client: My husband really isn't in favor of my mother coming to live with us.	I thought she'd been avoiding this discussion for some time. Now it's out, what do I do?
Student: He isn't?	
C: They never really got along.	
S: Is that making things hard for you right now?	I hope she'll tell me more. I hope this doesn't delay the discharge.
C: I don't know what to do. I'm in the middle!	
S: You really are, but I'm afraid you're going to have to make a decision soon.	Oh, oh, I stopped listening, but what I said is true.

Part 2: Analysis of Process Recording

Review the process recording.

    a. First, consider your contract with the client/family/group (or mutual understanding of what you are working on together); what was the contract for this session?

    b. Note anything important regarding the verbal and nonverbal communication between you and the client.

    c. Select and number 10 of your interventions from the process recording (an intervention is any statement of yours to the client(s)). Evaluate each of the interventions according to the following format:

Narrative	*Intervention Skill/Intent*	*Student Reactions*	*Comments/Alternative Intervention*

Narrative: the specific words of the interaction.

Intervention skill/intent: Label and identify the intervention skill that you used. What were you trying to accomplish?

Student reactions: Your thoughts and feelings about your intervention and the client's responses to it.

Comments/alternative intervention: Analysis and suggestions after the fact. (Did it work? Would you do it differently? If so, why and how.)

---

    d. Summary reflection: Highlight both the successful and less successful aspects of your intervention skills overall. If relevant, note how your feelings influenced the process. Identify any obstacles to your efforts to communicate with the client, including those that arose from lack of skill, client issues, client/family dynamics, or systems issues. Note the extent to which you think the objectives of the interview were met. Please remember that you are not expected to have all of these techniques under your control at this point in your development; even those of you who have done extensive interviewing have, no doubt, rarely examined your interventions at such a microscopic level. This assignment is meant to further develop your critical and analytic skills rather than demonstrate "perfect" interviewing skills. Finally, when you are practicing in the field, what strategies will you use for self-evaluation, when tools such as process recording or videotaping may not be feasible?

Part 3: Evaluating Skills Through Analysis of Videotaped Interviews

If you (or other students) have access to videotaping equipment (or if the school has available equipment), you may wish to tape yourself role-playing the social worker in one of the scenarios provided below while another student plays the client. You can then practice evaluating your interviewing skills on the tape by using the steps in the exercise above.

Scenarios for Videotaped Role Plays
Prepared by Micro Practice Faculty Group, School of Social Welfare, University at Albany, Albany, New York

General Note: You may change the gender or race of the social worker to match the characteristics of the student playing the role; however, please do not change the client's characteristics or situation.

Scenario 1: Mr. Grafton's Independence

Paul Grafton is a 77-year-old African American farmer whose wife, Vickie, died 2 years earlier. He has been very successful at farming and lives alone on a five-acre farm. Recently, a neighbor found Mr. Grafton lying helplessly on the ground near his mailbox. Two walking canes were found next to him. While the neighbor was assisting Mr. Grafton into the house, Mr. Grafton revealed that he has rheumatoid arthritis and poor eyesight. He has been unable to get around without the use of his canes. He also indicated that activities of daily living were becoming increasingly difficult to perform without his wife. Currently, he is experiencing financial difficulties and foreclosure seems imminent. The neighbor reports to you that Mr. Grafton is becoming increasingly depressed over these events and his failing health. He perceives himself, however, as an independent man who can handle these concerns if people would only leave him alone. He has no interest in altering his circumstances and clings doggedly to the present situation.

Scenario 2: Stress in the Workplace

Maria Cardinale is a 32-year-old Italian American woman who works as a nurse at an urban hospital. She is the divorced mother of an 8-year-old son and a 5-year-old daughter. Ms. Cardinale and her co-workers often talk about stress. Conversations usually concern how tense the staff feels when Dr. Jack, a physician, is on duty. Dr. Jack is a new physician who seems to elevate stress levels immediately. Either he assumes the nursing staff knows what he is thinking or he shouts orders in a condescending fashion. As a general duty nurse on the medical ward, Ms. Cardinale alternates between working 1 week of day shifts with 1 week of afternoons; she has 1 week of nights every 2 months as well, which she dreads and refers to as "torture time." Arranging child care for daytime and afternoons is difficult enough, but her week of night shifts (which start at 11:00 p.m.) is a "nightmare," which she worries about constantly. Once, a combination of understaffing, lack of sleep, and a hastily written medication order almost caused Ms. Cardinale to make a grave mistake. She thinks about this all the time.

Ms. Cardinale's work situation worsens when Megan is the charge nurse on duty. Megan is the kind of supervisor who assumes every other nurse is incompetent. She frequently hovers, making critical comments and second guessing the decision-making process. When Ms. Cardinale returns home from working with Megan and Dr. Jack, her stress level is so high that only pills or a couple of drinks can get her to sleep. When she does fall asleep, often her dreams are about work. Ms. Cardinale has decided to accept help from a professional social worker.

Scenario 3: The Intake Process

James has been on the road for the past 4 years ever since being discharged from a state alcoholism treatment program. He has worked very occasionally, panhandled frequently, and generally has been able to survive at a subsistence level. He has continued to drink after release from the program. James recently came to town in his wanderings and would like a little respite from the streets so he came to the Homeless and Travelers' Aide office. From there, he was sent to the "Bridge," a shelter for homeless adults, where he is being interviewed by the intake worker. The social worker's function is to do an initial assessment of the varied needs of each person who seeks shelter. He or she needs to complete an intake form for each client, which includes basic information about the client, client's family, prior living arrangements, and job information as well as mental and physical health history. He or she must also focus on engaging the client.

Scenario 4: Who Is the Client?

You are working in a child welfare agency and have been assigned a case involving three children who have been placed in foster care with their maternal grandmother. The children are 5, 9, and 11 years old and have been living with their grandmother for 6 months. They were placed after their alcoholic mother left them in the care of the 11-year-old over the weekend. Their mother has completed a treatment program and seems to be doing fairly well in remaining sober, getting on public assistance, living in her own apartment, and beginning to look for a job. The grandmother has called you to say that her daughter has been visiting the household and telling the children that she is going to take them back to live with her. The grandmother comes in to see you and expresses her alarm that her daughter could get custody of the children again. She feels her daughter is not ready to care for the children, that she still is not reliable as a parent, and that she has done the same thing before when she has come out of rehab. It didn't work out then, and the grandmother does not think it will work out now. She wants your assurance that the kids can stay with her.

8 ENDINGS AND TRANSITIONS

EXERCISE 33 *Letter to the Editor*

Kim Strom-Gottfried

Purpose

1. To understand the elements in a persuasive correspondence.
2. To effectively convey your thoughts in written form.
3. To use your experience as a social worker to influence larger systems.

Background

Social workers and the clients they serve are affected by social policies that were not of their making. Such policies are often shaped by public opinion, political pressure, and vocal interest groups, but we wonder if those involved in the policy-making process understand the impact they ultimately have. Social workers and service consumers are in an important position to educate people about the effects of social policies. They can debunk myths that shape public opinion and put a "human face" on social issues and bureaucratic decisions. The NASW Code of Ethics (Section 6.04) requires that social workers engage in political and social action to improve availability and access to services, to encourage social justice and to ensure that basic human needs are met.

One way to work for social change is through writing letters to newspaper editors and to elected officials. These letters can provide your perspective on impending legislation, comment on a social issue, or bring to light the real-life consequences of a policy decision. With the advent of fax machines and electronic mail, this is an easy and accessible method of conveying your opinion. Yet, as with verbal communication, the impact of letters is based not only on what you say but how you say it. The exercise below helps you to identify the elements of a persuasive letter then asks you to write such a letter and have it critiqued by a fellow classmate.

Instructions

In the first section, list the qualities that you feel make a letter effective in persuading the recipient to see a situation from your point of view.

Your text may have information to help in this segment of the exercise. It may also help to imagine yourself as a policymaker and consider what you would find appealing in a letter from a constituent. Reviewing letters to the editor of your local paper may also help you to identify characteristics of those that are persuasive and those that are not.

Next, select a topic you will write about and a recipient for your letter. You may want to comment about a current event in which you as a social worker have an opinion. You may want to give input on a legislative issue, or you may want to describe the effects of a policy on your clientele (without, of course, violating a client's privacy). If you have trouble coming up with ideas, think about some of the clients portrayed in this workbook. Imagine you are trying to shape public opinion about conditions affecting those clients. What would you want people to know? On the workbook page, or a separate sheet, write the letter as you would send it.

Following this, your instructor will divide your class into pairs. With your partner, review the criteria each of you has established for writing an effective letter. Is there anything you disagree on, or anything you want to add or delete? Now, exchange letters and read them. When you are done, briefly evaluate the letter's effectiveness, based on your reaction as a recipient and based on the criteria you established. Is there anything you would change? Why?

To conclude the exercise, consider sending the letter and establishing goals for using letter writing as a regular form of influence.

EXERCISE 33

Characteristics of a Persuasive Letter

Do's

Don'ts

_____   _____

_____   _____

_____   _____

_____   _____

_____   _____

_____   _____

_____   _____

_____   _____

_____   _____

_____   _____

_____   _____

_____   _____

_____   _____

_____   _____

_____   _____

_____   _____

_____   _____

Letter

Date _____

Address _____

Dear: _____

_____

_____

_____

_____

_____

_____

_____

_____

_____

_____

_____

_____

_____

_____

Sincerely,

(Your Signature)

EXERCISE 34 *Making Effective Referrals*

Kim Strom-Gottfried

Purpose

1. To acquaint you with the skills and knowledge needed for finding resources and making effective referrals.
2. To help you develop a "list" of local resources, based on the information you and your fellow classmates find.

Background

Social workers frequently make referrals. We do this when a client comes to us with needs we cannot address, when new issues arise in the course of our work that need attention by other experts, or when we are terminating services with the client but other needs still remain.

Effective referrals involve more than simply giving the client system a list of phone numbers. Social workers need to have knowledge about available resources, an understanding of the eligibility requirements, of what the service entails, the name and number of the contact person, and the steps needed to access services. Finding this information may not be easy! Whereas many communities offer directories of social services, these sources can often be dated or a poor reflection of the actual services available. You may use these guides as a starting point for resources, but they should not be your only source. Other ways to find out about resources include networking with social workers and professionals in other disciplines, checking phone books, consulting with clients about their experiences with various services, and asking your contacts at organizations, "Who else provides these types of services?"

Beyond this, social workers need to consider the particular client and the "fit" between that client and the prospective service. Perhaps the service has a waiting list and the client's need is urgent. Perhaps the service is located in an office park that is not accessible unless the client has a car. When making referrals, it is not enough just to know about the resource, but to consider the information and assistance a particular client system might need to access that resource.

Hepworth, Rooney, and Larsen (1997b) discuss steps in making referrals, including the following:

1. Discuss the prospective referral with the clients, so that they understand why the referral is being made and what choice(s) they have in accepting the referral.

2. Determine which resource(s) can match the client's needs, leaving the final choice of resource to the client.

3. Provide the client with necessary information about the resource, whom to speak with, how to make an appointment, what to expect, and so forth.

4. Offer the client the opportunity to contact the service from your office, or to contact them yourself to "bridge" the services.

5. Address apprehensions or concerns through problem solving (e.g., how to pay for a service, how to get there, who might accompany the client).

6. Follow up to assess the referral's effectiveness.

Instructions

1. Determine the client system for whom you are selecting services and the need for which you are making the referral (e.g., you could seek a support group for a gay teenager, low-cost legal assistance for a community group, or fund-raising assistance for a fledgling agency).

2. Locate at least two resources to fill this need, finding out about the nature of the service/resource, its availability, whether your client (hypothetically) is eligible for this service and how he/she/they would access the service.

3. On the attached forms, describe the services you found, the process you used to find them, and the factors that might facilitate or impede a client's ability to qualify for or use these services.

4. Be prepared to submit your forms to your instructor who may create a "directory of services." Also, be prepared to describe your experiences in the referral search.

5. Consider the following discussion questions:
   - What sources were helpful to you in locating resources? What sources were not?
   - Did you experience any "dead-ends" in your search?
   - How did you contact the services? If you visited in person, how did that shape your impressions of the organization?
   - Did any information you gathered differ from the original impression or information you had about an organization?
   - What might be some barriers for clients in accessing the services you contacted?
   - What feelings did seeking out these resources raise?
   - What gaps exist in the service delivery system in your area?
   - What overlaps or duplication of services appears to exist?
   - What suggestions do you have for organizations in making the public more aware of their services?

Reference

Hepworth, D. H., Rooney, R. H., & Larsen, J. A. (1997b). *Direct social work practice: Theory and skills* (5th ed.). Pacific Grove, CA: Brooks/Cole.

EXERCISE 34

Resource Sheet

Organization name:

_____

Address(es) and office location:

_____

_____

_____

Phone number(s):

_____

_____

_____

Fax:

_____

E-mail:

_____

Hours of operation:

_____

Contact person:

_____

Position/title:

_____

Back-up contact person:

_____

Position/title:

_____

What services does the organization or program provide?

_____

_____

_____

_____

_____

_____

_____

_____

Who does the organization or program serve?

_____

_____

_____

_____

_____

_____

_____

_____

_____

Eligibility criteria/fees:

_____

_____

_____

_____

_____

_____

_____

_____

_____

Steps for clients to take in accessing services:

_____

_____

_____

_____

_____

_____

_____

_____

_____

_____

Resource Sheet

Organization name:

_____

Address(es) and office location:

_____

_____

_____

Phone number(s):

_____

_____

_____

Fax:

_____

E-mail:

_____

Hours of operation:

_____

Contact person:

_____

Position/title:

_____

Back-up contact person:

_____

Position/title:

_____

What services does the organization or program provide?

_____

_____

_____

_____

_____

_____

_____

_____

_____

Who does the organization or program serve?

_____

_____

_____

_____

_____

_____

_____

_____

_____

Eligibility criteria/fees:

_____

_____

_____

_____

_____

_____

_____

_____

_____

_____

Steps for clients to take in accessing services:

_____

_____

_____

_____

_____

_____

_____

_____

_____

_____

EXERCISE 35 *Getting Closure on Unplanned Endings*

Kim Strom-Gottfried

Purpose

1. To help you understand the importance of closure.
2. To develop effective strategies for closure in a variety of unplanned case terminations.

Background

Termination refers to the ending of a social work relationship. Sometimes, the endings are planned—the 6-week group comes to an end, the family achieves its goals, the community group gets its grant, the client moves on to a new program, or the social worker resigns and transfers the case. Social work texts address planned terminations at some length, noting the tasks of termination: reviewing progress that was made in the case, examining future steps to be taken, celebrating achievements, addressing feelings of sadness or loss, and so on.

Sometimes, terminations are unplanned: when clients die, drop out, or are discharged unexpectedly, or when social workers have to leave their positions without properly terminating with some cases. Yet the tasks of termination are still important because they help to bring *closure* to the work that occurred. Closure allows social workers and clients the opportunity to look back on the work that occurred, to acknowledge feelings about the relationship or about the abrupt ending, to mutually understand what future work can occur, and to generally bring this particular work to an end. The lack of closure can leave people feeling unsettled, angry, confused, or "at loose ends." A poor termination can make it difficult for both the client and social worker to reinvest in future working relationships, whereas closure, even when the case did not conclude as was planned, can yield a feeling of satisfaction and a willingness to invest in future work.

Instructions

1. Your instructor will assign you to one of the following scenarios. In the time that is allotted, list ways that you would achieve the

goals of closure, even if the case had an abrupt ending. If you have extra time, begin to list ideas for some of the scenarios you were not assigned.

2. When instructed, get together with other class members who were assigned the same scenario as you were. Compare notes. Are you able to add some ideas to those you already listed?

3. In your group, evaluate the items you have listed. What are the pros and cons of some of the ideas that have been suggested? If you were going to follow a particular idea, what steps might you need to take to carry it out effectively? Think about not only *how* you would get closure, but *what* you would want to say.

4. Identify any dynamics of the cases that presented particular difficulty for you.

5. Select the one or two most feasible ideas generated by your group and be prepared to discuss them and/or demonstrate them for the class.

EXERCISE 35

Unplanned Endings

1. A teen you have placed in foster care has run away.

_____

_____

_____

_____

_____

_____

_____

_____

_____

2. A resident of your homeless shelter commits suicide.

_____

_____

_____

_____

_____

_____

_____

_____

_____

3. A hospital patient falls into a coma.

_____

_____

_____

_____

_____

_____

_____

_____

_____

4. Over the weekend, your client violates a rule of the program and is immediately discharged.

_____

_____

_____

_____

_____

_____

_____

_____

_____

5. You become ill and require immediate surgery followed by a lengthy recuperation.

_____

_____

_____

_____

_____

_____

_____

_____

_____

6. The community group you have been consulting with decides to disband because of infighting among the various constituencies.

_____

_____

_____

_____

_____

_____

_____

_____

_____

_____

7. Your agency abruptly notifies you that it has eliminated half of its programs, including yours.

_____

_____

_____

_____

_____

_____

_____

_____

_____

8. The group you have been facilitating for sexual abuse survivors ends abruptly when the trial they were preparing for is settled out of court.

_____

_____

_____

_____

_____

_____

_____

_____

_____

EXERCISE 36 *Classroom Terminations*

Kim Strom-Gottfried

Purpose

1. To provide opportunities for reflection of what you've learned in your class.
2. To provide opportunities for closure with other members of the "group."
3. To understand the ways the tasks of termination manifest themselves in the classroom, and how these can parallel social work practice situations.
4. To learn different methods for group closure that are adaptable for social work groups.

Background

As social workers, we go to a lot of effort to join with our clients and engage them as partners in the helping process. Sometimes, however, when it is time to bring that relationship to a close, we don't pay a lot of attention to how to end the relationship. This process and the tasks related to it are called *termination*. Among other things, termination involves reviewing the work that was done together, evaluating the gains that were made, and identifying future areas for growth. Sometimes, particularly in work with groups, termination also involves celebrations of various forms that are structured to acknowledge the achievements and difficulties that have been overcome. Celebrations shouldn't take the place of a serious look at the sad or painful aspects of termination, but they can be a poignant way to bring closure to the totality of the social worker-client relationship.

In addition to the exercises below, you may want to ask at your workplace or field site about any processes for termination they use with certain clients, programs, or groups. Perhaps you can add their ideas to those below!

Instructions

This exercise offers you a chance to experience one of a variety of closure activities. Your instructor will have the information needed to lead you through some of these experiences, and he or she may alter the activities to suit the needs of your class. For these reasons, do not read ahead about the exercises unless you are instructed to do so. At a later point, however, you may want to look at all of the termination exercises and think about how they might be adapted for use in your work with clients.

EXERCISE 36

Oh, The Places You'll Go

As your instructor reads this book, consider the following:

- How does the book's theme reflect issues of termination?

- What kinds of practice situations would lend themselves to using a story, for closure or as part of your intervention?

- What kinds of preparation are needed to do this kind of ending successfully?

- In what ways can "play" and "playfulness" be used effectively in social work practice?

Excerpts from this chapter reprinted by permission from Haworth Press, 1995, Haworth Press, Binghamton, NY. "Engagement and Termination in the Classroom," *Creative Activities for Beginning and Ending, 12,* 1/2, 39–54.

What'd It Get Ya?

Think back to the beginning of this course. What was the weather like? How did the room, the instructor, and your classmates seem to you on that first day? What was it like the first time you saw the syllabus and opened the book? In the space below, write down some of the impressions you had.

_____

_____

_____

_____

_____

_____

_____

_____

_____

_____

Now think about where you and your classmates are today. What do you know now that you didn't know then? In what ways will you be different as a social worker than you would have been without the course? In short, "What'd it get ya?"

_____

_____

_____

_____

_____

_____

_____

_____

_____

_____

_____

_____

Affirmation Exercise 1

Your instructor will provide you with an envelope and several slips of paper. Put your name on the envelope and pass it to the classmate to your right. You will now have an envelope with a classmate's name on it. When instructed, take one of the slips of paper and write something on it to (or about) the classmate whose envelope you are holding. You should not write your name on the slip, but you should write something affirming about the person whose envelope you hold. For example, you might write something you admire about that person, something you have learned from him or her, a way he or she has been helpful or inspiring to you, or something you wish for the person in the future.

When you are done, put the slip of paper in the envelope and pass it to the next person. Write another affirmation for the person whose envelope you receive next, and continue to do so until you get your original envelope back. Do not open it.

Your instructor will lead a discussion to bring closure to this exercise. Following the class, you may want to look at the feedback provided to you by your classmates. Are some of their thoughts or observations a surprise to you? In what ways are their statements helpful to you as you think about your contributions to the course you have just completed and to your future work as a social worker? What impact might such an exercise have on clients, for example, those who are leaving a program or "graduating" from a group?

Affirmation Exercise 2

Like the last exercise, this one will ask you to share positive feedback with other members of your class. Take a moment and think about various classmates and characteristics you respect about them, qualities you see in them, and so forth.

With your classmates, form a circle. Your instructor will begin the exercise by stating an affirming comment and tossing a ball of yarn to that student (while hanging on to the end of the string). The student who receives the yarn will make an affirming comment to another member of the class and toss it to that person, while holding on to the yarn. This continues until all members have received feedback. At the end, your instructor will make concluding comments and help you cut the yarn. Hang onto the pieces of yarn you held and attach them to your cap and tassel at graduation.

Some questions to think about as you conclude the exercise:

- Picture the web created after you shared your observations and the yarn with your classmates. What did that symbolize to you about your learning process in this class? What does it symbolize about systems? How might it reflect what you'll experience in social work practice?
- How might you adapt this exercise to use with groups?

Class Will

Wills are a method for people to leave what they've accumulated to those who remain. This "class will" is a chance for you to do the same for the students who will succeed you. Reflect for a moment on your experience in this class. What have you learned? What skills or abilities will you take with you? What wishes and wisdom do you have for students who will follow you in this course? What can new students in this class expect to learn?

On a piece of paper provided by your instructor, write down what you'll "leave" for future students. Be prepared to share these verbally with the class.

- How might this exercise be used or adapted as you think about termination in groups work?

REFERENCES

Anderson, J. E., & Brown, R. A. (1980, July). Notes for practice: Life history grid for adolescents. *Social Work,* pp. 321-323.

Anderson, R., & Carter, I. (1990). *Human behavior in the social environment* (4th ed.). New York: Aldine.

Arias, I. (1992). Behavioral marital therapy. In S. M. Turner, K. S. Calhoun, & H. Adams (Eds.), *Handbook of clinical behavior therapy* (2nd ed., pp. 437-455). New York: Wiley.

Asamoah, Y. (1995). Managing the new multicultural workplace. In L. Ginsberg & P. R. Keys (Eds.), *New management in human services* (2nd ed., pp. 115-127). Washington, DC: NASW Press.

Bandura, A. (1977). *Social learning theory.* Englewood Cliffs, NJ: Prentice Hall.

Beck, J. (1995). *Cognitive therapy: Basics and beyond.* New York: Guilford.

Bertalanffy, L. von (1981). *A systems view of man* (P. A. LaViolette, Ed.). Boulder, CO: Westview.

Bloom, M., & Fischer, J. (1982). *Evaluating practice: Guidelines for the accountable professional.* Englewood Cliffs, NJ: Prentice Hall.

Blythe, B. J., & Tripodi, T. (1989). *Measurement in direct practice.* Newbury Park, CA: Sage.

Brill, N. I. (1990). *Working with people: The helping process* (4th ed.). New York: Longman.

Bronfenbrenner, U. (1979). *The ecology of human development: Experiments by nature and design.* Cambridge, MA: Harvard University Press.

Chetkow-Yanoov, B. (1992). *Social work practice: A systems approach.* New York: Haworth.

Collins, P. M., Kayser, K., & Platt, S. (1994, March). Conjoint marital therapy: A practitioners approach to single-system evaluation. *Families in Society: The Journal of Contemporary Human Services,* pp. 131-141.

Dorfman, R. A. (1988). The case. In R. A. Dorfman (Ed.), *Paradigms of clinical social work.* New York: Brunner/Mazel.

Elks, M. A., & Kirkhart, K. E. (1993, September). Evaluating effectiveness from the practitioner perspective. *Social Work, 38*(5), 554-563.

Fischer, J., & Corcoran, K. (1994). *Measures for clinical practice.* New York: Free Press.

Foley, M. (1993, August 31). The poisons of life. *Charlotte Observer.*

Freud, S. (1965a). The dissection of the psychial personality. In J. Strachey (Ed.), *New introductory lectures on psychoanalysis* (pp. 57-80). New York: Norton.

Freud, S. (1965b). Anxiety and instinctual life. In J. Strachey (Ed.), *New introductory lectures on psychoanalysis* (pp. 81-111). New York: Norton.

Gambrill, E. (1997). *Social work practice: A critical thinker's guide.* New York: Oxford University Press.

Garbarino, J. (1992). *Children and families in the social environment* (2nd ed.). New York: Aldine de Gruyter.

Germain, C. B. (1991). *Human behavior in the social environment.* New York: Columbia.

Germain, C. B., & Gitterman, A. (1980). *The life model of social work practice.* New York: Columbia University Press.

Germain, C. B., & Gitterman, A. (1995). Ecological perspective. In R. L. Edwards (Ed.), *Encyclopedia of social work* (19th ed., Vol. 1, pp. 816-824). Washington, DC: NASW Press.

Gibbons, K. (1989). *A virtuous woman.* Chapel Hill, NC: Algonquin.

Glassman, U., & Kates, L. (1990). *Group work: A humanistic approach.* Thousand Oaks, CA: Sage.

Goldenberg, I., & Goldenberg, H. (1985). *Family therapy: An overview* (2nd ed.). Monterey, CA: Brooks/Cole.

Greene, R. R. (1993). *Human behavior theory: A diversity theory.* New York: Aldine de Gruyter.

Hanson, B. G. (1995). *General systems theory: Beginning with wholes.* Washington, DC: Taylor & Francis.

Hartman, A. (1978). Diagrammatic assessment of family relationships. *Social Casework, 59,* 467-474.

Hepworth, D. H., Rooney, R. H., & Larsen, J. A. (1997a). Assessing family functioning in diverse family and cultural contexts. In *Direct social work practice: Theory and skills* (5th ed., pp. 276-316). Pacific Grove, CA: Brooks/Cole.

Hepworth, D. H., Rooney, R. H., & Larsen, J. A. (1997b). *Direct social work practice: Theory and skills* (5th ed.). Pacific Grove, CA: Brooks/Cole.

Holmgren, N. (1990). Social Security. In J. Mukand, *Vital lines: Contemporary fiction about medicine.* New York: Ballantine.

Ivey, A. (1994). *Intentional interviewing and counseling: Facilitating client development in a multicultural society* (3rd ed.). Belmont, CA: Brooks/Cole.

Kadushin, A., & Kadushin, G. (1997). *The social work interview: A guide for human service professionals* (4th ed.). New York: Columbia University Press.

Kelly, J. (1968). Toward an ecological conception of preventive interventions. In J. Carter (Ed.), *Research contributions from psychology to community mental health* (pp. 75-99). New York: Behavioral Publications.

Lippitt, R., Watson, J., & Westley, B. (1958). *The dynamics of planned change.* New York: Harcourt, Brace & World.

Marlow, C. (1993). *Research methods for generalist social work.* Pacific Grove, CA: Brooks/Cole.

Martin, P. Y., & O'Connor, G. G. (1989). *The social environment: Open systems applications.* New York: Longman.

McCollum, E. E., & Beer, J. (1995, March/April). The view from the other chair. *Family Therapy Networker,* pp. 59-62.

McPhatter, A. (1993). Assessment revisited: A comprehensive approach to understanding family dynamics. In J. Rauch, *Assessment: A sourcebook for social work practice* (pp. 31-45). Milwaukee, WI: Families International.

Merkel, W. T., & Searight, H. R. (1992). Why families are not like swamps, solar systems, or thermostats: Some limits of systems theory as applied to family therapy. *Contemporary Family Therapy, 14*(1), 33-49.

Okun, B. F. (1997). *Effective helping: Interviewing and counseling techniques* (5th ed.). Pacific Grove, CA: Brooks/Cole.

Pincus, A., & Minahan, A. (1973). *Social work practice: model and method.* Madison: University of Wisconsin.

Rooney, R. H. (1992). *Strategies for work with involuntary clients.* New York: Columbia University Press.

Rooney, R. H., & Bibus, A. A. (1996). Multiple lenses: Ethnically sensitive practice with involuntary clients who are having difficulties with drugs or alcohol. *Journal of Multicultural Social Work, 4*(2), 59-73.

Schuyler, D. (1991). *A practical guide to cognitive therapy.* New York: Norton.

Shaw, M. (1980). *Role-playing.* La Jolla, CA: University Associates.

Shulman, L. (1992). *The skills of helping individuals and groups* (3rd ed.). Itasca, IL: F. E. Peacock.

Toseland, R. W., & Rivas, R. F. (1995). *An introduction to group work practice* (2nd ed.). Needham Heights, MA: Allyn & Bacon.

Tracy, E. M., & Whitaker, J. K. (1990, October). The social network map: Assessing social support in clinical practice. *Families in Society,* pp. 463, 466.

Tripodi, T. (1994). *A primer on single-subject design for clinical social workers.* Washington, DC: NASW Press.

Wielkiewicz, R. M. (1995). *Behavior management in the schools: Principles and procedures* (2nd ed.). Boston: Allyn & Bacon.

Zastrow, C., & Kirst-Ashman, K. K. (1997). *Understanding human behavior and the social environment* (4th ed.). Chicago: Nelson-Hall.

INDEX